Music Technology and the Project Studio

Music Technology and the Project Studio: Synthesis and Sampling provides clear explanations of synthesis and sampling techniques and how to use them effectively and creatively. Starting with analog-style synthesis as a basic model, this textbook explores in detail how messages from a MIDI controller or sequencer are used to control elements of a synthesizer to create rich, dynamic sound. It explores a variety of synthesis techniques including oscillator sync, ring modulation, frequency modulation, multiple wavetable synthesis, physical modeling, and granular synthesis, with a special focus on the use of expressive MIDI messages, envelopes, and low-frequency oscillators to modulate the parameters of these synthesis techniques. Since samplers and sample players are also common in today's software, the book explores the details of sampling and the control of sampled instruments with MIDI messages. Effects that can be applied to the audio generated by both synthesizers and samplers are also covered, including compression, gating, equalization, delay, chorus, flanging, phasing, and reverb.

This book is not limited to any specific software and is general enough to apply to many different software instruments. Overviews of sound and digital audio provide students with a set of common concepts used throughout the text, and "Technically Speaking" sidebars offer detailed explanations of advanced technical concepts, preparing students for future studies in sound synthesis.

Music Technology and the Project Studio: Synthesis and Sampling is an ideal follow-up to the author's *An Introduction to Music Technology*, although each book can be used independently.

The Companion Website includes:

* Audio examples demonstrating synthesis and sampling techniques
* Interactive software that allows the reader to experiment with various synthesis techniques
* Guides relating the material in the book to various software synthesizers and samplers
* Links to relevant resources, examples, and software.

Dan Hosken is Professor of Music at California State University, Northridge where he teaches courses in music technology and composition. He is the author of *An Introduction to Music Technology*, published by Routledge.

Visit the companion website at www.routledge.com/cw/hosken2.

Music Technology and the Project Studio

Synthesis and Sampling

Dan Hosken

California State University, Northridge

Routledge
Taylor & Francis Group

NEW YORK AND LONDON

First published 2012
by Routledge
711 Third Avenue, New York, NY 10017

Simultaneously published in the UK
by Routledge
2 Park Square, Milton Park, Abingdon, Oxon OX14 4RN

Routledge is an imprint of the Taylor & Francis Group, an informa business

© 2012 Taylor & Francis

The right of Dan Hosken to be identified as author of this work has been
asserted by him in accordance with sections 77 and 78 of the Copyright,
Designs and Patents Act 1988.

All rights reserved. No part of this book may be reprinted or reproduced
or utilized in any form or by any electronic, mechanical, or other means,
now known or hereafter invented, including photocopying and recording,
or in any information storage or retrieval system, without permission in
writing from the publishers.

Trademark Notice: Product or corporate names may be trademarks or
registered trademarks, and are used only for identification and explanation
without intent to infringe. Apple, GarageBand, Logic Pro, and Soundtrack
Pro are trademarks of Apple Inc., registered in the US and other countries.

Library of Congress Cataloging in Publication Data
  Hosken, Daniel W. (Daniel William)
  Music technology and the project studio: synthesis and sampling/Dan Hosken.
  p. cm.
  Includes bibliographical references and index.
  1. Software synthesizers. 2. Software samplers. I. Title.
  ML74.3.H67 2012
  786.7–dc22   2011008653

ISBN: 978–0–415–87828–9 (hbk)
ISBN: 978–0–415–99723–2 (pbk)
ISBN: 978–0–203–80490–2 (ebk)

Typeset in Bembo and Helvetica Neue by
Florence Production Ltd, Stoodleigh, Devon, UK

Printed and bound in the United States of America
on acid-free paper by Sheridan Books, Inc.

Contents

Illustrations

FIGURES

TABLES

Preface

With the rapid virtualization of synthesizers and samplers over the last several years, music creators have more options than ever for generating sound in the form of a vast array of software instruments. A computer in a project studio might have anywhere from several of these software instruments to dozens, each of which may take a different approach to generating sound. The challenge, then, for a music creator in a project studio is to figure out how to harness these resources to create rich, complex timbres to better serve their music.

My goals in writing this book were to provide a clear explanation of the common elements found in software instruments, to explore these elements and their interactions in detail, and then to expand beyond these common elements to explore a variety of other sound synthesis techniques. By themselves these sound generation techniques represent *potential* sound. It is up the music creator to provide the necessary notes and other expressive information—usually in the form of MIDI messages stored in DAW/ Sequencers—for these software instruments to actually make sound. An additional goal of this book, then, is to explicitly explore the relationship between these MIDI messages and the synthesis and sampling elements that they control.

In order to begin delving deeply into the details of synthesis and sampling, it is expected that the reader will already have an understanding of the basics of sound, audio, MIDI sequencing, and synthesis at the level found in my book *An Introduction to Music Technology*. The early chapters of *Music Technology and the Project Studio: Synthesis and Sampling* include an overview of sound, digital audio, and MIDI taken at a relatively fast pace that can serve as review material for those who have taken a music tech course before or as a fast introduction for those who already have significant experience with music technology.

ABOUT THIS BOOK

To achieve the goals I have outlined above, I start first with chapters on **Sound** and **Digital Audio**. These two chapters provide the necessary background for the discussion of timbre that occurs throughout the rest of the book. As mentioned above, these chapters contain some review material as well as more detailed information. Both of these topics are quite deep and could be explored in much greater detail. However, I've limited the information in these chapters to those topics that I think are directly relevant to the discussion of synthesis and sampling found in the remainder of the book. There are several sources for further exploration of these topics found in the bibliography, including works by Loy (2006), Cook (1999), Pierce (1992), Steiglitz (1996), and Pohlmann (2005).

Chapter 1, **Sound**, also contains the first "Technically Speaking . . ." sidebars. I use these sidebars to present more technical detail than is found in the main body of the text. For readers encountering this material for the first time, the "Technically Speaking . . ." sidebars can be skipped initially and revisited once the material in the main body of the text has been mastered.

The third chapter provides an overview of **MIDI, Sequencing, and Software Instruments**. Throughout this book, software synthesis and sampling is considered in the context of software instruments controlled by MIDI messages in a DAW/Sequencer, and this chapter provides a fast-paced overview of these topics. For a reader who has significant experience with sequencers and software instruments or who has read my previous book, *An Introduction to Music Technology*, this material provides a review of these topics.

Chapter 4, **Synthesis, Sampling, and MIDI Control**, introduces a model for synthesis based on the core elements of oscillators, filters, and amplifiers, and explores how the data contained in various MIDI messages are mapped to these elements. This pattern, in which a synthesis technique or element is introduced along with typical MIDI mappings, is replicated throughout the text. The end of the chapter presents the core concepts involved in sampling.

Chapter 5, **Modulation and Dynamic Sound**, expands the basic synthesis and sampling models to include envelopes and LFOs (Low Frequency Oscillators), along with an introduction to modulation routing which connects MIDI messages with envelopes, LFOs, and other synthesizer elements. With the full synthesis model having been developed in Chapters 4 and 5, Chapter 6, **Oscillators and Filters**, goes into some detail about interactions between oscillators, such as oscillator sync and ring modulation, and explores the various filter types beyond the standard resonant low pass filter.

Chapter 7, **Synthesis Techniques**, expands beyond oscillators and filters to explore a variety of synthesis techniques including multiple wavetable, additive, frequency modulation, physical modeling and granular synthesis. For each technique, the parameters that are suitable targets for modulation are discussed along with likely modulation sources. This chapter also discusses synthesis programming applications that allow the user to create unique synthesis techniques, as opposed to traditional software instruments in which the synthesis elements (oscillators, filters, etc.) and their possible configurations are fixed.

Chapter 8, **Effects**, describes the various types of effects that can be applied to synthesized/sampled sound as well as to recorded sound. These effects include compression, equalization, delay, flanging, phasing, and reverb. Because software instruments are typically used within a DAW/Sequencing environment, this chapter also discusses signal routing including insert and send effects. Care is taken in this chapter to explore some non-typical applications of these effects including using sidechain routing with a gate to impose a rhythm on a synthesized sound and using extreme reverb settings to yield unusual effects.

Chapter 9, **MIDI in Detail**, delves deeply into the MIDI standard to explore the kinds of messages available and how these messages are put together. This chapter acts as a complement to the introduction to MIDI messages found in Chapter 3 and the various uses of MIDI messages as modulation sources discussed throughout the other chapters. The information in this chapter can deepen the reader's understanding of the language used to control synthesis, and this information can be used directly in synthesis programming applications introduced in Chapter 7.

TO THE INSTRUCTOR

The focus of this book is the creation of complex and powerful timbres using the various techniques of synthesis and sampling. The target student is a musician creating music with computers who wants to learn how to use their sampling and synthesis resources more effectively and more creatively. There are a number of books already available that touch on this topic, but in my experience they are either too closely tied to pushing buttons in a single program or too technically involved for the average student to apply the concepts to their software instruments. This book is designed to be general enough to apply to many different software instruments and is written at a technical level that allows the student to master the concepts and apply them without being overwhelmed.

To achieve these goals I had to make a variety of decisions concerning content and organization. For example:

- **Software versus hardware instruments**—Many music technology students are acquainted solely with software instruments, often to the point that they don't even realize that there is a "synth" generating the sound in their software. As a result, I generally assume that the reader is using a software instrument. Nevertheless, the synthesis and sampling concepts presented in this text are generally applicable to both software and hardware.
- **Starting with an analog model**—Though a great deal of progress has been made since the first commercial analog synthesizers were developed in the 1960s, the basic elements of the analog model remain prominent in many modern software instruments, and most DAW/Sequencers include an analog-style synth as part of their basic package. As a result, I have chosen to start with that model and approach more complex sound generation techniques from that basis. This model also allows me to address some critical issues in sound design, such as the relationship between loudness and brightness through the application of low pass filters and filter envelopes, and the dynamic nature of sound through the application of envelopes and LFOs.

- **Technical details**—This is a text designed for musicians who use technology, so I tried to strike a balance between ease of understanding and technical depth. Most of the somewhat technical sections have been placed in the "Technically Speaking . . ." sidebars, but there remain a few essential equations in the body of the text itself. For example, I felt that an understanding of the various types of decibels required the recognition that they are logarithms of ratios, so the various decibel formulas are presented in the main body of the text. In addition, I feel that it is important for students who will go on to more advanced work in sampling and synthesis to begin to grasp the technical aspects of this creative work that will allow them to access concepts and techniques of greater complexity.

- **Mainstream software versus experimental software**—Most of this text is written with the expectation that the reader will be using mainstream commercial software instruments such as those that are packaged with most DAW/Sequencers and those that can be purchased as plug-ins. I chose to focus on these types of software instruments because they are widely available and widely used. However, much of this information can be applied to more experimental software, such as Csound, Max/MSP, Pd, or Reaktor, that allow you to build synthesis and sampling algorithms from the ground up. I label these programs "synthesis programming applications" in the text and give a detailed example using both Csound and Max/MSP in Chapter 6. For similar reasons, I have chosen to focus on MIDI control of software instruments rather than an alternative protocol such as OSC (Open Sound Control). Links to information concerning synthesis programming applications and OSC are available on the text's website.

- **Review material**—Even though I assume in this text that the reader has already taken a typical broad introductory course in music technology, instructors of introductory courses with a more "electronic music" focus may want to use this text instead of a more traditional introductory text. To accommodate this, I have included some review material in the first three chapters, especially Chapter 3. I present this material more quickly than I would in an introductory text and introduce more advanced concepts as well. This approach also allows students taking a sequence of courses to review essential information.

I welcome feedback and criticism from my fellow music technology instructors in order to improve future versions of this book. Please send such feedback to **dwhosken@alum.mit.edu**.

TO THE STUDENT

This book is written for *you*, as a music creator, to help you use sampling and synthesis techniques more effectively and more creatively in your music. Software instruments abound in the modern project studio representing tremendous potential to enhance your music with rich, nuanced timbres. The question is how to move beyond the presets that *everyone* uses to create sounds that represent your own unique style? *Music Technology and the Project Studio: Synthesis and Sampling* explains the inner workings of synthesizers and samplers, providing you with the keys to unlocking their sonic potential.

Just about every piece of music creation software comes with an analog-style software synthesizer, so the book uses this as a basic synthesis model and explores in detail how MIDI messages generated by your keyboard controller are used to control elements of the synthesizer to create dynamic sound. Samplers and sample players are also very common in today's software, so the book explores the details of sampling and the control of sampled instruments with MIDI messages.

The book goes on to explore a variety of powerful techniques for synthesizing sound including oscillator sync, ring modulation, frequency modulation, multiple wavetable synthesis, physical modeling, and granular synthesis, with a special focus on the use of controllers, envelopes, and LFOs (low-frequency oscillators) to modify the parameters of these synthesis techniques. In addition, the book covers effects that are found in most software including compression, gating, equalization, delay, chorus, flanging, phasing, and reverb.

It is expected that you already have some experience with DAW/Sequencers and software instruments. However, the first few chapters of the book include an overview of sound, digital audio, and MIDI sequencing that can bring you up to speed on these topics and prepare you to dive into the rest of the text.

The goal of this book is help you as a *musician* to better use the sampling and synthesis resources in the project studio. Nevertheless, an understanding of some of the technical aspects of synthesis and sampling is necessary to master the various techniques. Much of the technical material is contained in the "Technically Speaking . . ." sidebars, but there are some essential technical details in the body of the text. Grasping these details will enable you to better understand the software instruments that you use *and* those you will encounter in the future.

Unlike some books, this one doesn't focus on a specific piece of software. Instead, the concepts are presented in such a way that they can be applied to many different synths and samplers. Every software instrument has its own particular "take" on the common techniques for digitally generating sound and may use slightly different terminology than what you will encounter here. My hope is that this book will prepare you for these variations and allow you to approach a new synth or sampler with the knowledge of what it will likely be able to do and the ability to understand and appreciate its unique features.

WEBSITE

Naturally, a book about using technology to create sound would be incomplete without actual sound. The website for this book contains audio examples of the techniques discussed here and working interactive software that will allow you to explore these techniques in a hands-on way. Visit www.routledge.com/textbooks/9780415997232.

In addition, I strongly encourage you to use the software instruments available in your DAW/Sequencer to explore these concepts. After all, the goal here is for you to combine the information in this book with your synths and samplers to create rich, complex timbres that better serve your music.

ACKNOWLEDGEMENTS

I want to thank Constance Ditzel, my editor at Routledge, for her support and her boundless patience in bringing this project to fruition. I also want to thank Denny Tek, Mhairi Bennett, and the rest of the team at Routledge/Taylor & Francis for their invaluable assistance. Thanks also to Rosie White at Florence Production Ltd. and Amanda Crook for excellent copy-editing and many useful suggestions.

Along the way, I had the benefit of candid suggestions and useful criticisms from several anonymous reviewers. As always, I am grateful for the thoughtfulness, expertise, and collegiality that can be found in abundance in the field of music technology.

I am also indebted to the students who have taken my classes during my decade-plus of teaching at California State University, Northridge. Many of the pedagogical ideas that inform this text have come directly from my experiences with this passionate learning community.

As always, my work is made possible by the support of my family. The steady encouragement of parents over the years has given me the confidence to pursue my goals, the love and joy from my children has given me the inspiration to try to match their astronomical energy levels, and the never-ending patience and love of my wife, Rebekka, has given me the time and courage to devote myself to the task of writing yet another book.

Dan Hosken
April 2011

Introduction

The focus of this book is the exploration of synthesis and sampling techniques to create rich, complex, and satisfying timbres. The goal is to take you beyond your synth's presets so that both your music *and* your sound are your own. With the rapid migration of synthesis and sampling from hardware boxes to software plug-ins, most of this activity now takes place using software instruments in a DAW/Sequencer. A DAW/Sequencer is software that is part Digital Audio Workstation and part MIDI sequencer—popular DAW/Sequencers include Pro Tools, Logic, Digital Performer, Cubase, and Sonar. Much of the book will assume that you are working with software instruments, but the information carries over easily to hardware synthesizers and samplers as well.

Most DAW/Sequencers come with a variety of software instruments, and many more are available from other companies. These instruments can be split into two broad categories: synthesizers that use elements such as oscillators and filters to generate sound, and samplers that use pre-recorded audio as the basis for their timbres. Of the synthesizers, most DAW/Sequencers will come with at least one analog-modeling synth—a synth that uses virtual versions of analog synthesizer elements—and perhaps a few others that utilize other synthesis techniques. Even a modest collection of these virtual instruments usually represents a wide variety of sound-generation techniques that span the fifty-plus year history of synthesized and sampled sound.

This book is designed to help you understand the sonic resources available in your collection of software instruments so that you can get the most out them. There are a tremendous number of ways to configure synthesizer and sampler elements, and one book cannot possibly cover each configuration in detail. However, most softsynths share a common synthesis vocabulary involving such elements as oscillators, filters, envelopes, LFOs (low frequency oscillators), and modulation routings. Understanding these elements and their interactions in detail will help you figure out what's going on with most software instruments. In addition to those common elements and their interactions, there is a set of non-analog-modeling synthesis techniques that are found in many softsynths, including multiple wavetable synthesis, frequency modulation, and physical modeling. This book thoroughly covers the basic synthesis and sampling elements and their interactions, along with many of the other common synthesis techniques implemented in today's software instruments.

WHAT'S IN THE BOOK?

The book opens with three important preparatory chapters. Chapter 1 discusses the properties of sound as seen in the waveform and spectrum views. You will see these properties referenced over and over throughout the book. Chapter 2 discusses digital audio, audio file types, and digital audio signal levels. Chapter 3 provides an overview of MIDI hardware, MIDI data, MIDI sequencing, and the relationships between DAW/Sequencers and software instruments. It is assumed that you have had some previous experience with DAW/Sequencers and software instruments and are looking here to take your existing knowledge to the next level. As a result, this preparatory material is covered swiftly with the goal of refreshing your memory, filling in any knowledge gaps, and providing a common vocabulary that will be used throughout the rest of the book.

After these initial chapters, we begin to explore synthesis and sampling techniques. Chapter 4 presents a basic synthesis model and overview of sampling. This and subsequent chapters consistently stress the relationship between the MIDI messages sent from controllers or sequencer MIDI tracks and the parameters that shape the sounds of synthesizers and samplers. Chapter 5 focuses on making synthesized and sampled sounds dynamic by expanding the basic model to include various forms of modulation, including envelopes and LFOs. Throughout the rest of the book, attention is paid to synthesis parameters as modulation targets and MIDI messages and modulation routings as essential elements of dynamic sound design. Chapter 6 covers interactions between multiple oscillators, such as oscillator sync and ring modulation, and expands our stable of filter types and parameters.

Up to this point in the book, most of the techniques discussed could fall under the category of analog-modeling techniques. With Chapter 7, we move past analog modeling and look at other types of synthesis found in software instruments. Chapter 7 concludes with a discussion of synthesis programming applications such as Reaktor, Max/MSP, and Csound. Synthesis programming applications allow you to actually create software instruments that utilize any synthesis or sampling technique imaginable. Chapter 8 discusses the kinds of plug-in effects commonly available in DAW/Sequencers and their application to synthesized and sampled sounds as well as to recorded and imported audio. Finally, Chapter 9 provides a detailed look at MIDI messages with a focus on how they are used to control the elements of hardware and software synthesizers.

Throughout the book there are a number of "Technically Speaking . . ." sidebars that deal with technical issues in greater detail than in the body of the text. These sidebars frequently involve some math, though nothing more complicated than logarithms. Even in the body of the text, there are a few occasions where a mathematical expression or two was deemed necessary. This kind of material is especially valuable if you continue on with your study of synthesis and digital signal processing in more depth, or from an electrical engineering or computer science perspective. Nevertheless, it is not necessary to master a great deal of math to understand and utilize the concepts discussed in this book.

There are three sources of audio in a DAW/Sequencer: 1) recorded audio; 2) imported audio (e.g., loops); and 3) synthesized or sampled audio. This book focuses on synthesis and sampling, and does not cover microphones, recording techniques, loops, or audio editing. These are valuable concepts and techniques for making music with your DAW/Sequencer, but there are already several good books that cover these topics. In the end these three sources of audio can be treated in the same way when it comes to processing and mixing. Using a hardware synth or sampler requires a few extra steps—plugging the audio outs from your synth into your audio interface and routing that to a track—but once that audio is inside the DAW/Sequencer it can be treated just like any of the other audio sources.

I believe that if you grasp the synthesis and sampling concepts in this book, you will be better able to use your software instruments to create powerful, effective timbres to express your music.

CHAPTER 1

Sound

The focus of this book is the creation of rich, complex timbres using software instruments that employ various synthesis and sampling techniques. The output of these instruments is first carried as digital audio from the software to the audio interface and then as sound from the speakers or headphones to your ears. Sound and digital audio, then, are fundamental topics that underlie the creation of these rich, complex timbres.

Both sound and digital audio are deep subjects that would require several books many times the size of this one to fully explain. The goal of these first two chapters is more modest: to provide an overview of essential sound and digital audio concepts necessary to create sounds through synthesis and sampling.

The way the material in this book is presented assumes that you have some experience with music technology and thus some understanding of sound and digital audio. As a result, the material in these chapters is presented in a relatively brief fashion to review important concepts and provide a common basis for the terminology that will be used throughout the book.

SOUND GENERATION, PROPAGATION, AND PERCEPTION

A sound wave can be thought of in three different phases: generation, propagation, and perception. First, a sound wave is generated by a vibrating source, such as a drumhead, a string, buzzing lips, or a speaker cone, that comes in contact with an elastic medium, such as air. The vibrating source creates regions of air pressure that are higher and lower than normal air pressure as the molecules in the air are periodically pushed together. The regions of higher air pressure are called **compressions** and the regions of lower air pressure are called **rarefactions** (see Figure 1.1).

Once air molecules have been pushed together by the vibrating source, creating a compression, their energy is passed on to other air molecules and the compression moves, or **propagates**, through the medium. In its wake, the compression leaves a rarefaction,

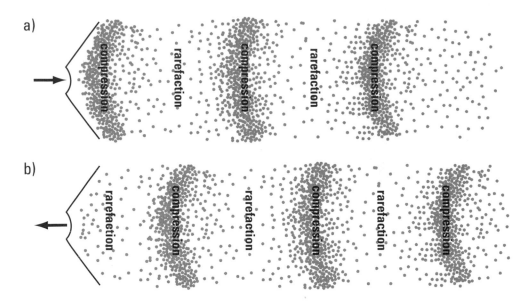

Figure 1.1 Side cutaway view of a speaker cone: a) the forward motion of the speaker cone causes a compression; b) the backward motion of the speaker cone causes a rarefaction

a region of lower than normal air pressure. As the vibrating source continues to move back and forth, more compressions and rarefactions are produced that also propagate through the medium. This series of moving compressions and rarefactions form a sound wave, also referred to as a compression wave or a longitudinal wave.

The actual medium through which a sound wave travels affects the propagation of the sound wave. For example, sound waves travel faster through water than through air and faster still through a metal such as steel. The speed of sound in the air is also dependent on the air temperature, with higher temperatures yielding faster speeds. Different gases besides the normal air mixture will also have different speeds of sound. The higher speed of sound in helium is responsible for the well-known helium-voice effect. Sound waves do not travel through the vacuum of space because there isn't a sufficient density of molecules for a compression to propagate by passing its energy on to other molecules.

The final phase of a sound wave is, of course, our perception of it. In fact, it is arguable that a sound wave is not actually "sound" until someone perceives it, leading to the well-known question: "If a tree falls in a forest and no one is around to hear it, does it make a sound?" Human perception of sound waves starts with the sound waves entering our ears and leads eventually to a response from our brains. The study of perception is called **psychoacoustics**, and the study of our brain's evaluation of what we perceive is called **music cognition**.

While we won't spend time in this book discussing the human perceptual and cognitive apparatus in much detail, it is important to note that our ears and brain influence strongly what we actually hear. Throughout this chapter we will be discussing the relationship between the physical properties of sound and the perceptual properties of sound, and noting the many ways in which they are not the same.

SOUND PROPERTIES AND THE WAVEFORM VIEW

The view in Figure 1.1 of a speaker cone generating a series of compressions and rarefactions helps us understand the physical basis of sound generation and propagation, but it doesn't tell us much about the sound itself. In a musical context we are interested in such perceptual properties as pitch, loudness, articulation, and timbre.

To help us see the physical properties of a sound wave that give rise to the perceptual properties we're interested in, it is helpful to look at the sound wave graphed as the change in air pressure (*y*-axis) over time (*x*-axis). We will refer to this as the **waveform view** of sound, though some sources refer to this as the "time domain representation" (see Figure 1.2).

Frequency and Pitch

One of the physical properties that we can see in the waveform view is the amount of time between compressions in a sound wave. This amount of time is the **period** of the waveform and is measured in the number of seconds per compression-rarefaction cycle (see Figure 1.3). The **frequency** can then be derived from the period by noting that we measure frequency in cycles per second, or **Hertz (Hz)**, which is the inverse of the period:

$f = 1/T$, where f stands for frequency and T for the period

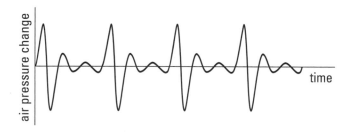

Figure 1.2 The waveform view of sound: a trumpet sound graphed as the amount of air pressure change over time. Notice the repeating pattern

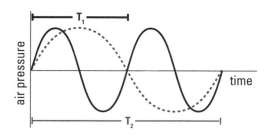

Figure 1.3 Two waves with the same amplitude but different frequencies graphed on the same axis. Period T_2 is twice as long as Period T_1 resulting in half the frequency

For example, if the period was 2 seconds per cycle, its frequency would be 0.5 Hz (cycles per second) and if the period was 0.01 seconds per cycle, its frequency would be 100 Hz.

One of the perceptual properties of a sound wave with a regular frequency is **pitch** (frequency is also central to our perception of timbre, which we'll discuss a little later in the chapter). While a sound wave with a period T has a frequency f calculated from the above formula, we can't perceive all frequencies as pitch. Our perception of frequency is limited to approximately 20 Hz to 20 kHz (kilohertz), or 20,000 Hz. Below 20 Hz (**infrasonic**) we don't perceive the wave as a pitch, though we may perceive some kind of pulse if the sound wave is complicated enough. Above 20,000 Hz (**ultrasonic**), we don't perceive frequencies as sound, though they may still have an impact on us. For example, doctors use compression waves at ultrasonic frequencies to break up kidney stones. As we age, the upper limit of our frequency perception naturally diminishes, and people who have sustained hearing damage may have a dramatically reduced upper frequency limit.

Another distinction between the perceptual property of pitch and the physical property of frequency can be found in the way we perceive musical intervals. We hear two musical intervals as being the same size when they have the same frequency ratio between the highest and lowest pitches, not when they are the same number of Hertz apart. The simplest example is the octave. The frequency ratio between pitches that are an octave apart is 2 to 1, notated as 2:1. This ratio holds regardless of the octave. As a result, the absolute size of an octave gets larger as we go up in pitch. For example, if we start with the A that has a frequency of 110 Hz, the octave above it would be the A with a frequency of 220 Hz. The octave above that would be 440 Hz and the octave above that would be 880 Hz. Thus the octaves grow in absolute size—110 Hz, 220 Hz, and 440 Hz—but we perceive them as being the same size. The same holds true for all of the other musical intervals as well. This will be discussed further under "Tuning and Temperament" below.

Figure 1.4 shows the frequencies and pitches across the range of the piano. Pitches are often given in a pitch-class/register notation, with C4 being middle C, B3 being one semitone below that and C5 being one octave above middle C. As you'll see in Chapter 3, many MIDI applications use C3 as middle C. Notice that the lowest frequency

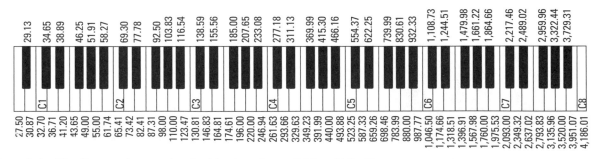

Figure 1.4   The frequencies associated with piano keys. C4 is middle C

on a piano is near the bottom of our hearing range, but the highest frequency is only a little over 4,000 Hz. The frequencies above that are usually a part of the timbre of a pitch with a lower fundamental frequency (see below).

Amplitude and Loudness

Another physical property that we can see in the waveform view is **amplitude**, which is related to the amount of air pressure change above normal in a compression and below normal in a rarefaction (see Figure 1.5). In general, the more energy you put into a sound—the harder you pluck, strike, bow, or blow—the more the air molecules are pressed together in a compression and thus the greater the amplitude. As a result we perceive amplitude as loudness.

As with frequency, we cannot perceive every change in amplitude, so there is a lower limit to our perception of sound wave amplitude below which we cannot hear the sound, and an upper limit above which we experience physical pain. This lower limit is an experimentally derived value and represents the quietest sound that the average person can hear. Also, as with frequency, we perceive changes in amplitudes as being equal when the *ratios* of the amplitudes are equal rather than when the differences between the amplitudes are equal. Just as this perception of frequency ratios leads us to measure the distance between frequencies as musical intervals, our perception of amplitude ratios leads us to measure amplitude differences using the relative measurement of decibels of sound pressure level, or **dB SPL**.

dB SPL measures the ratio of the amplitude of a sound wave relative to the amplitude of the quietest sound we can hear. Here is the decibel formula for amplitude:

$$dB\ SPL = 20\ \log_{10}(A/A_{ref})$$

where A is the amplitude of the sound wave we're measuring and A_{ref} is the amplitude of the quietest sound we can hear. When the sound wave that we're measuring has the same amplitude as A_{ref}, the formula yields the following:

$$dB\ SPL = 20\ \log_{10}(A_{ref}/A_{ref}) = 20\ \log_{10}(1) = 0\ dB\ SPL$$

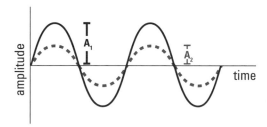

Figure 1.5   Two waves with the same frequency but different amplitudes graphed on the same axis

This value is referred to as the **threshold of hearing**. The level at which sound causes pain is referred to as the **threshold of pain** and is usually given as approximately 120 dB SPL, though some sources cite 130 or even 140 dB SPL. A dB SPL level of 120 dB results from an amplitude ratio of 1,000,000 to 1. Table 1.1 gives some dB SPL levels for some common sounds.

Another commonly discussed aspect of a sound wave is the **intensity** of a sound. Where pressure is a measurement of force per unit area, intensity is a measurement of power per unit area and is proportional to the square of the amplitude. The decibel formula for the sound intensity level, or dB SIL, is similar, but not identical, to the formula for dB SPL:

$$\text{dB SIL} = 10 \log_{10} (I/I_{ref})$$

where I is the intensity of the sound we're measuring and I_{ref} is the intensity of the quietest sound we can hear. Since intensity is related to the square of the amplitude, the ratio of intensities from the threshold of pain to the threshold of hearing is 1,000,000,000,000 (1 trillion) to 1. The dB formula for amplitudes is used when comparing amplitudes, pressures, and voltages, and the dB formula for intensity is used when comparing characteristics such as intensity and power.

Table 1.1 Sound sources and related sound pressure levels

Sound source	Sound pressure level
Rock music peak	150 dB
Jet engine at 30 meters away	140 dB
Threshold of pain	120 dB
Symphonic music peak	120–137 dB
Amplified rock music at 1–2 meters	105–120 dB
Subway train at 60 meters away	95 dB
Piano played loudly	92–95 dB
Train whistle at 150 meters away	90 dB
Telephone dial tone	80 dB
Chamber music in small auditorium	75–85 dB
Piano played at moderate levels	60–70 dB
Normal conversation at arm's length	45–55 dB
Whisper	30 dB
Threshold of hearing	0 dB

Source: Data from Sallows, 2001 and ASHA (American Speech-Language-Hearing Association), no date.

The following are some potentially useful results from these decibel formulas:

- A doubling of amplitude yields a change of 6 dB ($20 \log_{10} (2)$).
- Each additional doubling of amplitude results in 6 more dB.
- A doubling of intensity yields a change of 3 dB ($10 \log_{10} (2)$).
- Each additional doubling of amplitude results in 3 more dB.
- Halving the amplitude yields a change of −6 dB ($20 \log_{10} (0.5)$).
- Halving the intensity yields a change of −3 dB ($10 \log_{10} (0.5)$).
- Ten times the amplitude yields a change of 20 dB.
- Ten times the intensity yields a change of 10 dB.

It is important to note that decibels are used for many different kinds of measurement in music technology, so you have to know what is being compared to know just what the decibel value means. In the next chapter we'll use dB FS when discussing digital audio recording, and various kinds of decibels will be used in several other places in the book.

Even though decibels are very useful in expressing physical properties in more perceptually relevant ways, our perceptions of loudness differ somewhat from even these decibel calculations. For example, while a 3 dB increase represents a doubling of the intensity, a 10 dB increase (ten times the intensity) is perceived as a doubling of loudness. In practice 3 dB is about the smallest change that can be perceived, though in very quiet environments a change of 1 dB may be perceivable.

Pitch-Dependent Loudness

Up to this point we've been discussing pitch and loudness as if they were independent of one another. However, we are more sensitive to some frequencies than others, meaning that we may perceive one frequency at a particular dB SPL as being louder or softer than another frequency *at the same dB SPL*.

Figure 1.6 shows the so-called "equal-loudness contours" where the x-axis is frequency, the y-axis is dB SPL, and the curves represent our perceptions of equal loudness. Historically, equal-loudness contours have been referred to as "Fletcher–Munson curves" after the researchers who first conducted this type of research in the 1930s. If pitch/frequency and loudness were independent, the equal-loudness lines would be flat. Notice that the equal-loudness curves are labeled by the dB SPL level at which they intersect 1 kHz.

From this figure, you can see that we are most sensitive to frequencies between about 2 kHz and 5 kHz—in that range the equal-loudness curves dip down noticeably, indicating that it requires fewer dB SPL in that range of frequencies to sound as loud as it does at other places in the audible frequency range. To determine the dB SPL levels necessary for two frequencies to sound equally loud, you would identify the curve that intersects a given frequency and dB SPL point and follow the equal-loudness curve until it intersects with the other frequency of interest. For example, if you have a 1,000 Hz tone at 20 dB SPL, a 100 Hz tone would have to be almost 50 dB SPL to sound as loud.

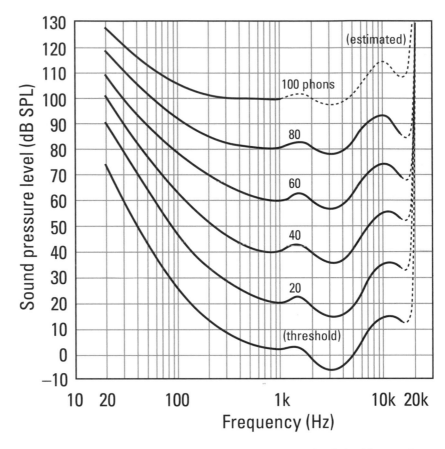

Figure 1.6 Equal-loudness contours (based on ISO 226:2003). The dashed lines indicate estimated values

Envelope and Articulation

The waveform amplitude discussed above is determined by looking at an individual cycle or a few cycles of a waveform, which corresponds to a very small timeframe. Just to take a few examples, the lowest frequency in the audible range, 20 Hz, has a period of 1/20, or 50 milliseconds (0.05 seconds); the 110 Hz A at the bottom of the bass clef staff has a period of 1/110, or about 9 ms (0.009 seconds); and the 440 Hz A (the tuning A) has a period of about 2.3 ms (0.0023 seconds). By comparison, the durations of an eighth note, a sixteenth note, and a thirty-second note at quarter-note equals 60 are:

(0.5 beats/60 beats per minute) * 60 seconds per minute = 0.5 seconds (500 ms)

(0.25 beats/60 beats per minute) * 60 seconds per minute = 0.25 seconds (250 ms)

(0.125 beats/60 beats per minute) * 60 seconds per minute = 0.125 seconds (125 ms)

As you can see, even the relatively fast thirty-second notes have a duration more than twice as long as the period of the lowest frequency we can hear as a pitch. As a result, to understand the way the amplitude of a sound wave changes over the course of a musical note, we must "zoom out" and look at timeframes quite a bit longer than the periods of individual waveform cycles. Once we zoom out, we can observe another of the important physical properties of a sound: the amplitude envelope (see Figure 1.7).

The shape of an **amplitude envelope** is determined by the way the amplitude of the sound changes over time, with this shape providing a container, or envelope, for the individual waveform cycles. We perceive this shape as the **articulation** of an individual note. While an arbitrary sound might have an envelope shape that changes very little over time, such as traffic noise, or changes constantly over time, such as machinery in a factory, musical sounds tend to fall into one of two categories: bowed/blown or struck/plucked.

Bowed or blown envelopes are characteristic of instruments that can sustain, such as bowed strings, brass, and woodwinds. Though these can also have a variety of shapes, a common model for bowed or blown envelopes is the **ADSR**—Attack, Decay, Sustain, Release—envelope (see Figure 1.8a). The amount of time represented by the attack segment of a bowed or blown envelope indicates how quickly an instrument goes from making no sound to the maximum volume for that note; the decay segment indicates a short fall-off from the maximum volume; the sustain level indicates how far the note falls in volume from its maximum; and the release time indicates how long it takes for the sound to finally fall away to nothing.

A loud, accented note would likely have a short attack time, whereas a soft, legato note would have a longer attack time. Similarly, a staccato note would have a short release time as the note is quickly stopped, whereas a legato note would likely have a longer release time. As you can see, the lengths of the various segments as well as the overall shape—bowed or blown here—are perceived as the note's **articulation**.

Struck or plucked envelopes are characteristic of instruments in which energy is put into the system through striking or plucking and then the sound is allowed to decay or release to nothing (see Figure 1.8b). Struck or plucked instruments include drums, cymbals, guitars, harps, pizzicato strings, and pianos. The notes of these

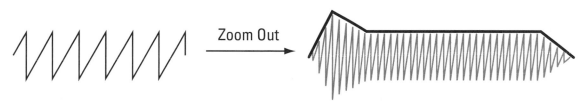

Figure 1.7 A "zoom out" from individual cycles of a waveform to see the amplitude envelope. Only the top of the envelope is usually shown because many waveforms are the same on the top and on the bottom. The frequency is extremely low—20 Hz—so you can still see the individual waveforms within the envelope

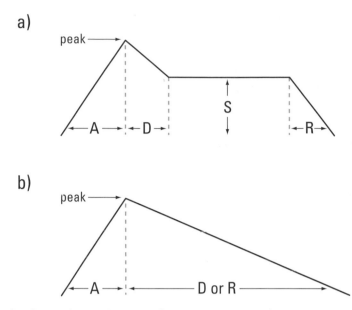

Figure 1.8 Amplitude envelopes: a) an Attack-Decay-Sustain-Release (ADSR) amplitude envelope characteristic of bowed or blown instruments; b) an Attack-Decay/Release amplitude envelope characteristic of struck or plucked instruments

instruments are not always allowed to simply die away: drums can be rolled, piano notes repeated or stopped, and guitars muted. Nevertheless, their natural amplitude envelope shape is struck or plucked. Instruments such as pianos and vibraphones have "sustain" pedals, but those pedals merely keep the sound from being damped right away; if left to ring, these sounds will decay or release to nothing, though they may do so relatively slowly.

The bowed/blown and struck/plucked models represent a substantial simplification from the complex amplitude behavior of most sound waves or of a sound wave comprised of many notes at once or in succession. Nevertheless, they provide useful models for amplitude shapes. When we discuss synthesis later in the book, you will see that these envelope models allow us to shape the amplitudes of synthesized notes to create simulations of natural amplitude shapes.

Waveform and Timbre

Zooming back in to look at individual cycles again, we can observe the physical property of the shape of the **waveform** itself. The perceptual property related to the waveform is **timbre**. Unfortunately, apart from a few standard waveforms that are seldom seen in real-world sounds, it is difficult to determine much about the timbre of a sound by looking at its waveform. One generalization that you can make is that the more sharp angles a waveform has the brighter its timbre is likely to be. This is a very approximate kind of measurement, subject to many other details, but it can be a useful rule of thumb. We can see this in practice by looking at the standard waveforms: sine, triangle, square, sawtooth, pink noise, and white noise (see Figure 1.9). These waveforms are standard by virtue of the fact that they served as the basis for patches in early synthesizers and are still found today in softsynths that mimic, or model, analog synths.

The **sine waveform** (see Figure 1.9a) is the simplest waveform, representing the smoothest possible transition from compression to rarefaction. The **triangle waveform** (see Figure 1.9b) is also relatively simple, but its sharp, 90-degree turn at the top and bottom indicate that it will have a brighter timbre than the sine wave. In practice, digital waveforms can't have such sharp angles because they will contain frequencies that can't be represented in a digital system. This will be discussed further in the next chapter under "Aliasing." We can think of these sharp-angled waveforms as ideals that digital synths will get as close to as possible.

The **square waveform** (see Figure 1.9c) has not one but two sharp 90-degree turns at the top and two at the bottom, yielding a timbre that is brighter still. Finally, the **sawtooth waveform** (see Figure 1.9d) has angles at the top and bottom that are more acute than 90-degrees, yielding a timbre that is the brightest of this group.

The noise waveforms are not really waveforms at all—in fact, noise is partially defined by its lack of a repeating pattern. Nevertheless, various types of noise are often used as sound sources for synthesis. **Pink noise** (see Figure 1.9e) is a relatively pleasant kind of noise where **white noise** (see Figure 1.9f) is fairly harsh. Both have more sharp turns than the other standard waveforms.

Thus far I have been using only the vague term "brightness" to distinguish between these waveforms. Because they are so central to analog-modeling synths it is useful to listen to them carefully by themselves and in musical contexts to learn and remember just what each waveform sounds like. After a little practice this is no more difficult than distinguishing between acoustic timbres such as a flute and a clarinet. To get a better understanding of timbre, we will turn to the overtone series and the spectrum view of sound.

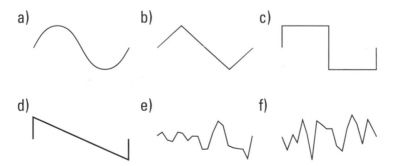

Figure 1.9 Standard waveforms: a) sine; b) triangle; c) square; d) sawtooth; e) pink noise; f) white noise

THE OVERTONE SERIES

When a note is played on an instrument, the rate at which the waveform repeats is the frequency that we perceive as the pitch. However, there are other frequencies present in the sound that are perceived not as pitch but as color, or timbre. The frequency heard as pitch is called the **fundamental frequency** and the other frequencies are referred to as overtones, harmonics, or partials.

The terms **overtones** and **harmonics** imply a specific relationship between those frequencies and the fundamental frequency—namely, that they are integer multiples of the fundamental. The term **partials**, on the other hand, doesn't specify any particular relationship between the frequencies present in the sound and the fundamental frequency is just considered the first partial. Partials is the preferred term because it is more general and allows for the possibility that the partials will not be related to a fundamental frequency.

A timbre whose partials are integer multiples of the fundamental frequency is said to be harmonic, and its partials follow the overtone series. Figure 1.10 shows the overtone series for a harmonic timbre with a fundamental frequency of 110 Hz. Each of the partials has a frequency equal to the partial number times the fundamental frequency. As a result, if the fundamental frequency is denoted by f, the overtones series based on f will consist of the partials f, $2f$, $3f$, $4f$, $5f$, $6f$, $7f$, etc.

Though the partials are shown in traditional music notation and their pitch is indicated in pitch-register notation with C4 as middle C, the overtone series is *not* an enormous chord but rather a set of frequencies that combine together to give a sense of pitch and timbre. The filled-in notes indicate a significant discrepancy between the

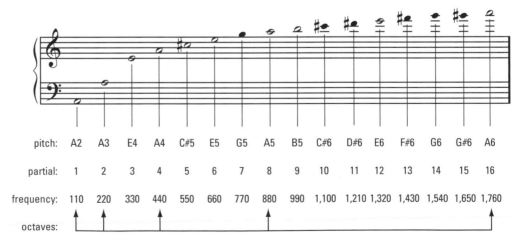

Figure 1.10   The first 16 partials of the overtone series built on A2

Source: from Holmes, 2008

frequency of that partial and the frequency associated with that note on a keyboard. Compare these frequencies to those of Figure 1.4.

Tuning and Temperament

The frequency ratios between "notes" in the overtone series produce "pure" intervals—intervals without any beating, or pulsing. As you can see from Figure 1.10, the frequency ratio between partials 2 and 1 is 2:1, as is the ratio between partials 4 and 2, 8 and 4, and 16 and 8—each is an octave. In fact, you can simply use the partial numbers themselves to generate the ratios for ideal (pure) intervals. The interval of a fifth, then, results from a frequency ratio of 3:2 (partial 3 to partial 2), a fourth from a frequency ratio of 4:3, a third from a ratio of 5:4, and a minor third from a ratio of 6:5.

The frequencies on the keyboard shown in Figure 1.4 differ somewhat from those calculated using ideal intervals because the tuning of a piano is "tempered" by tuning it away from the ideal intervals found in the overtone series. The reason for this tempering is that tuning to ideal intervals would work for a single key, but would fail as the music modulated to other keys. The intervals in increasingly distant keys would diverge significantly from the ideal frequency ratios to the point where they would be nearly unrecognizable.

To make the intervals the same in all keys, the system of **equal temperament** was developed, in which the ratio between each semitone is made to be identical. As a result, a fifth in any key consists of seven semitones of exactly the same size, yielding a ratio of 1.498:1 as opposed to the ideal 3:2 ratio or 1.5:1 (see the sidebar "Technically Speaking . . . equal-tempered ratios" on page 18); a fourth in any key has a ratio of 1.335: 1 as opposed to the ideal 4:3 or 1.333:1; a major third has a ratio of 1.26:1 as opposed to the ideal 5:4 or 1.25:1; and so on. Each type of interval on a piano, except for the octave, is slightly off from the ideal ratio, but each instance of a particular interval is off in exactly the same way, so they sound the same in any key.

To represent interval sizes that are larger or smaller than equal tempered intervals we divide the equal tempered semitone into 100 equal parts called **cents**. This division allows us to determine just how different the equal-tempered intervals are from the ideal intervals found in the overtone series. Table 1.2 shows several intervals along with their ideal ratios, their ideal size in cents, their equal-tempered ratios, their equal-tempered size in cents, and the "error" in cents introduced by equal temperament. See the sidebar "Technically Speaking . . . semitones and cents" on page 19 for the formula for calculating cents from an interval ratio.

Many composers over the years have developed an affinity for various tuning systems, such as Just Intonation, that seek to correct the errors introduced by equal temperament, and there are many tuning systems in use for keyboard instruments that are somewhat different from equal temperament. In addition, it is common even in nominally equal-tempered music for singers and instrumentalists to adjust their intonation on a chord-by-chord basis to come closer to the ideal ratios.

TECHNICALLY SPEAKING . . . EQUAL-TEMPERED RATIOS

Technically speaking . . . semitones in equal temperament are related by a single constant ratio, making each semitone on an equal-tempered keyboard the same perceptual size, which wasn't true before equal-tempered tuning. This means that the *ratio* between C# and D is the same as the *ratio* between C and C#. They will not be the same number of Hertz apart, but they will sound the same. If we represent this ratio by a, then the frequency of D would be a times the frequency of C#, and C# would be a times the frequency of C:

$$D = a \times C\sharp \text{ and } C\sharp = a \times C, \text{ so } D = a \times a \times C = a^2 \times C$$

Every semitone that we go up is an additional factor of a times the previous semitone's frequency. By the time we get to an octave, we've multiplied by a twelve times:

$$C4 = a^{12} \times C3$$

Since frequencies double every octave, we get:

$$C4 = 2 \times C3 = a^{12} \times C3,$$

so $2 = a^{12}$ meaning that $a = 2^{(1/12)}$, or the twelfth root of 2,

and $2^{(1/12)} \approx 1.0595$ (where $\approx$ means "is approximately equal to").

Every increase of a semitone in pitch, then, is a factor of $2^{(1/12)}$ times the frequency of the previous semitone. This results in different frequency ratios for musical intervals than those calculated from the overtone series. The advantage is that equal-tempered intervals are the same in every key.

To figure out the ratio for a given interval, you use the number of semitones in the interval with the following formula:

Interval ratio for n semitones $= 2^{(n/12)}$

For a perfect fifth, this would yield $2^{(7/12)}$, which is a ratio of 1.498:1. This is only a little bit different than the ideal ratio of 3:2, or 1.5:1. Other intervals lead to larger differences between ideal and equal-tempered ratios.

TECHNICALLY SPEAKING . . . SEMITONES AND CENTS

Technically speaking . . . we measure musical intervals smaller than a semitone in cents. In traditionally notated music, the smallest pitch step is the semitone. However, many kinds of music, such as the Blues, use pitches that are in between semitones ("blue" notes), and in synthesis it is sometimes desirable to detune an oscillator up or down from a particular semitone. In addition, composers using alternate tuning systems use cents to designate the size of the intervals they are using.

There are 100 cents to the equal-tempered semitone and 1,200 cents to the octave. Like semitones, all cents are the same perceptual size so that each successive change of one cent would be the same factor times the previous frequency. If some frequency f_1 is one cent higher than f_0, and f_2 is one cent higher than f_1 and two cents higher than f_0, then using c to represent the ratio for one cent:

$$f_2 = c \times f_1 \text{ and } f_1 = c \times f_0, \text{ then } f_2 = c \times c \times f_0 = c^2 \times f_0$$

Since there are 100 cents per semitone, you'd have to multiply 100 c's together to get the factor of a semitone, and 1,200 c's together to get an octave:

$$C\sharp = c^{100} \times C, \text{ so } C4 = c^{1200} \times C3$$

Using the familiar factor of 2 for an octave:

$$C4 = 2 \times C3 = c^{1200} \times C3,$$

$$\text{so } 2 = c^{1200} \text{ and } c = 2^{(1/1200)}, \text{ or the twelve-hundredth root of two}$$

$$\text{and } 2^{(1/1200)} \approx 1.00058$$

So if frequency f_n is n cents above frequency f_0, then:

$$f_n = f_0 \times 2^{(n/1200)}$$

This works just as well for negative cents (down in frequency) because a negative exponent indicates division by that factor, which is what you would expect in order to go down in frequency. To check this formula, you can use $n = 100$ for an increase of one semitone and you get the familiar ratio for equal-tempered semitones:

$$2^{(100/1200)} = 2^{(1/12)}, \text{ or the twelfth root of two}$$

To figure out how far apart two frequencies are in cents, you can rearrange the previous formula, apply the logarithm base 2, and use logarithm properties to solve for n:

$$n = 1200 \times \log_2 (f_n/f_0) = (1200/\log_{10} 2) \times \log_{10} (f_n/f_0)$$

$$n = 3986.3 \times \log_{10} (f_n/f_0)$$

You can test this by using the ratio of two for f_n and f_0 an octave apart and you should get $n = 1,200$ cents.

Technically Speaking

For two frequencies that are both in equal temperament, this formula will result in multiples of 100. We can also use this formula for two frequencies that are not in equal temperament to compare them to equal-tempered intervals. For example, the equal-tempered minor third (three semitones) is 300 cents in size, while the pure minor third from the overtone series has a ratio of 6:5 ($f_n/f_0 = 1.2$). Using the formula, we find that the minor third from the overtone series is about 315.64 cents in size. The equal-tempered minor third, then, is about 16 cents "flat" from the pure ratio found in the overtone series. The size of the smallest frequency change that we can detect is about 3.5 cents (about 0.2 percent) and varies up from there depending on both the frequency and the loudness of the sounds (Gelfand, 2010, p. 175).

Table 1.2 Equal-tempered and pure interval ratios

Interval	Ideal ratio	Ideal interval size	Equal-tempered ratio	Equal-tempered interval size	Equal-tempered "error"
Major Second	9:8 = 1.125:1	204	1.122:1	200	4 cents flat
Minor Third	6:5 = 1.2:1	316	1.189:1	300	16 cents flat
Major Third	5:4 = 1.25:1	386	1.26:1	400	14 cents sharp
Fourth	4:3 = 1.333:1	498	1.335:1	500	2 cents sharp
Fifth	3:2 = 1.5:1	702	1.498:1	700	2 cents flat
Minor Sixth	8:5 = 1.6:1	814	1.587:1	800	14 cents flat
Major Sixth	5:3 = 1.667:1	884	1.682:1	900	16 cents sharp
Major Seventh	15:8 = 1.875:1	1,088	1.888:1	1,100	12 cents sharp
Octave	2:1	1,200	2:1	1,200	None

THE SPECTRUM VIEW

While the overtone series shown in Figure 1.10 is useful for understanding the nature of timbre, it does little to tell us the exact frequencies for the partials or their amplitudes. In addition, many sounds are not harmonic and hence don't follow the overtone series. For these inharmonic sounds, the overtone series is irrelevant. To represent the partials present in a wide variety of sounds, we can use the spectrum view of sound.

The **spectrum view** plots frequency versus amplitude to show us the precise frequencies and their amplitudes that are present in a timbre. Figure 1.11 shows the spectrum for a trombone note with a fundamental of 110 Hz (A). Notice that the partials are harmonic—they follow the overtone series—and their amplitudes vary quite a bit. Figure 1.12 shows the spectrum for a bell whose partials are inharmonic and thus do not follow the overtone series. The dashed lines in Figure 1.12 show where the harmonic partials would be if they were present.

The spectra for the standard waveforms are shown in Figure 1.13. When we discussed them earlier in the chapter, we distinguished them on the basis of the "sharpness" of the angles in their waveforms, which corresponded to their "brightness." You can see in Figure 1.13 that a greater sharpness of the angles in the waveforms corresponds roughly to more energy in the upper partials, providing a more precise basis for the intuitive judgments made earlier in the chapter.

The sine wave has the simplest spectrum with just a single partial (see Figure 1.13a). As a result, the sine wave may appear a bit useless. However, in the more complex spectra discussed above and below, each partial can be thought of as a separate sine wave. Complex spectra, then, can be thought of as a sum of sine waves with the

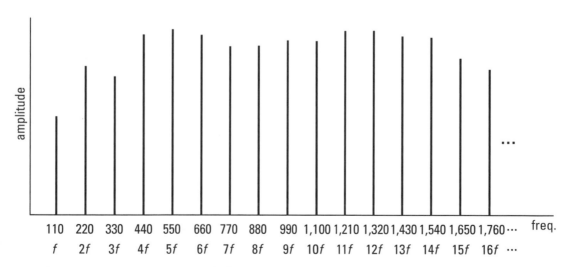

Figure 1.11   The spectrum view of sound with frequency on the *x*-axis and amplitude on the *y*-axis. The fundamental is A2 (110 Hz) and 16 total partials are shown, with the ellipses indicating that the partials continue. The relative amplitudes of the partials are based on a recording of a trombone

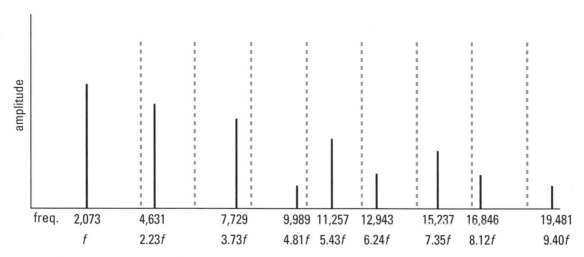

Figure 1.12 Inharmonic spectrum of a small bell. Note that the partials are not whole number multiples of the fundamental. Dashed lines indicate the positions of whole number multiples of the "fundamental"

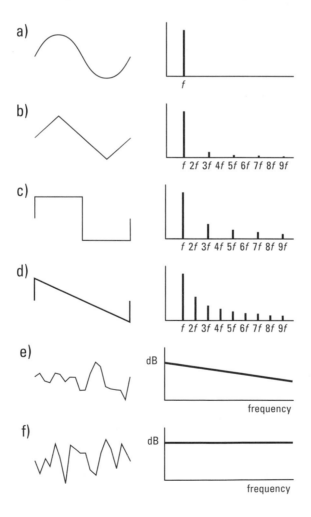

Figure 1.13 Standard waveforms and their spectra: a) sine wave; b) triangle wave; c) square wave; d) sawtooth wave; e) pink noise; f) white noise

appropriate frequencies and amplitudes. This is the heart of **Fourier's Theorem**, which states that any periodic waveform can be constructed by adding together sine waves with the appropriate frequencies, amplitudes, and phases (more on phase below). Fourier's Theorem gives rise to the concept of additive synthesis, in which an arbitrary spectrum can be constructed by adding together sine waves. Additive synthesis will be discussed later in the book in Chapter 7: Synthesis Techniques.

The triangle wave has only odd partials (1, 3, 5, etc.) and their relative amplitudes fall off as one over the square of the partial number (see Figure 1.13b). So, the relative amplitude for the third partial is $1/3^2$ or $1/9$, the relative amplitude for the fifth partial is $1/5^2$ or $1/25$, the relative amplitude for the seventh partial is $1/7^2$ or $1/49$, etc. This matches our aural judgment of the waveform as being only somewhat more complex than a sine wave because the amplitudes of the partials above the fundamental fall off so quickly.

The square wave also has only odd partials, but the amplitudes of those partials fall off as one over the partial number (see Figure 1.13c). So, the relative amplitude for the third partial is $1/3$, for the fifth partial $1/5$, etc. Since these partials fall off more slowly than the triangle wave, there is more energy in the upper partials, resulting in a brighter sound. The square wave also has a somewhat hollow quality due to the missing even partials and has a sound similar to a clarinet in its lowest register or a guitar that is plucked an octave above where it's fretted.

The sawtooth wave has both even and odd partials whose amplitudes fall off as one over the partial number (see Figure 1.13d). So the relative amplitude for the second partial is $1/2$, for the third $1/3$, for the fourth $1/4$, etc. It has all the partials of the square wave at the same relative amplitudes plus all of the even partials. The richness of the sawtooth spectrum is one of the reasons that it is such a common basic waveform for an analog-modeling synth patch.

The noise "waveforms" do not have spectra with clear partials—that's one of the reasons that they are noisy. Their spectra are best represented as distributions of energy across the spectrum. The pink noise distribution falls off as the frequencies go up because it has equal energy per octave (see Figure 1.13e). Since octaves get larger in absolute size as they go up in frequency, the amplitude of the energy in the pink noise spectrum has to fall off to keep the same amount of energy in each octave. The white noise distribution stays flat across the spectrum because it has equal energy per band of frequency (see Figure 1.13f). So it has the same energy between 100 and 200 Hz as between 1,000 and 1,100 Hz, whereas pink noise has the same energy between 100 and 200 Hz as between 1,000 and *2,000* Hz. Since we perceive equal frequency ratios, not equal frequency differences, as being the same, white noise sounds bright and harsh, where pink noise is more mellow.

Unlike simple synthetic waveforms, natural sounds change subtly in timbre over time. For example, most acoustically produced timbres get brighter as they get louder and darker as they get softer. In other words, the increase or decrease in energy in an acoustic system leads to an increase or decrease in the energy in the upper partials. This phenomenon is difficult to see in the spectrum view, which represents a timbre frozen in time. The **spectrogram** view graphs time (*x*-axis) versus frequency (*y*-axis) with the amplitudes of the frequencies shown as lighter or darker, or in different colors. Figure 1.14 shows the spectrogram view (also called the "sonogram" view) of a vocal utterance in which the pitch stays the same, but the vowels change. Notice that the spectrogram view shows how the upper partials change over time.

Phase

When discussing Fourier synthesis above, I mentioned the physical property of phase. **Phase** refers to the position in the waveform at which the waveform starts. Phases are often given in degrees with a phase shift of 360 degrees returning the waveform to its normal starting point. Phase may also be given in radians with 2π (2 times pi) radians returning the waveform to its normal starting point.

Figure 1.15a shows a sine wave starting conventionally with the amplitude at zero and then rising. This corresponds to an initial phase of 0 degrees. Figure 1.15b shows the sine wave starting with an amplitude of one and then falling. This corresponds to a phase difference of one-quarter of the waveform's period, or 90 degrees. You may notice that this is equivalent to a cosine wave. Figure 1.15c shows a sine wave starting with an amplitude of zero and then falling. This corresponds to a phase difference of one-half of the waveform's period or 180 degrees.

Phase becomes important when waveforms are combined together. For example, combining a sine wave at some frequency with a second sine wave at the same frequency but 180 degrees out of phase results in the two sine waves canceling each other out (**phase cancellation**) and no sound. In the discussion of the triangle wave spectrum above, we saw that the amplitudes of its partials (odd ones only) are proportional to one over the square of the partial number (1/1, 1/9, 1/25, 1/49, etc.). However, in

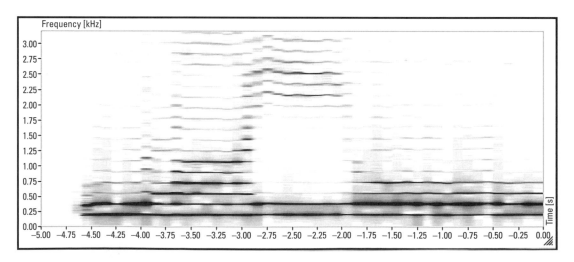

Figure 1.14 Spectrogram of a voice saying "oo-ah-ee-oh" on the same pitch. Time is shown horizontally, frequency vertically, and amplitude by the intensity of the line. All four vowels are shown left to right

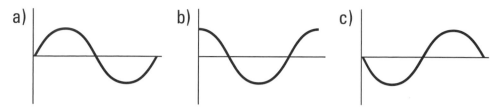

Figure 1.15 Different phases of a sine wave: a) starting phase of 0 degrees; b) 90-degree phase difference; c) 180-degree phase difference. a) and c) would cancel each other out if they were added together

addition, every other partial starting with the third is 180 degrees out of phase, a property often shown by a negative sign in front of the amplitude. The negative amplitude factor would cause a sine wave to start from zero amplitude and go downward first just as the sine wave in 1.15c that is 180 degrees out of phase with 1.15a. The proper amplitudes for the odd partials in a triangle wave then are 1, −1/9, 1/25, −1/49, 1/81, −1/121, etc.

Phase shows up in many instances in music technology. For example, filters affect not only the spectrum of the sound being processed, but also the relative phases of the partials in the sound. The property of "linear phase" in such sound processing is desirable to prevent problems due to phase cancellation or phase distortion. Phase also shows up in frequency modulation synthesis, which can generate partials with negative frequencies. These negative frequency partials act like positive frequencies that are 180 degrees out of phase and combine with partials of the same frequency, resulting in some amount of phase cancellation depending on the relative amplitudes of the partials in question. Phase changes can be an explicitly desirable phenomenon such as with a phaser effect. A phaser changes only the phases of the partials in the audio that it's processing, resulting in controllable phase cancellation when combined with the original signal that colors the sound in an interesting way.

SOUND PROPERTIES SUMMARY

The perceptual and physical properties discussed in this chapter are summarized briefly in Table 1.3.

Table 1.3   Perceptual and physical properties of sound

Perceptual properties	Physical properties
Pitch	Fundamental frequency
Loudness	Amplitude
Timbre	Waveform *and* spectrum
Articulation	Amplitude envelope

CHAPTER 2

Digital Audio

In the previous chapter, we explored the various physical and perceptual properties of sound. In this chapter, we'll look at the digital representation of sound. Digital audio that is imported from CDs, downloaded from the Internet, or generated by software instruments is already digital. However, recorded sound must first be digitized before it can be stored and manipulated in a DAW/Sequencer. To understand digital audio in all contexts, we will consider what is actually done to an audio signal when it is digitized. First, it is useful to consider the big picture and briefly discuss the audio recording path.

THE AUDIO RECORDING PATH

As we saw in the last chapter, sound is acoustic energy comprised of a series of compressions and rarefactions propagating through the air. Before it can be digitized it must be captured as an electrical signal, which involves the conversion of energy from one form to another—acoustical energy to electrical energy. The device that accomplishes this is a **transducer**. The transducer that converts sound into an electrical signal is a microphone. There are many books on recording that go into microphones in some detail. Since the focus of this book is on synthesized and sampled sound, we won't cover that here.

The microphone's analog electrical signal is carried to a pre-amp where the signal is made larger and then to an Analog to Digital Converter, or **ADC**. The pre-amp and ADC are standard parts of an audio interface to a computer, though in higher-end settings the pre-amp may be a separate box. When using USB microphones, these functions are all combined into the electronics of the microphone itself. When digital audio is played back from a computer it first runs through a Digital to Analog Converter, or **DAC**, at which point it becomes an analog audio signal that is amplified and converted back into acoustic energy by a speaker—another transducer. The DAC is also part of an audio interface, and the amplifier and speakers may be combined together into powered monitors. Figure 2.1 shows this audio recording path.

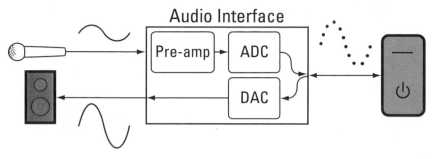

Figure 2.1 The audio recording path. The speaker shown is a powered monitor

SAMPLING AUDIO

When an analog audio signal reaches an ADC, the ADC's job is to convert that audio into digital audio through sampling and amplitude quantizing. **Sampling** involves measuring the amplitude of the incoming analog waveform at a regular rate called the **sampling rate** (see Figure 2.2). The sampling rate for CD-quality digital audio is 44,100 samples per second, or Hertz. Other common sampling rates include 48 kHz, 88.2 kHz, 96 kHz, and 192 kHz. The standard sampling rate for video applications is 48 kHz and 96 kHz is commonly used in recording studios. The inverse of the sampling rate is referred to as the **sampling period**, which is about 0.023 milliseconds (0.000023 seconds) for a 44.1 kHz sampling rate. By comparison, the period of the highest frequency that we can hear, 20 kHz, is about 0.05 ms (0.00005 seconds), about twice as long.

Measuring only some amplitude points of a continuous signal means that many more points are not being measured—in fact, theoretically, an infinite number of points are being ignored. Naturally, ignoring an infinite number of amplitude points must have some consequences for the digital signal. The limitation placed on a digital signal by the finite (not infinite) sampling rate is that the digital signal can only properly represent

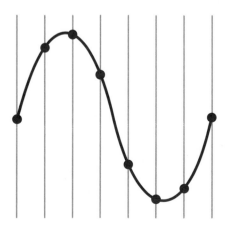

Figure 2.2 A waveform sampled in time. The distance between the vertical grid lines is determined by the sampling rate. The higher the rate, the closer the grid lines are together

frequencies up to half of the sampling rate. This limiting frequency is called the **Nyquist frequency**. For CD-quality digital audio:

Nyquist frequency = 0.5 * 44,100 Hz = 22,050 Hz

Fortunately, the top of our hearing range is 20,000 Hz, which is below the Nyquist frequency, so all of the frequencies that we can hear are properly represented in CD-quality digital audio.

Aliasing

If we try to record frequencies above the Nyquist frequency, the audio interface will filter them out before they reach the ADC. However, it is possible to synthesize digital audio in software such that it has partials above the Nyquist frequency. In that case **aliasing**—also called **foldover**—occurs, in which the frequencies above the Nyquist frequency are mirrored to "alias" frequencies below the Nyquist frequency. If those partials are harmonic, their alias frequencies will probably not be and may then conflict with harmonic partials below the Nyquist frequency causing harmonic distortion. If a frequency, f_{over}, is above the Nyquist frequency, NF, then its alias frequency, f_{alias}, would be mirrored below the Nyquist frequency by as much as f_{over} was above the Nyquist frequency:

$$f_{alias} = NF - (f_{over} - NF) = 2NF - f_{over}$$

If the Nyquist frequency was 22,050 Hz and f_{over} was 25,050 Hz, then f_{alias} would be $(2\star22,050) - 25,050 = 19,050$ Hz. Figure 2.3 shows a harmonic spectrum with partials that alias and may clash with legitimate, non-aliased harmonic partials.

Another way to think about aliasing is that it is the DAC's job to reconstruct an analog waveform from digital samples. If it doesn't have enough samples of a waveform

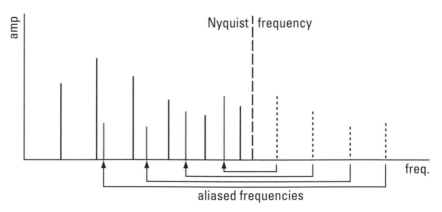

Figure 2.3 A spectrum with aliasing frequencies. Dotted lines above the Nyquist frequency indicate the original frequencies and gray lines below the Nyquist frequency indicate aliased frequencies

then it can't properly reconstruct it. Figure 2.4a shows a sine wave at a frequency above the Nyquist frequency with dots representing the samples. When that digital sine wave is converted to an analog signal by the DAC, it is reconstructed into the sine wave in Figure 2.4b, which is the simpler path through those samples. One interpretation of the sampling theorem, which gives rise to the Nyquist frequency, is that you must have at least two samples for every period of a frequency in order to properly represent that frequency in a digital audio signal. As a result, you must sample a waveform at twice the rate of the highest frequency, which is equivalent to the Nyquist frequency limitation.

When discussing waveforms in the last chapter, I mentioned that digital waveforms can't actually have such sharp angles as are usually shown for them. Perfectly sharp angles in a waveform effectively require an infinite number of partials. Since any partials above the Nyquist frequency would be aliased, digital waveforms are limited to the number of partials that would not alias given likely fundamental frequencies. Waveforms that don't alias are referred to as **band-limited waveforms** because their bandwidth does not exceed the limits of the digital system. Figure 2.5 shows a band-limited version of a square wave.

One of the possible advantages of higher sampling rates is that there would be less chance of aliasing for synthesized sounds. As mentioned above, audio interfaces filter out any frequencies above the Nyquist frequency when recording, so there won't be any aliasing in that recording even at lower sampling rates. Another argument in favor of higher sampling rates is that the anti-alias filtering can be done at frequencies far out of the range of human hearing. For the CD-quality 44.1 kHz sampling rate, simple

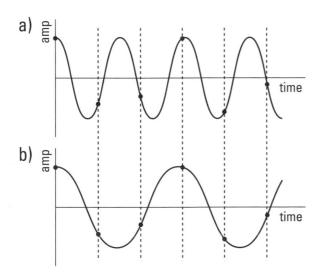

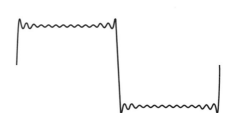

Figure 2.4 Aliasing: a) original waveform with frequency above the Nyquist frequency—dots and dotted lines indicate samples; b) aliased waveform

Figure 2.5 Band-limited square waveform lacking sharp corners. Its spectrum stops at the 25th partial, so it won't alias at 44.1 kHz, unless the fundamental is above 880 Hz (A5)

anti-alias filtering would be done at least partially in the very upper reaches of the hearing range because filters cannot suddenly cut off frequencies without affecting the timbre dramatically. However, this particular issue can also be taken care of through common techniques such as oversampling.

QUANTIZING AUDIO

When the ADC measures the amplitude of the incoming analog waveform in each sampling period, it must assign a single amplitude value to that sample (see Figure 2.6). This process is referred to as amplitude **quantizing** (the term "quantizing" is also used to mean something very different in the context of MIDI sequencing). In order to assign an amplitude value to a sample, it must have a pool of amplitude values to choose from. Since these values will be stored digitally, the pool of amplitude values is specified as some number of binary digits, or bits. The number of bits used for each sample is referred to as the **sample resolution**, also called bit depth or sample width. The related term **bitrate** is the sampling rate times the resolution.

The CD-quality standard resolution is 16 bits, which allows for 2^{16}, or 65,536, different amplitude values. The current standard for recording is 24 bits, which allows for 2^{24}, or 16,777,216, different amplitude values. Even at the higher 24-bit resolution, there will always be some error in the quantizing in which the actual amplitude value falls in between the possible integers. This is similar to the issue of a finite sampling rate ignoring an infinite number of possible samples in between each sample. Here, an infinite number of amplitude values are ignored between each amplitude value available for the given resolution. The consequence of ignoring all the in-between amplitude values is that there is a small regular amount of error that shows up as very low-level noise, referred to as **quantization noise**.

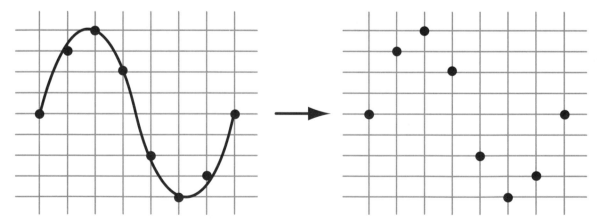

Figure 2.6 A waveform sampled in time *and* quantized in amplitude. The distance between the horizontal grid lines is determined by the sample resolution. The actual amplitude of the waveform and the number assigned by the ADC may be slightly different as shown in the figure

One of the advantages of a larger resolution, such as 24 bits, is that the signal can be much farther above the error than is the case with smaller resolutions. The **signal-to-error ratio** is approximately:

S-to-E ratio in dB = 6.02n + 1.76, where n is the number of bits being used

When the signal is at a maximum, n is equal to the number of bits of resolution—16 or 24—and this equals the overall dynamic range of the digital system. That would yield an ideal dynamic range of about 98 dB for 16-bit systems and about 146 dB for 24-bit systems. When fewer bits are being used—when the signal is smaller—the signal is closer to the error noise. If the amplitude of the signal were one-sixteenth of the maximum, you would be using 12 bits in a 16-bit system yielding a signal-to-error ratio of 74 dB, or 20 bits in a 24-bit system yielding a signal-to-error ratio of 122 dB. With 24 bits instead of 16 bits, you can have a quieter signal whose level is still farther above the level of the quantization noise.

It is common to record audio at 24 bits and later reduce it to 16 bits for release on CD or other distribution medium. However, when you go from 24 to 16 bits you introduce quantization error into the signal that is now closer to the signal levels in 16 bits than it was in at 24 bits. In addition, this quantization error may be correlated to the signal itself, resulting in quantization noise that changes as the signal changes. Changing noise is more likely to be heard than a steady low-level noise that is unrelated to the signal. As a result, when going from 24 to 16 bits, you would use **dither**, a steady low-level noise that masks the correlated quantization noise. When executing this conversion in a DAW/Sequencer, dither is usually provided as an option and is useful in most cases to prevent quantization noise from being distracting in the final mix.

DIGITAL SIGNAL LEVELS

Sample resolution also has an effect on recording and output levels. When you record in a DAW/Sequencer, you use the gain knobs and possibly pad switches on your audio interface to control the level of the analog signal going into the ADC. If the analog signal is too large, the ADC will **clip** the signal, resulting in a flat top or bottom on what was originally a more rounded waveform (see Figure 2.7). This results in unpleasant and almost always unwanted digital distortion. The same problem can occur at the output of the DAW/Sequencer when many tracks may be processed and mixed together.

Recording Levels

To avoid clipping while recording you use the gain knobs on the audio interface to set the incoming levels to an average operating level that may vary depending on whether you're recording at 16 or 24 bits. Levels in a digital system are given in **dB FS**, for decibels full scale. The formula for dB FS is related to the decibel formula for amplitude

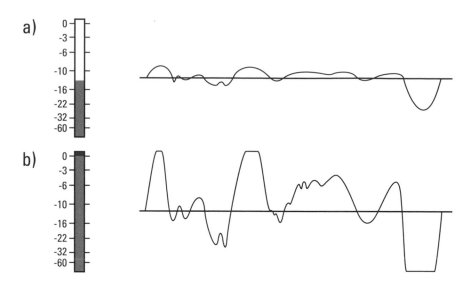

Figure 2.7   Two recording levels and the resultant waveforms: a) good level and clean waveform; b) distorted level and clipped waveform

given in the previous chapter and relates the digital amplitude level of the signal being recorded to the maximum amplitude level available in the system:

$$\text{dB FS} = 20 \log_{10} (A_{sig}/A_{max})$$

where A_{sig} is the amplitude of the signal you're monitoring and A_{max} is the maximum amplitude value available in the system—32,768 for 16 bits and 8,388,608 for 24 bits. These are half of the total amplitude values because they represent the amplitude of a bipolar waveform that goes above *and* below zero. When $A_{sig} = A_{max}$, the dB FS level will be $20 \log_{10} (1)$, which is equal to 0 dB FS. Levels above 0 dB FS result in clipping at the input and the output. Since the logarithm of a number less than one ($A_{sig} < A_{max}$) is negative, the signal level should always be a negative dB FS value.

There is no universal standard for average dB FS recording levels, but common ones include −12, −18, and −20. There is a tradeoff here between the distance from the operating level up to the point of clipping and the distance from the operating level down to the error noise. Lower operating levels give you more **headroom** before you clip, enabling you to tolerate more sudden spikes in the sound being recorded, but the lower levels bring your signals closer to the noise. Recording at 24-bit gives you a distinct advantage here because you can record at a lower operating level, such as −18 dB FS, and still have your signal significantly above the error noise. Recording at 16-bit would suggest an operating level of something more like −12 dB.

Mixing Levels and Output Levels

Just as you must take care not to exceed 0 dB FS while recording, you must also avoid exceeding 0 dB FS at the output. However, after the audio has been digitized/recorded (A to D) and before the signal is sent out to the audio interface (D to A), most DAW/Sequencers process and mix audio in a higher resolution 32-bit floating-point format. The advantage to a floating-point representation is that it has a much wider dynamic range. As a result, it's virtually impossible for a signal on a DAW/Sequencer track to clip while it's being processed or mixed. It's only at the output that the signal must be constrained to be below 0 dB FS.

It's possible, then, to have every audio and instrument track in your DAW/Sequencer showing clipping and still have a good output signal as long as the fader on the output bus is set low enough to bring this signal below the 0 dB FS mark. This extreme situation could result in an output fader that is set for a great deal of gain reduction, such as −40 dB or more. In practice, it is probably better to keep individual tracks below the point of clipping so that the meters can provide useful information—a constantly peaked track meter can't tell you much about variations in the signal level for that track.

AUDIO FILE FORMATS

Once audio has been digitized, it must be stored on the computer in some file format that determines what information is in the file and how that information is organized. Broadly speaking there are two types of digital audio file formats: uncompressed and compressed.

Uncompressed Audio Files

In **uncompressed audio files** digital audio samples are stored as a series of 16- or 24-bit integers or 32-bit floating-point numbers. Information is embedded in the file that specifies the sampling rate, the resolution, the number of channels (e.g. two channels for stereo), and the length of the file. Some file formats also include data such a loop points for use by samplers. DAW/Sequencers record, mix, and process using uncompressed audio files, though they may import and export compressed files.

The two most prominent uncompressed audio file formats are AIFF (.aif) and WAVE (.wav). The Broadcast WAVE format, a variant on the WAVE format, is the default file type for many DAW/Sequencers. Apple Core Audio format (.caf) and Windows Media Audio format (.wma) support both compressed and uncompressed audio. Each of the above file formats supports the full range of sample rates and resolutions. Uncompressed files are also referred to as **PCM** (Pulse Code Modulation) files in reference to the way that the audio is digitized.

The size of an uncompressed file can be calculated from its sampling rate and resolution along with a few conversions. The file size for a CD-quality digital audio file can be calculated as follows:

44,100 samples/second × 2 bytes per sample = 88,200 bytes/second

88,200 bytes/sec × 1 KB/1,024 bytes × 1 MB/1,024 KB × 60 sec/min
= 5.05 MB/min × 2 channels (stereo) = 10.1 MB/min

The file size for 96 kHz, 24-bit is:

96,000 samples/second × 3 bytes per sample = 288,000 bytes/second

288,000 bytes/second × 1 kB/1,024 bytes × 1 MB/1,024 kB × 60 sec/minute
= 16.5 MB/minute × 2 channels (stereo) = 33 MB/minute

You can obtain the sizes for mono files by skipping the last multiplication by 2 in each calculation and the sizes for surround sound files by multiplying by the number of overall channels in the last step instead of 2.

It is also useful to know the bitrates of uncompressed audio to compare to the bitrates of compressed audio. For 44.1 kHz, 16-bit audio, the bitrate is $44,100 \times 16 \times 2$ channels = 1.4 Mbps (Megabits per second), and for 96 kHz, 24-bit audio, the bitrate is $96,000 \times 24 \times 2$ channels = 4.6 Mbps.

Compressed Audio Files

The audio in compressed file formats has been processed in such a way so as to reduce the overall data size. The simplest reduction method would be to reduce the sampling rate and/or the resolution. Unfortunately, this results in poor quality audio. There are two basic types of compression: lossy and lossless.

In **lossy compression**, some data is removed permanently in order to reduce the data size. The difference between lossy compression and simply reducing the sampling rate and resolution is that lossy compression algorithms use perceptual encoding techniques to eliminate only the audio that is not perceptually significant. That is, lossy compression gets rid of audio we can't hear or audio that's not very prominent. Lossy compression has been successful enough that it has become one of the dominant ways that music is delivered, though it is not without its detractors.

Lossy compressed files are usually characterized by the bitrate of the resultant file. Common bitrates include 128 kbps (kilobits per second) and 256 kbps with file sizes of approximately 1 MB/minute and 2 MB/minute respectively. This represents an 80–90 percent reduction in file size with generally acceptable sonic results.

The most famous lossy compression is MP3 (.mp3), but there are several file formats that support lossy compression:

- MP4 format (.mp4, .m4a) supports AAC (Advanced Audio Coding) compression.
- Apple Core Audio Format (.caf) supports AAC and MP3 compression.
- Windows Media Audio format (.wma) supports lossy compression.
- Ogg format (.ogg, .oga) supports Vorbis compression.

In **lossless compression**, no data is permanently removed; the audio data is just packed more cleverly to save space. Unlike lossy compression, *all* of the original information in the audio file is preserved, leading to no loss at all of audio quality. The drawback to lossless compression is that the data reduction is only about 50 percent, though it varies quite a bit depending on the actual material being compressed.

File formats that support lossless compression include the following:

- MP4 format (.mp4, .m4a) supports Apple Lossless Audio Codec (ALAC).
- Apple Core Audio Format (.caf) supports Apple Lossless Audio Codec (ALAC).
- Windows Media Audio format (.wma) supports Windows Media Audio Lossless compression.
- Ogg format (.ogg, .oga) supports the Free Lossless Audio Codec (FLAC).

You may notice that there are several audio file formats that support uncompressed, losslessly compressed, and lossy compressed files, including CAF, WMA, and Ogg. These formats are referred to as **container formats** that act as wrappers for a variety of digital audio encodings.

Loop File Formats

In addition to the file formats discussed above, there are several file formats for loops. Loops can be run-of-the-mill AIFF or WAVE files, or one of the specialized loop formats such as Acid Loops, Apple Loops, or REX files. A loop that is stored as a simple AIFF or WAVE file is not technically any different than any other AIFF or WAV file. These files are only distinguishable from other AIFF or WAVE files in that they are designed to be repeated as a "loop" and are usually an integral number of bars long, such as 2 or 4 bars.

The specialized loop formats are a bit different. They are proprietary in that a single company controls each format—Sony controls the Acid Loop format, Apple controls the Apple Loop format, Propellerhead Software controls the REX format—and they contain special data for use by the music creation software. Despite the proprietary control, these loop formats can be used in a variety of applications.

Both **Acid Loops** and audio **Apple Loops** are regular uncompressed audio files, WAVE and CAF respectively, that include extra information, referred to as **metadata**, that contains the location of attacks, or transients within the audio file. This information allows software to identify virtual slices of the audio file that can be made to line up with the bars and beats of a project, even if the project tempo is different than the original loop tempo. This is accomplished by automatically stretching or compressing the audio so that the beats of the loop line up with the project timeline. The software maintains this alignment even when the tempo is later adjusted by again stretching or compressing the audio.

Acid Loops were originally designed to be used with the Acid software, but can be used in other pieces of software as well. When WAVE files are turned into Acid Loops, they are referred to as "Acidized" WAVE files. Apple Loops are supported primarily by Apple software: GarageBand, Logic, and Soundtrack Pro.

There are also special Apple Loops called Software Instrument Apple Loops (SIALs). These loops consist of MIDI data coupled with software instrument and channel strip information. When used in Apple software, the MIDI data just becomes a region on an instrument track assigned to the specified software instrument. These loops are limited to Apple software, but they are very powerful and flexible and don't suffer from any of the time stretching or time compression artifacts that audio loops do.

REX files are a bit different than Acid or Apple Loops. A REX file starts as a regular file format (AIFF, WAVE, etc.), but is then processed using Propellerhead Software's ReCycle. When REX files are played back, instead of stretching or compressing the audio in between the transient markers, the slices are treated independently. When the project tempo is slower than the original loop tempo, the slices are pulled farther apart, and when the project tempo is faster than the original loop tempo, the slices are further overlapped. There is some overlap built into the slices, so the slices aren't separated by silence until the tempo is slowed down by quite a bit. When REX files are played back in Propellerhead's Reason software, MIDI information is generated to trigger each of the slices. As a result, the slices can be reordered or reconfigured in Reason into an entirely new loop just by manipulating the MIDI messages.

Figure 2.8 shows the same loop as a WAVE file and as a REX file before and after a tempo change. In both a) and b), the WAVE file is on the top and the REX file is on the bottom. In Figure 2.8a, the project tempo is the same as the original loop tempo

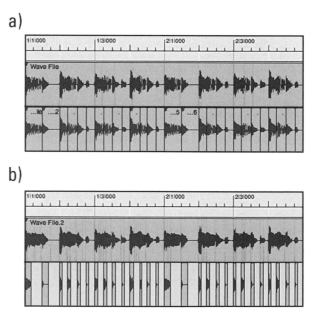

Figure 2.8 The same loop as a WAVE file and a REX file: a) project tempo is same as original loop tempo; b) project tempo is 1/3 of original loop tempo

and both loops sound fine. The REX file sounds continuous even though it is separated into slices, because the slices are slightly overlapped. In Figure 2.8b, the project tempo has been reduced to about 1/3 of the original loop tempo. The WAVE file is still continuous, but because it has been stretched so much, the sound quality is severely degraded. In the REX file, each slice is unchanged in length so the slices are separated by silence. Each slice sounds good by itself, but the slices together sound unnatural because of the silence between them. For both file types, extreme changes of tempo result in sound problems.

Now that we've covered the basic principles of sound and digital audio necessary to the study of sound creation through synthesis and sampling, we turn to the DAW/Sequencer environment and an overview of MIDI, MIDI sequencing, and software instruments.

CHAPTER 3

MIDI, Sequencing, and Software Instruments Overview

In a DAW/Sequencer environment, audio produced by a software instrument is triggered and controlled by MIDI messages either stored in a MIDI/instrument track or coming directly from a MIDI controller. The starting point for synthesized and sampled audio, then, is the MIDI (Musical Instrument Digital Interface) specification.

The MIDI spec (pronounced like "speck") describes how musical controllers, such as keyboards, can be connected to each other and to computers, and how the notes and other information from those controllers are encoded as messages and communicated through these connections. In a DAW/Sequencer, these messages are stored in a MIDI track where they can be edited, combined with other MIDI messages, and played back along with other MIDI and audio tracks. This is, of course, the act of MIDI sequencing.

When a sequence is played back, the MIDI notes and other messages are sent to software or hardware synths and samplers that use those messages to create audio. From there, this audio can be processed and mixed just like recorded or imported audio. So, while MIDI is itself not audio, it is essential to the generation of synthesized audio. Figure 3.1 illustrates this path from a MIDI controller to audio output.

The MIDI specification was developed in the early 1980s as a way for digitally controlled synthesizers to pass notes and other information to each other and to and from digital sequencers and personal computers (microcomputers). Digital synths, personal computers, and MIDI formed the basis of the composing workstation during much of the 1980s. The MIDI sequencing software developed in the 1980s to control

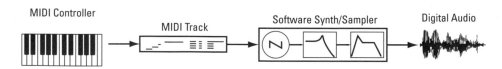

Figure 3.1 The data path from MIDI controller to DAW/Sequencer MIDI track to software instrument to digital audio

hardware synthesizers and samplers from a computer was expanded in the 1990s to include digital audio recording, editing, and processing, and in the 2000s to include software synthesizers and samplers. This software has become our modern DAW/Sequencer. The most prominent exception to this line of software evolution is Pro Tools, which started as audio recording and editing software in the 1980s and then expanded in the 1990s and 2000s to include MIDI and software instruments.

There are a few alternatives to MIDI, the most prominent of which is Open Sound Control (OSC). However, protocols such as OSC are not as universally supported as MIDI and are used most often in experimental settings with such synthesis software as Max/MSP, Pd, and Reaktor. Even when using non-instrument controllers such as Wii remotes or game pads to control synthesizers and samplers, the data from those controllers is often, though by no means always, converted to MIDI first.

Before delving in the details of the sound producing and sound modifying elements in samplers and synthesizers, I will first provide an overview of the basic concepts behind MIDI hardware, MIDI messages, MIDI sequencing, and the relationship between DAW/Sequencers and software synths and samplers. I've kept the discussion of MIDI relatively brief here because many students are already familiar with at least some MIDI hardware, such as keyboard controllers, and some MIDI sequencing including using virtual instruments. Naturally, there is much more to be said on these topics, but this overview will cover the essential ground. I will discuss MIDI messages more extensively in Chapter 9: MIDI in Detail.

MIDI HARDWARE

The MIDI specification can be divided into two parts: hardware and messages. The hardware side of MIDI includes standard cables, ports, computer interfaces, and such MIDI devices as controllers, modules, keyboard synthesizers, and workstations.

Controllers, Modules, and Keyboard Synthesizers

Most of the MIDI-compatible devices available can be categorized as controllers, modules, or keyboard synthesizers.

A **controller** is a device that can *only* send MIDI messages when its keys are played and can't generate any sound of its own. With the migration of sound generation from hardware synthesizers and samplers to software synthesizers and samplers, a large market has developed for keyboard controllers, many with knobs and sliders for manipulating the parameters of software synthesizers. To match the portability of laptops, many of these keyboards are quite small, with only two octaves or so of keys.

A **module** is a device that can generate sound when it receives MIDI messages but has no keys to play, and hence can't output MIDI messages. A module is usually designed as a rectangular box that can be installed in a rack for convenience in a studio or stage setting. Calling a device a "module" doesn't say anything about how it goes about producing sound; these devices can use any of the sound generation methods discussed in the next several chapters.

The term **keyboard synthesizer** is ambiguous, but for the purposes of this discussion, it refers to a device that can both send MIDI messages when its keys are played and generate sound when it receives MIDI messages. A keyboard synthesizer can be thought of as a controller and a module combined together. It's worth noting that in this context "synthesizer" simply refers to an electronic sound-producing device and does not refer to the specific method by which the sound is generated; in fact, most keyboard "synthesizers" use samples as the basis for their sounds.

While "module" always refers to a rectangular box that generates sounds, "controller" can also mean the device that is the primary means of MIDI input to the computer. For example, if you have a keyboard synthesizer attached to your computer, you could say that it is your "controller," even though it also generates sound.

Workstations

Some keyboard synthesizers have additional features that elevate them to the level of a **workstation**. In addition to sending MIDI messages and producing sound, a keyboard workstation might include an onboard MIDI sequencer, multiple audio effects, and the ability to record digital audio samples or even entire tracks. It is important to note that the audio recording capacity available in keyboard workstations is more limited than that of a computer-based DAW.

With the combination of sequencing, sound-generation capability, effects, and perhaps sound recording and playback, the keyboard workstation can be an all-in-one solution for creating and performing music. In a home setting or a project studio setting, a computer would generally be used for MIDI sequencing, audio processing, and audio recording. However, in a live setting keyboard workstations offer an alternative to using a computer onstage. In addition, a keyboard performer may find a workstation to be more easily triggered and controlled than a live computer rig.

There are other hardware workstations that are not keyboard based, but instead use drum pads as their primary interface. The most famous example of this is the Akai MPC, which has been a staple of hip-hop production for many years. The drum pads are used to trigger sampled sounds, and the order in which the pads are pressed is stored within the device as part of a MIDI sequence. A device such as an MPC can be used as a standalone workstation or in conjunction with a keyboard synthesizer, keyboard workstation, or computer.

Because workstations generally include a self-contained sequencer, they have their own clock. When used by themselves, this is fine, but when they are integrated into a computer-based project studio or with other devices that have their own clocks, some method of synchronization between the clocks is needed. Chapter 9: MIDI in Detail introduces some MIDI messages that can be used for this purpose, including MIDI Timing Clock and MIDI Time Code.

Basic MIDI Connections: Ports and Cables

For most of the history of MIDI, messages were transmitted from synth to synth or computer to synth only through MIDI cables that were connected to MIDI ports on the devices and to computer interfaces. Though most modern MIDI devices continue to have MIDI ports for this purpose, most of them also have standard USB ports as well. Thus you can connect most MIDI devices to your computer the same way you connect a printer.

The evolution from MIDI ports, cables, and computer interfaces to standard USB connectors is well under way, but there are still many slightly older devices that don't have USB ports, and USB is still used primarily for device-to-computer connections rather than device-to-device connections. As a result, though it is decidedly "old school," it is still essential to understand MIDI ports, cables, and computer interfaces.

The MIDI spec requires a particular connector (a five-pin "DIN") for the cables and the jacks on a MIDI-compatible device, which means that the connection hardware is independent of manufacturer—there is no "Yamaha MIDI cable" or "Korg MIDI jack." The jacks on a MIDI-compatible device have different functions and are referred to as ports. The three standard ports are In, Out, and Thru (see Figure 3.2).

The **In Port** on a MIDI device receives MIDI messages from other devices such as controllers, keyboard synthesizers, and computer interfaces. The **Out Port** on a MIDI device outputs the messages that are generated by that device. Controllers, keyboard synthesizers, and computer interfaces send primarily note messages, expressive messages, and program (patch) messages out of this port, though they can also send system messages. Modules also have Out Ports for sending configuration data in the form of system messages.

If you want to use one keyboard to control a second keyboard or module, you would connect a MIDI cable from the Out Port of Keyboard One (the master) to the In Port of Keyboard Two (the slave; see Figure 3.3). Unlike most computer cables, MIDI cables are uni-directional instead of bi-directional, so you need separate cables for MIDI input and output. To avoid confusion when setting up MIDI connections, simply remember that Out Ports always connect to In Ports.

The third common MIDI port, the **Thru Port** allows one keyboard to send messages to two or more other keyboards by **daisychaining** them together. If you want to play

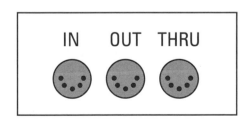

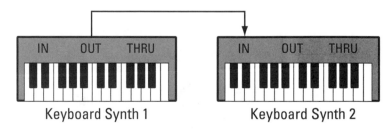

Figure 3.2 In, Out, and Thru MIDI ports found on most MIDI devices

Figure 3.3 MIDI connection that allows messages to flow from Keyboard Synth 1 (master) to Keyboard Synth 2 (slave)

Keyboard One and have the messages sent to Keyboard Two *and* to Keyboard Three, you would first connect the Out Port of Keyboard One to the In Port of Keyboard Two and then the Thru port of Keyboard Two to the In Port of Keyboard Three (see Figure 3.4). The Thru Port of Keyboard Three could then be connected to the In Port of another device and so on. To keep the function of the Thru Port straight, just remember: "whatever comes in goes thru."

This was a particularly important practice in the early days of MIDI when daisy-chaining was the only way to control multiple MIDI synths from one synth or a computer. It is not often used in a modern project studio.

So far, we've only discussed connecting synthesizers together, but a computer is usually a central element in a MIDI network.

Computer Connections

Computers do not have MIDI jacks on them, so either the synth must be able to connect to a computer through a standard USB cable or a special interface must be used. As mentioned above, most controllers and many modules and keyboard synthesizers can connect to the computer directly through a USB cable. This arrangement is simple and is particularly useful for mobile music creation using a laptop and a small keyboard controller.

For MIDI devices that cannot connect to a computer via USB, a **MIDI interface** with standard MIDI jacks is needed. The simplest of these interfaces connects to the computer via a USB cable and has one MIDI In Port and one MIDI Out Port. To connect a controller or keyboard synth such that messages generated by the keyboard reach the computer, you would connect a cable from the Out Port of the controller or keyboard synth to the In Port of the interface. To connect a keyboard synth or module such that it receives MIDI messages sent from the computer, you would connect a cable from the Out Port of the MIDI interface to the In Port of the keyboard synth or module.

Figure 3.5 shows a single keyboard synth attached to a computer through an external MIDI interface. Since the audio is being generated outside of the computer by the keyboard synth, the audio outputs of the synth needs to be routed back to the computer through an audio interface. This way the audio from the keyboard synth can be treated

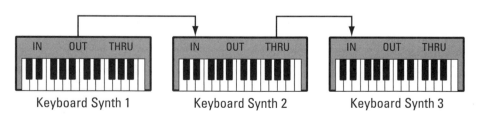

Figure 3.4 Daisychained MIDI connections that allow messages to flow from Keyboard Synth 1 (master) to Keyboard Synth 2 (slave) and Keyboard Synth 3 (slave)

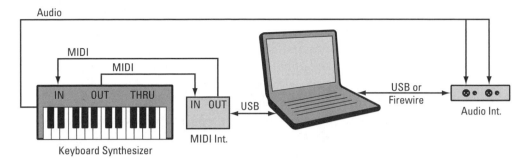

Figure 3.5   A computer and a keyboard synthesizer connected through a USB MIDI interface. The audio from the keyboard synth is routed back into the computer through an audio interface

within the DAW/Sequencer as just another digital audio source and processed/mixed along with recorded audio, loops, and audio from software instruments.

In addition to dedicated MIDI interfaces, many controllers, modules, and keyboard synths that connect directly to the computer via USB also have standard MIDI jacks, allowing you to connect other MIDI devices to the computer through those jacks. The same is true of external audio interfaces that have MIDI In and Out ports. In that case, the audio and MIDI interfaces in Figure 3.5 would be combined in one box.

The various MIDI interfaces discussed so far have one MIDI input port and one MIDI output port. In order to connect more than one device to a computer using MIDI cables, you would need a multiport MIDI interface.

A **multiport MIDI interface** is an external interface that possesses more than one In Port and Out Port. Although it is possible to connect a computer to more than one module or keyboard synthesizer through daisychaining, as discussed above, it is not possible to have fully independent control over each device that way and daisychaining is seldom used today. To have independent control from the computer over a keyboard synth or module, a computer must be connected to that keyboard or module by a separate MIDI cable attached to a separate MIDI Out Port. A multiport MIDI interface provides this independent control over connected devices.

In addition to MIDI device connections, many multiport interfaces have the ability to take in SMPTE time code and convert it to MIDI Time Code. The acronym SMPTE (pronounced "Simp-tee") stands for the Society of Motion Picture and Television Engineers, and SMPTE time code is used to synchronize video, audio, and MIDI devices together. This is useful in some large live performance or studio settings, but modern film scoring is most often done using digital video files played back directly in a DAW/Sequencer. SMPTE time code and MIDI Time Code will be discussed further in Chapter 9: MIDI in Detail.

In the past, a project studio used by a commercial composer would have a MIDI interface with four or more inputs and outputs, and larger studios would have 8-in/8-out interfaces or even multiple 8-in/8-out interfaces connected together. The migration of sound generation from hardware instruments to software instruments has significantly reduced the need for more than just a few MIDI ports in a project studio, and many require no MIDI ports at all thanks to direct USB connection of controllers, modules, and keyboard synthesizers.

Peripheral devices such as external MIDI interfaces and USB keyboards may require the installation of driver software so that the operating system can communicate with the external device. However, many USB controllers are "class compliant" with the existing USB specifications and require no additional drivers at all beyond the capabilities of the operating system. Audio interfaces that possess MIDI ports often require drivers, as do more complicated multiport MIDI interfaces.

Alternate Controllers

The controllers that we've discussed so far have been keyboard controllers, but there are many other ways to provide MIDI information to a computer. A general definition for a MIDI controller is a device that converts physical actions into MIDI messages. There are many controllers modeled after non-keyboards that fit that definition, including guitar controllers, wind controllers, trumpet controllers, and percussion controllers (see Figure 3.6). For non-keyboard players, alternate controllers can be an excellent way to apply their particular performing skills to electronic performance and provide input to MIDI software.

Many of the instrument-style controllers have special sound modules that are designed to produce sounds that respond well to that instrument's control. For example, guitar controllers are usually sold along with guitar synthesizer modules that respond to each string individually and track guitar specific gestures such as string bending, and wind synthesizer modules are often programmed to respond to parameters such as lip pressure and breath pressure.

These alternate controllers often utilize a larger number of expressive MIDI messages than keyboard controllers because they use a variety of sensors to detect performance aspects such as breath pressure in a wind controller. Expressive messages and their use in controlling synthesizers and samplers will be central to the next several chapters.

There are also many control devices that don't look like musical instruments at all but can be powerful controllers for shaping sound. These include devices that allow for touchscreen control, infrared sensing, and various other physical sensors (see Figure 3.7). In addition, many control devices that were designed for videogames make excellent musical input devices as well. These include standard joysticks that can be used to control the spatial position of sound, game pads that have many buttons and small joysticks, Wii Remotes that contain accelerometers and an infrared light detector, and Microsoft's Kinect that utilizes camera-based motion sensing.

Alternate Receivers

Just as not every controller must be a keyboard, not every device that receives MIDI messages must be a sound generator. For example, there are theatrical lighting boards that can receive MIDI messages to change lighting scenes or intensities, software that

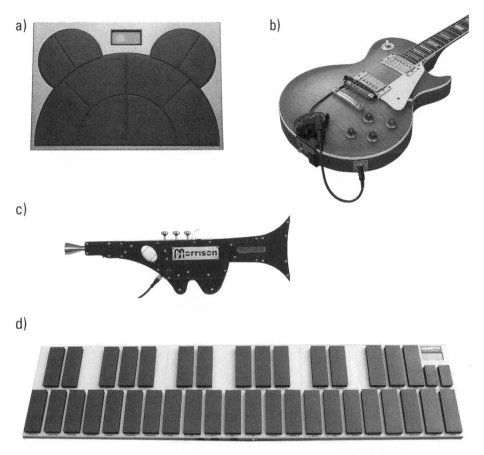

Figure 3.6 Non-keyboard musical controllers: a) Alternate Mode DK 10 percussion controller (courtesy of Alternate Mode, Inc.); b) Roland GK-3 guitar converter (special thanks to Roland Corporation); c) Morrison Digital Trumpet brass controller (courtesy of www.morrisondigitaltrumpet. com); d) Alternate Mode MalletKAT Pro mallet controller (courtesy of Alternate Mode, Inc.)

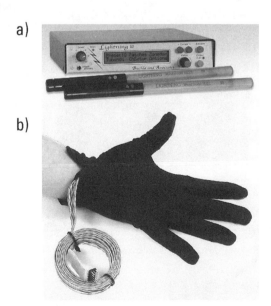

Figure 3.7 Alternate musical controllers: a) the Buchla Lightning III infrared wand controller (courtesy of Buchla and Associates); b) the I-CubeX TouchGlove sensor with six pressure-sensitive pads for the I-CubeX environment (courtesy of Infusion Systems Ltd., www.InfusionSystems.com)

causes visual images to respond to MIDI messages (used by DJs/VJs in clubs), and some experimental performers have even hacked devices such as a Roomba vacuum cleaner to respond to MIDI messages. Figure 3.8 shows a fountain that can be controlled by MIDI and thus can be synchronized to music.

To accommodate such unusual MIDI receivers, the MIDI standard includes specialized protocols for controlling external hardware, including MIDI Machine Control (MMC) and MIDI Show Control (MSC). MMC and MSC are described only briefly below because they are quite specialized and the commands that make up these protocols are more relevant to computer programmers—they aren't typically manipulated directly by the user.

Many hardware audio recorders can be controlled from a DAW/Sequencer or MIDI hardware through **MIDI Machine Control** (MMC). MMC was created to allow MIDI systems to interface with hardware audio recorders. The commands available through MMC range from simple start and stop to commands for producing MIDI time code.

MIDI Show Control (MSC) was created to allow MIDI devices to integrate with multimedia systems for controlling sound effects, lighting, and pyrotechnics. One example of MIDI Show Control in action is the "Waterworld" live stunt show at

Figure 3.8 A MIDI-controllable water fountain (courtesy of Erich Altvater, Atlantic Fountains)

Universal Studios Hollywood in which live action is synchronized with sound, music, lighting, and pyrotechnics (Richmond Sound Design, Ltd., 2010).

Now that we've covered the basics of MIDI connections (see Figure 3.9 for a summary), it's time to consider the messages that flow over these connections.

MIDI MESSAGES

The purpose of the MIDI connections discussed above is to transmit MIDI messages from one device to another. Eventually, these messages arrive at a sampler or synthesizer, which uses these messages to generate audio. There are four basic kinds of MIDI messages: note messages, expressive messages, program (patch) messages, and system messages. Of these, note messages and expressive messages are the primary sources of synthesizer and sampler control during performance or sequencer playback. The note messages are the most basic and most important of the MIDI messages.

Note Messages

Each note played on a keyboard controller is split into two separate messages: a **note-on** message generated when a key is pressed down and a **note-off** message generated when a key is released. If the press and release of a key were packaged in the same message, then a synth receiving those messages could never be played in real time, because the controller would have to wait until a key was released to send a note message to the synth.

Since the notes *are* split into two messages, the keyboard controller sends a note-on message to the synth as soon as a key is pressed allowing the synth to start generating sound immediately. The result is real-time performance. When the key is released, the

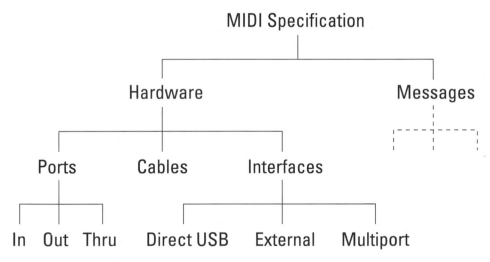

Figure 3.9 Summary of MIDI hardware

controller sends a note-off message and the synth stops the note. This is sometimes referred to as "gating" the synth: the note-on opens the gate and the note-off closes it.

In addition to gating the synth, note-on and note-off messages include several important pieces of information. A **note-on** message contains three pieces of information: the channel, the key number, and the velocity. The **channel** is important if the receiving synth can play multiple timbres, or patches, at the same time—if it is **multitimbral**. In that case, a note's channel number ensures that only the patch assigned to that channel on the synth will be played by that note. Most hardware synths and samplers are multitimbral, but many software instruments are not, so the channel is important when your synth is a piece of hardware and may or may not be important if your synth is software. I'll discuss the concept of the MIDI channel at greater length in Chapter 9: MIDI in Detail.

The **key number** is normally used to indicate the pitch of the note being played, though some patches (timbres) on a synth or sampler are not pitched, such as drum kit patches. The key numbers in a note-on message range from 0 to 127 with 60 indicating middle C (C3), and each change of one in the key number indicating an increase or decrease of a semitone (61 is C#3/Db3, 62 is D3, 48 is C2, 72 is C4, and so on). The strangeness of the range—0 to 127—is due to the way the information is encoded in binary in the message (see Chapter 9: MIDI in Detail).

As mentioned in the chapter on sound, pitches are often given in pitch-register notation, in which regular pitch names (C, D, E, etc.) are coupled with a number that denotes the specific octave, or register, of the note. This notation appears both in texts such as this and in software such as sequencing or notation programs. In textbooks on music theory and acoustics, middle C is shown as C4. However, in MIDI contexts, middle C is often shown as C3. The reasons for this aren't entirely clear, but, regardless, you have to get used to the contradiction and possible confusion. Most pieces of software allow you to change the register indicator for middle C between C3 and C4, with C3 being the more typical "MIDI" setting. When discussing MIDI, I will use C3 for middle C. Earlier in the text, in the context of acoustics, I used C4 as middle C.

The **velocity** value in a note-on message is determined by how quickly the key is depressed and, like the key number, ranges from 0 to 127. Some inexpensive keyboard

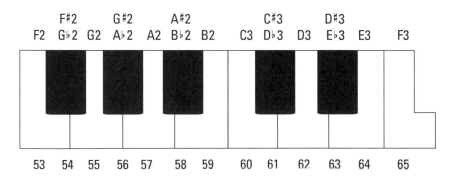

Figure 3.10   Some key numbers and their pitch-register designations (middle C is C3 here)

controllers that are not velocity sensitive will send a dummy value, such as the mid-point value 64, instead. The velocity reflects how much energy you put into depressing the key and is often mapped in a synth to the loudness of the sound, and perhaps the brightness as well.

The **note-off** message that is generated when a key is released also contains three pieces of information: the channel, the key number, and the release velocity. The **channel** number is used by a multitimbral synth to ensure that a note sounding on a particular patch is turned off. If the software synth is not multitimbral, then the channel isn't important, but will still be part of the message.

The **key number** allows the synth to determine which of the sounding notes is to be turned off. Without this, notes sounding on the same patch couldn't be turned on and off independently. It is important that the channel and the key number of a note-on message be matched by the channel and key number of a subsequent note-off message. Otherwise the note could play indefinitely as a "stuck" note until you select "all notes off" in your DAW/Sequencer or turn off a hardware synth.

The **release velocity** in the note-off message is a measure of how quickly the note is released, and its value ranges from 0 to 127. The idea behind release velocity is that a performer can control the end of a note with the release velocity just as they can control the beginning of the note with the velocity. This is a logical concept, but it is seldom used in practice.

One of the reasons that the release velocity is not usually relevant is that many controllers do not send actual note-off messages at all, but rather note-on messages with a velocity of zero. If the controller does not always send a release velocity value, then it makes little sense to program synthesizers to respond to them. In addition, variable key release is a less intuitive performance gesture than variable key attack. The reason that note-on messages with a velocity of zero are often used in the place of actual note-off messages has its roots in the MIDI hardware transmission speed and a concept called "running status," which will be discussed in Chapter 9: MIDI in Detail. For now, it's enough to know that the release velocity isn't of much use.

Expressive Messages

There are three types of expressive MIDI messages that can be used to control synthesis parameters: pitch bend, pressure, and control change messages. In general, these messages allow for a continuous change in the sound over the course of a note, or over the course of many notes. As a result, while there is only one note-on and one note-off message per note, there may be many expressive messages sent to change the sound of the synth while that note is playing.

Pitch Bend Messages

Pitch bend messages are sent by moving a dedicated wheel or joystick on a keyboard controller, and the purpose of the **pitch bend** messages is, of course, to bend the pitch up or down from the pitch given in the note-on message. Pitch bend messages contain three pieces of information: channel, fine bend value, and coarse bend value. As discussed with the note messages, the **channel** number allows a multitimbral synth to direct the message only to the desired patch. All notes on that patch will bend, but not notes on any other patch.

Both the **fine bend** and **coarse bend** values range from 0 to 127, like the key number and velocity above. However, the two bend values really combine together to create a larger bend range. The reason for the larger range is that we are quite sensitive to changes in pitch and if there were only 128 steps (0 to 127), we might hear the pitch change in small steps, which would ruin the illusion of a continuous pitch bend.

Offhand, you might think that combining two numbers that can each take on 128 values might yield 256 values. However, when the actual bits for each digital value are combined, there are really 16,384 different values (128 × 128; see "Technically Speaking . . . MSB and LSB" in Chapter 9: MIDI in Detail). You can pitch bend both down and up, so pitch bend all the way down is 0, no pitch bend is 8,192, and pitch bend all the way up is 16,383. However, for convenience, in most DAW/Sequencers this range is shown with pitch bend all the way down as −8,192, no pitch bend as 0, and pitch bend all the way up as 8,191.

While the pitch bend message determines whether the pitch is bent part of the way up or down or all the way up or down, it doesn't actually determine how far that bend is in musical terms. That's up to the receiving synthesizer. A typical default for the **pitch bend range**, also referred to as the **pitch bend sensitivity**, is two semitones up and two semitones down, with anything from 0 semitones to 24 semitones (two octaves up or down) commonly available on synths and samplers. This range can be set using sliders or knobs or with a special MIDI message that sets the pitch bend range (more on that in Chapter 9: MIDI in Detail).

If a synth was programmed for the normal default of +/− two semitones, then a pitch bend message value of −8,192 would represent a bend down of two semitones, −4,096 a bend down of one semitone, +4,096 a bend up of one semitone, and 8,191 a bend up of two semitones. If a synth was programmed for a range of +/− twelve semitones (one octave), then −8,192 would cause a bend down of an octave, −4,096 a bend down of a tri-tone (six semitones), +4,096 a bend up of a tri-tone, and +8,191 a bend up of an octave (see Figure 3.11).

A continuous bend of the pitch is accomplished with a relatively large number of pitch bend messages, each representing a new amount of pitch change from the pitch given by the key number of the note-on message. It is important to recognize that pitch bend messages are not directly connected to note messages in any way. You can send pitch bend messages from a controller to a synth without pressing down any keys at all—there will be no sound, but the messages will be legitimately sent and received. You can also bend the pitch over the course of several notes such that a musical passage is slowly transposed up a major second (or to whatever value is set for the synth's pitch bend range). This message independence is a feature of most MIDI messages and allows for tremendous flexibility along with some occasional confusion.

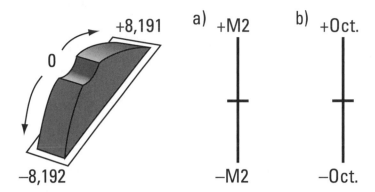

Figure 3.11 The pitch bend wheel and its maximum and minimum values mapped with a pitch bend sensitivity of a) +/− 2 semitones, and b) +/− an octave

Pressure Messages

You can send **pressure**, or **aftertouch**, messages from a keyboard controller by first playing a key and then pressing into the keyboard. The harder you press, the larger the pressure value that is sent in the message. You can change the amount of pressure you apply over the course of the note to change the affected synthesis parameter in a continuous way. Not every controller is capable of sending aftertouch messages, though some that aren't allow you to send aftertouch messages with a slider instead. There are two types of pressure messages: channel pressure and polyphonic key pressure.

The **channel pressure**, or monophonic aftertouch, message contains just two pieces of information: the channel and the pressure value. The **channel** acts as before to target the message to a particular patch of a multitimbral synth. The **pressure value**, which ranges from 0 to 127, may be mapped to a variety of synthesis parameters as determined by the patch programming on the synthesizer. Common applications include vibrato and low pass filter cutoff, which determines the brightness of the timbre.

Like channel pressure messages, you send **polyphonic key pressure**, or poly aftertouch, messages by first playing a key and then pressing into that key. The difference is that the poly pressure message allows for independent pressure values for each key. To accomplish this, the poly pressure message contains three pieces of information by adding a **key number** to the channel and pressure value. This would allow you, for example, to play a chord and have different pressure values for each chord member. If the pressure value was mapped to the cutoff of a low pass filter, this would mean that each note in the chord could have a different brightness that changed as desired over the course of the note.

Though poly pressure messages suggest some intriguing possibilities for modifying, or modulating, a synthesized sound over time, they are not widely used. Very few controllers can send poly pressure messages and very few synths are designed to receive them. Poly pressure is thus similar to the release velocity of a note-off message in that they both suggest interesting sound design possibilities but have never really caught on.

Control Change Messages

The third type of expressive MIDI message is the **control change** message. The control change message contains three pieces of information: channel, control number, and control value. The channel functions, as previously discussed, to allow a multitimbral synth to route the message to the proper patch ensuring that only notes played on that patch will be affected by the message.

The **control number** ranges from 0 to 127 and is used by the synth to determine what synthesis parameter is to be altered. The presence of this number means that the control change message is really 128 separate expressive messages. Though this seems like a large number, there are only a handful of control numbers that are used on a regular basis and the number of different control change messages that can be sent by a keyboard controller is limited to the number of knobs, sliders, and pedals that are mapped to those controllers.

Control change number 1, or CC1, is the **Modulation Wheel controller**, and is usually sent by a dedicated modulation wheel or a joystick that combines pitch bend and modulation. Like all control change messages, CC1 includes a **control value** that ranges from 0 to 127. The synth's programming determines the effect that CC1 has on the timbre. CC1 is most often used to control vibrato, but can also be used to control other synth elements, such as a low pass filter, which affects the brightness of a sound.

CC7 is the **Channel Volume controller** and is used to set the overall level for each channel of a synth or each instrument track in a DAW/Sequencer, much like the faders on a mixing board control the volume of each mixing board channel.

CC11 is the **Expression controller**, which allows you to create local swells and fades relative to the overall channel volume set by CC7. Using CC11 for crescendos and diminuendos allows you to change the overall level of the channels or tracks with CC7 without disrupting the crescendos and diminuendos created with CC11. Not all synths implement CC11; in these cases it is necessary to use CC7 for both the local volume changes and the overall channel or track volume changes.

CC11 values below the 127 maximum result in a reduction in the overall track volume from the level set by CC7. For example, a series of CC11 messages whose values increase from 64 to 127 would result in a crescendo up to the volume set by CC7. This will be covered further in Chapter 9: MIDI in Detail.

CC10 is the **Pan controller**, which allows you to position the synth sound in the stereo field and affects either a pan control at the output of the synth channel or the pan setting for the instrument track. A CC10 value of 0 would be hard left, a value of 64 would be in the middle, and a value of 127 would be hard right. Many types of sounds can be panned continuously across the stereo field, while some types of sounds such as some drum kits and sound effects can only be positioned by CC10 before they sound.

Another useful control change message is CC64, the **Damper Pedal (Sustain) controller**, which is usually sent by a footswitch attached to the keyboard controller. CC64 is a **switch controller** in that it has only an "on" state and an "off" state. The controllers discussed above are all **continuous controllers** that can take on any value between 0 and 127. For CC64, any control value between 64 and 127 would be "on" and any control value between 0 and 63 would be "off." After CC64 has been turned on for a particular channel, any note-off messages received on that channel are "deferred" until CC64 is turned off.

There are many other controllers including a Breath controller (CC2) and a variety of "sound controllers" (CC70 through CC79). Sound controllers, as the name suggests, are designed to affect aspects of a synth patch, such as Brightness (CC74) or Timbre/Harmonic Intensity (CC71). Despite the apparent utility of the sound controllers, there is no requirement that a synthesizer must implement them. Even the General MIDI 2 standard, which provides full definitions for them, only "recommends" their implementation in General MIDI 2 compatible devices. Some of these messages will be discussed in the following chapters on synthesis, and more information can be found in Chapter 9: MIDI in Detail.

Program (Patch) Change Messages

A program change, or patch change, message is sent to a synthesizer or sampler from a DAW/Sequencer or from a keyboard synth or controller in order to change the way the synth or sampling elements are configured. Such a configuration is referred to as a patch—a holdover from analog modular synthesizers whose modules had to be connected by patchcords to make any sound whatsoever. The actual **patch number** in the message refers to the memory storage location for a particular timbre on a synth or sampler.

Patch change messages are more important when you're using a hardware synthesizer or sampler with a DAW/Sequencer. In that case, you store patch change messages in the DAW/Sequencer so that you don't have to call up the patches directly on the synth and you can change patches in the middle of a sequence. When using software synths and samplers, you're more likely to choose the timbre directly from the interface of the software instrument itself, which is easy since it's just another window on the computer screen. Patch change messages will be discussed further in Chapter 9: MIDI in Detail.

System Messages

Unlike the messages discussed above, MIDI system messages are not directed at a specific channel but rather apply to the entire receiving MIDI device. System messages are used for a wide variety of purposes such as communicating messages to a specific synthesizer (System Exclusive), receiving time code from external sources such as video decks (MIDI Time Code), and transmitting timing messages between MIDI devices (MIDI Timing Clock).

Like the program change messages, system messages are less commonly used with software instruments because the parameters are readily accessible from the graphical interface and tempo synchronization with a DAW/Sequencer is handled internally. With the widespread use of digital video files within DAW/Sequencers for video scoring and

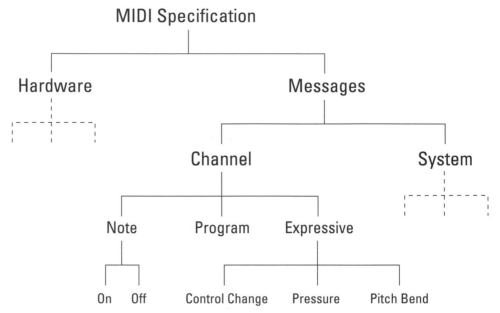

Figure 3.12 Summary of MIDI messages

Table 3.1 MIDI messages discussed in this chapter

Message type	Information in message		
Note-on	channel	key number	velocity
Note-off	channel	key number	release velocity
Pitch bend	channel	fine bend value	coarse bend value
Channel pressure (aftertouch)	channel	pressure value	[nothing else]
Poly pressure	channel	key number	pressure value
Control change	channel	control number 1 = Modulation Wheel 2 = Breath Pressure 7 = Channel Volume 10 = Pan 11 = Expression 64 = Sustain Pedal 71 = Sound controller #2: Timbre/Harmonic Intensity 74 = Sound controller #5: Brightness	control value
Program (patch) change	channel	program number	[nothing else]
System messages	variable information		

sound design, the use of MIDI Time Code has become less common. System messages are covered more thoroughly in Chapter 9: MIDI in Detail.

MIDI SEQUENCING

Now that we've looked at the various types of MIDI hardware, how they can be connected to each other and to a computer, and some of the messages that flow over those connections, we'll look at the most important software application involving MIDI.

MIDI sequencing involves **inputting** MIDI messages, organizing and **editing** MIDI messages, and **outputting** MIDI messages. However, before discussing the mechanics of note entry and editing, it is useful to first look at the user interface features common to most sequencers.

Multi-track Audio Recording Paradigm

The standard interface for MIDI sequencing is derived from multi-track audio recording. Multi-track audio recording, of course, involves recording *audio* from different instruments on separate tracks so that they can be edited and processed separately and later mixed together. MIDI sequencers allow you to organize MIDI messages on separate **tracks**, with the output of each track assigned to a software or hardware instrument (see Figure 3.13). If the assigned instrument can play more than one timbre a time (multitimbral), then the track is assigned to a particular **MIDI channel** on that instrument. Additionally, if the instrument is a hardware synth or sampler, a **patch** may be chosen in the sequencer for the assigned channel on that instrument. Also, by analogy with audio recording, each MIDI track typically has a record-enable button, a mute button, and a solo button (more on those features later when MIDI playback is discussed).

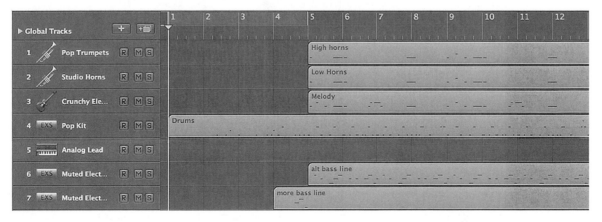

Figure 3.13a   Arrange window from Logic Pro 9 (screen shot reprinted with permission from Apple Inc.)

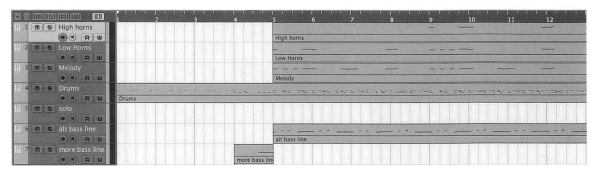

Figure 3.13b   Tracks window from Cubase Studio 4 (courtesy of Steinberg Media Technologies)

Other sequencer interface features that were derived from audio recording practice are the **transport** controls, consisting of play, stop, pause, rewind, fast-forward, and record (see Figure 3.14). Though these interface features originated when sequencers were MIDI only, it is particularly convenient now that MIDI and digital audio regularly coexist in DAW/Sequencers.

Measuring Time

Another important feature of the common sequencer interface is the method for measuring time. When a sequencer is being used to compose or arrange, the preferred time format involves measures and beats. In addition, some system is needed for subdividing beats so that note values smaller than a quarter note can be represented. Many sequencers first subdivide the beat into smaller units, such as sixteenth notes, and then further divide those into some number of ticks (see Figure 3.15).

The number of beat subdivisions (four for sixteenth notes) times the number of ticks per subdivision yields the sequencer's **PPQN**, or parts per quarter note. For example, if the beat is subdivided into sixteenth notes and there are 240 ticks per sixteenth note, the PPQN would be 960. The PPQN varies from sequencer to sequencer and can usually be changed by the user.

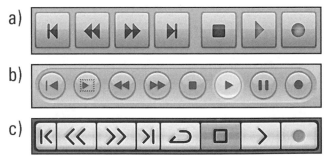

Figure 3.14   Transport controls from various DAW/Sequencers: a) Pro Tools LE 8 (©2011 Avid Technology, Inc.); b) Logic Pro 9 (screen shot reprinted with permission from Apple Inc.); and c) Cubase Studio 4 (courtesy of Steinberg Media Technologies)

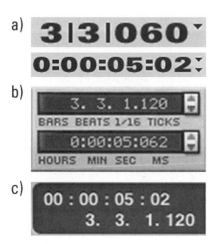

Figure 3.15   Clocks from various DAW Sequencers showing the same time: a) Digital Performer 6—measure time and SMPTE time (courtesy of MOTU); b) Reason 4 —measure time and real time (courtesy of Propellerhead Software); and c) Logic Pro 9—measure time and SMPTE time (screen shot reprinted with permission from Apple Inc.)

Displaying Pitch

The pitch in a MIDI note message is transmitted as a numerical value (the key number), but it is displayed in various windows in a MIDI sequencer in pitch-register notation. As mentioned above, in many MIDI applications and MIDI devices, middle C (key number 60) is represented as C3, as opposed to the C4 that is the standard in other areas of music and acoustics. The register numbers change at the Cs: a half step below C3 is B2 and an octave above C3 is C4.

MIDI Editors

The term **editor** in a sequencing program refers to a particular view of the MIDI information. You've already seen one of the standard MIDI editors, the **tracks editor**, also called the arrange window or the project window. The tracks editor is useful for manipulating one or more tracks of a sequence on the time scale of a measure or more. You don't typically edit notes themselves in this view, though some sequencers allow you to zoom in from the tracks view and edit individual notes.

To edit MIDI messages more precisely, there are a variety of common "note-level" editors that show each note in a track or in multiple tracks. It is important to recognize that the editors all access the same MIDI messages: if you change a note in one editor, it will change in all of the other editors that display notes as well. Here are several note-level editors commonly found in DAW/Sequencers (see Figure 3.16):

- A **piano roll editor** shows MIDI notes as horizontal bars whose height represents pitch and whose length represents duration. Piano roll editors may also show controllers and other MIDI messages as well.
- A **list editor** displays MIDI information as a list of messages. This editor is the most precise editor in that every MIDI message has its own line and each piece of information in the message can be changed individually.

- A **drum editor** is similar to a piano roll editor, but it specializes in collecting together notes that represent drum kit elements and displaying them in such a way that drum patterns become clear.
- A **notation editor** allows you to see information in common music notation. A notation editor is an excellent view for seeing and editing pitch, but usually a poor view for rhythm.

The **mixer window** in a sequencer is somewhat different than the other editors. The editors discussed above show MIDI messages organized by a timeline. A mixer window provides a graphical representation of volume, pan, and a few other settings only for the time currently shown on the sequencer's clock (see Figure 3.17).

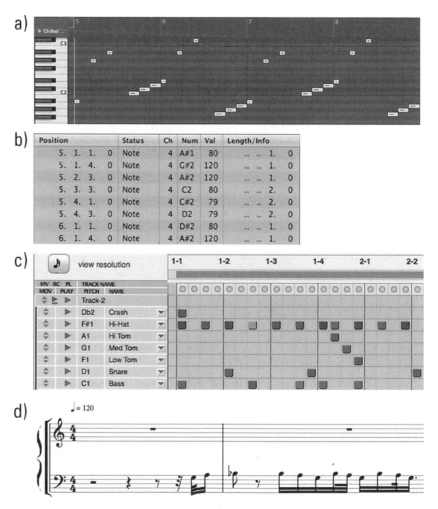

Figure 3.16 Various MIDI editors: a) piano roll editor from Logic Pro 9; b) list editor from Logic Pro 9 (screen shots reprinted with permission from Apple Inc.), c) notation editor from Digital Performer 6; and d) drum editor from Digital Performer 6 (courtesy of MOTU)

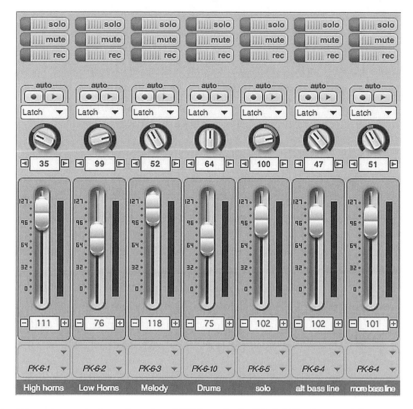

Figure 3.17 The mixer window showing MIDI tracks in Digital Performer 6 (courtesy of MOTU)

The strength of the mixer window as a MIDI editor is that it provides you with an intuitive interface for entering volume and pan information. In addition to a slider to control volume and a knob or slider to control pan, a mixer window allows you to automate pan knob and volume slider movements.

MIDI Input

There are a variety of ways to input MIDI messages into a sequencer, including real-time entry, step-time entry, and manual entry. In addition, there are a number of entry modes that affect what happens to existing data or where in time the recording takes place.

Real-time entry involves playing live to a metronome while the sequencer is recording, often with a one- or two-bar countoff before the recording starts. Real-time entry can also be used to record expressive messages, such as pitch bend. The advantage to real-time entry is that it allows you to be expressive in your playing style in terms of articulations and timing (swing or some other groove). The drawback to real-time entry is that every wrong note or misplayed rhythm is also recorded along with your expressive performance. Fortunately, you can edit the pitches and timing in one of the editors or apply one of the "corrective" functions discussed below in "MIDI Editing" to clean up the performance.

Step entry involves selecting the pitch and the duration separately so that the notes are put in step by step. To step enter notes, you choose the duration using a letter or a number on the computer keyboard and play the pitch on a MIDI keyboard. Passages that are entered with step entry can sound overly precise and often require further editing to create an effective performance.

Manual entry involves inputting data using a virtual tool such as a "pencil" tool. While this method of entry is occasionally useful for adding in a note or two, it is most widely used to enter automation information such as pan, volume, mod wheel, and pitch bend.

For both real-time entry and step entry, there are several different modes that determine how existing information in the target track is handled. Here are some of the common entry modes (your sequencer may have different names for these functions):

- In **replace mode** old information is deleted when new MIDI messages are being recorded.
- In **overdub** or **merge mode**, the new information is merged with the existing information. New information may also be placed "on top" of the old information in a separate container called a region or clip.
- In **Punch-in/punch-out mode** you define a punch-in point and a punch-out point. Messages can only be recorded between those points, not before the first or after the second.
- In **Loop mode** you specify a time range that will repeat continuously while you're recording. Some sequencers allow each pass to be stored as a separate "take" so that you can choose the best take later. Combined with merge, loop mode can allow you to build up a complex drum part, one drum/cymbal at a time.

MIDI Editing

Once MIDI messages have been entered into a sequencer, you can edit them in various editing views, such as the tracks editor or piano roll editor, to create the performance that you desire.

Standard editing functions such as **cut**, **copy**, and **paste** are available in MIDI editors, though there are more graphically oriented ways of accomplishing these same tasks, such as dragging selected messages for cut-and-paste and dragging selected items with a modifier key pressed, such as option or alt, for copy-and-paste. A different version of cut, called **snip** by some sequencers, removes both the messages *and* the time that was selected, thereby closing the gap. Just as snip is an extension of cut, **splice** is an extension of paste, in which the previously cut or copied messages push the existing messages later in time.

When dragging selected messages it is often useful to **constrain dragging** to either the vertical direction—changing pitch when dragging notes—or the horizontal direction—changing position in time. This is usually accomplished by dragging the selected items with the shift key held down. In addition, sequencers typically allow for an editing mode in which notes and other events are snapped to a time grid automatically.

The pitch and timing of groups of MIDI messages can also be modified by automated functions such as transpose, quantize, and humanize. MIDI note messages can be **transposed by interval** quite easily by simply adding a number of semitones to each key number. You can also make more complex pitch changes such as changing the mode from major to minor or combining the transposition by interval and **mode change** to transpose a sequence from, say, C major to F harmonic minor. The sequencer accomplishes this by mapping key numbers for each pitch-class in the first key to the appropriate key numbers for each pitch-class in the new key. For example, to change the tonic of the key, Cs (. . . 48, 60, 72 . . .) would be mapped to F♯s (. . . 54, 66, 78 . . . for F♯s), and to change the mode of the key, Es (. . . 52, 64, 76 . . .) would be mapped to As (. . . 57, 69, 81 . . .).

The timing of MIDI messages can be altered in a variety of ways: by shifting all selected messages earlier or later in time; by creating a backward version (retrograde) of selected messages; or by **quantizing** the selection. Quantizing involves automatically "correcting" the timing of MIDI messages that were entered in real time by moving selected messages to the nearest time point on a specified grid. Quantizing can often be performed in a **non-destructive** way where removing the quantization allows you to recover the original timing.

You have to be careful when quantizing a real-time performance, because you can easily eliminate the very expressive characteristics you were trying to obtain by recording in real time in the first place. Most quantize functions have one or more parameters that allow you to decide the strength of the quantization, which means that you can cause selected notes to move *toward* a grid point, but not all the way *to* a grid point. Other parameters allow you to focus the quantization on notes near beats and ignore notes that lie in between and vice versa.

There are several variants of quantize, including input quantize, swing quantize, and groove quantize. **Input quantize** snaps notes to the grid while they are being recorded. **Swing quantize** takes notes of a specified value (usually eighth notes) and delays the second note to create the characteristic uneven eighth notes of swing. **Groove quantize** shifts note timings and velocities in a pattern to create a different feel (groove) than the original timings/velocities (see Figure 3.18).

Some sequencers have a feature that is the opposite of the quantize function: **humanize**. Where quantize is used to "correct" MIDI messages that were input in real time, humanize can be used to selectively "mess up" MIDI messages that were entered through step entry. For example, if a group of notes all have a velocity of 80, you can give them random variations in velocity of +/−5, so the resultant velocities will be somewhere between 75 and 85.

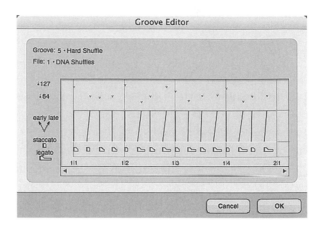

Figure 3.18   Groove quantize window in Digital Performer 6. Groove quantize alters the velocity, timing, and duration of selected notes according to the pattern shown (courtesy of MOTU)

MIDI Output

At its simplest level, MIDI output involves rewinding a sequence back to the beginning and pressing play in the transport controls. Other common playback features include the ability to mute and solo tracks and to change tempo.

Mute and solo are complementary functions that affect which track will play back. The **Mute** function, shown as a button labeled "M," allows you to silence one or more tracks during playback. The **Solo** function, shown as a button labeled "S," allows you to hear one or more tracks during playback. Ironically, you can "solo" more than one part at a time. These are valuable compositional and troubleshooting tools.

Tempo can be static for the entire sequence, set by entering a number into a tempo field, or can be changed dynamically by using a special **tempo track**. In addition to traditional expressive uses, tempo changes can be used to align the bars and beats of the sequence with the bars and beats of an audio track or with specific events in digital video (see Figure 3.19). These tempo changes now form a **tempo map** of the video, and new notes and other messages can be locked to it by recording to the metronome that now follows these tempo changes.

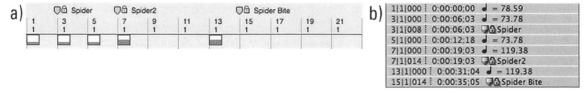

Figure 3.19   Demonstration of adjusting a sequencer's tempo to markers when working with video: a) timeline with aligned markers due to b) tempo changes

In addition to the MIDI sequencing interface and functions discussed above, there are some configuration concepts that are important to sequencing, including MIDI Thru and Local Control.

MIDI Thru and Local Control

When you connect a keyboard synth or controller to a computer and begin recording on a sequencer track, you want the notes that you play on the keyboard to sound like the patch you've chosen for the track. For this to happen, the sequencer must route the MIDI messages generated by your keyboard to the instrument you selected for the sequencer track. This routing is referred to as **MIDI Thru** (not to be confused with the Thru port on a synth; see Figure 3.20).

When the output is a software instrument, the MIDI messages are passed to it internally. When the output is a hardware synth, the messages are routed to the MIDI output of the computer. If the target hardware or software instrument is multitimbral, then the incoming MIDI messages must be routed to the correct channel of the target instrument as well. The MIDI Thru function is used by a variety of programs including sequencers and notation software.

If you're sequencing using a keyboard synth—meaning that it both generates MIDI messages from its keys *and* converts incoming MIDI messages into sound—you have to be concerned about the keyboard synthesizer's **Local Control** setting. When you purchase a keyboard synthesizer, plug it in, and turn it on, it will generate sound when you play the keys. This happens because there is a direct connection between the keys and the "sound engine"—the part of the synth that converts MIDI messages into sound. This direct connection is referred to as the Local Control and in this case, the Local Control is "on."

If you connect this synth to a computer running a sequencer and record-enable a track whose output is a channel on the same synth, then the synth will receive two note-on messages for each key that you play. One note-on message will come directly from the keys via the Local Control. The second note-on message will come from the

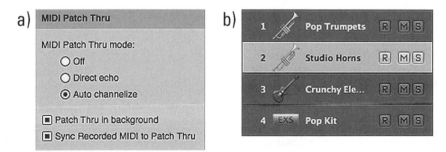

Figure 3.20　a) MIDI Patch Thru preference window in Digital Performer 6 (courtesy of MOTU); and b) track selected for patch thru in Logic Pro 9 (screen shot reprinted with permission from Apple Inc.)

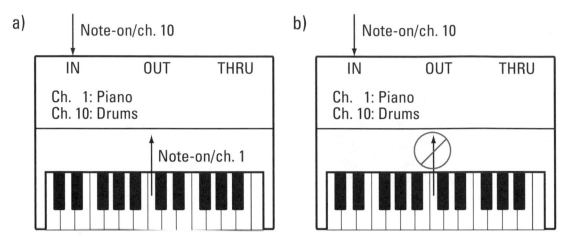

Figure 3.21 a) A key played on a keyboard synth results in two note messages being sent to its sound engine: one directly from the key via Local Control and the other from the sequencer via MIDI Thru. Both drum and piano patches are heard; b) with the Local Control "off," a key played on a keyboard synth results in only one note message being sent to its sound engine from the sequencer via MIDI Thru. Only the drum patch is heard. This is the desired setting for sequencing

sequencer via MIDI Thru. Depending on the output channel setting on the sequencer track, the two note-on messages may be on different channels, resulting in two different patches being heard for every key that is played (see Figure 3.21a). This can be distracting if, for example, you're trying to sequence drums, but you're also hearing a piano patch due to the Local Control.

To avoid this problem, you need to turn the **Local Control "off"** on the keyboard synth so that the sound engine only receives the messages coming through your sequencer via MIDI Thru (see Figure 3.21b). Local Control "off" is the desired setting for sequencing with a keyboard synthesizer. Local Control is not an issue when using a hardware module or purely software sound sources.

Standard MIDI Files

The act of sequencing involves storing data in a computer. Like all computer programs, DAW/Sequencers store their data in some file format. The actual sequence file or session file containing the MIDI messages is usually stored in an exclusive file format that can be read only by that particular program. These exclusive file formats contain the MIDI messages, but also include information specific to that sequencer, such as track settings, mixer settings, information on audio files used in the project, and audio processing plug-ins.

To transfer MIDI information from one program to another you use an interchange file format called a **Standard MIDI File** (**SMF**, file extension **.mid**). SMFs are widely readable by notation programs, sequencers, and other music software. Standard MIDI files come in three types:

- Type 0: All data is stored in one track; simplest, most transferable format.
- Type 1: Data is stored in multiple tracks; used for most situations.
- Type 2: This type contains one or more independent single-track patterns; seldom used.

Type 0 SMFs are useful for simple MIDI players, both hardware and software. Type 1 SMFs are used by music applications that organize MIDI messages into separate tracks including sequencing and notation programs. If you're going to transfer a file from one MIDI application to another, you will generally use a Type 1 SMF.

Standard MIDI Files store MIDI messages, of course, but they also store information such as track names, tempo, time signature, key signature, and the amount of time between events. SMFs do *not* store information concerning audio files, plug-ins, or any data that is specific to a particular DAW/Sequencer. As a result, an SMF represents only a portion of the data used in many projects. Nevertheless, it is very useful for transferring MIDI data between software.

In addition to sequencers, notation programs also support SMFs. However, SMFs store data that is most useful to performance programs such as sequencers and omit data that is important to notation programs. For example, the Standard MIDI File doesn't store articulations, slurs, crescendos, or page layout information. SMFs won't even indicate the difference between a G♯ and an A♭ because the notes are stored as note-on/off messages that indicate pitch with a key number, which would be the same for both of those spellings. If you save a notation file as a Standard MIDI File and then import it back into the same program, all of the layout information will be lost. Increasingly, notation programs support MusicXML, which includes notation-specific data.

DAW/SEQUENCERS AND SOFTWARE INSTRUMENTS

Now that we've reviewed the physical connections of MIDI hardware, the messages that are transmitted over those connections, and the basic functioning of MIDI sequencers, we'll turn our attention to the ways in which DAW/Sequencers interact with software synthesizers and samplers. In addition, we'll briefly touch on the topics of latency, polyphony, and multitimbral capacity. Softsynths interact with DAW/Sequencers in one of three modes: as a plug-in, as a ReWire slave, or as a standalone program, perhaps on another computer.

Plug-in Softsynths

As a **plug-in**, a softsynth is fully integrated into the DAW/Sequencer and loads when the project file loads. The DAW/Sequencer in this situation is referred to as the **host application**. As a plug-in, a softsynth appears as an instrument track with controls similar to an audio track. Some DAW/Sequencers use a separate MIDI track for its MIDI messages while others integrate MIDI messages and instruments on the same track.

There are a variety of **plug-in formats** for softsynths and each DAW/Sequencer supports one or more of them. The most common plug-in types are Apple Audio Units (**AU**), Microsoft's DirectX Instrument (**DXi**), Steinberg's Virtual Studio Technology instrument (**VSTi**), and Digidesign's Real-Time Audio Suite (**RTAS**). The formats supported by your DAW/Sequencer dictate which plug-in formats you can use. VSTi softsynth plug-ins are probably the most widely supported, with AU common on Apple computers, DXi in a number of Windows programs, and RTAS plug-ins being used by Pro Tools software.

There are several other formats that are usually used in more specialized circumstances: TDM plug-ins for the high-end Pro Tools HD systems, and DSSI and LV2 plug-ins for the Linux operating system. In addition, there are a variety of **plug-in wrappers** that allow one type of plug-in to work on a system that doesn't accept that type. For example, a VST-to-RTAS wrapper would allow you to use VST instruments within Pro Tools LE.

ReWire Softsynths

Some softsynths aren't available as plug-ins, so the DAW/Sequencer must communicate to the softsynth in another way. **ReWire** is a technology developed by Propellerhead Software primarily as a way for DAW/Sequencers to communicate with Propellerhead's softsynth rack, Reason, which is not available as a plug-in. However, ReWire can be used by other softsynths as well.

If two pieces of software are connected via ReWire, one is referred to as the **ReWire master** and the other as the **ReWire slave**. This is similar to the host/plug-in relationship discussed above, except that the ReWire master and slave are running as separate applications. ReWire allows audio and MIDI to be exchanged between the two applications along with synchronization information. If both ReWire applications have transport controls, then pressing "play" in one app will cause the other to play as well.

One of the more typical scenarios is that the ReWire master is a DAW/Sequencer in which MIDI information is sequenced and sent via ReWire to a ReWire slave. The ReWire slave is a synthesizer/sampler that receives the MIDI messages and generates

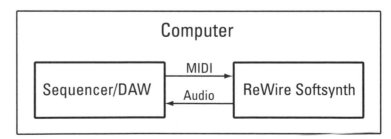

Figure 3.22   Two programs on one computer communicating through ReWire. MIDI messages flow from the ReWire master to the ReWire slave and audio flows back from the ReWire slave to the ReWire master

sound. The sound is passed back from the ReWire slave to the ReWire master and can then be mixed and processed using the DAW/Sequencer's capabilities (see Figure 3.22).

Standalone Softsynths

Some softsynths run in a standalone mode in which they are simply independent applications. Two applications connected via ReWire are running separately, but the ReWire technology creates a special connection between them. Often a synth can run either as a plug-in or in standalone mode depending on the needs of the user. A DAW/Sequencer can send MIDI messages to a standalone softsynth through a special inter-application connection that is either built into the system, such as the Mac's Inter-application Communications bus (IAC bus), or is supplied by third-party software, such as SubtleSoft's MIDIPipe or the Maple Virtual MIDI Cable.

You might run a softsynth as a standalone application because the MIDI messages are coming from outside the computer directly from a controller keyboard or from another computer. Some project studios use separate computers for sequencing and sound generation. This configuration is shown in Figure 3.23. In this configuration, a DAW/Sequencer on one computer is sending MIDI messages out through a MIDI interface. The Out Port of that interface is connected to the In Port of a MIDI interface connected to a second computer. Those messages are received by a softsynth running as a standalone application on the second computer, which then generates audio. Since sampling is one of the dominant ways of electronically producing sound, these standalone softsynths are likely to be samplers.

Frequently, the audio from the softsynth is sent out of its computer through an audio interface to an audio interface connected to the DAW/Sequencer's computer. This audio can then be mixed and processed in the DAW/Sequencer. In this scenario, the computer on which the softsynth is running as a standalone application dedicates its processing power and RAM only to the generation of sound and not to sequencing, mixing, or processing, which is taken care of by the first computer. For situations involving a large number of samples or complex sound synthesis that requires a great deal of CPU power, this configuration can be very useful.

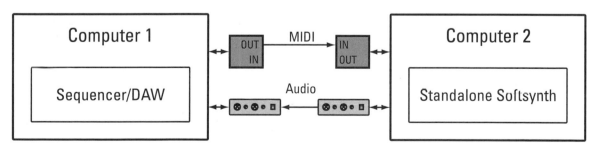

Figure 3.23 Two programs on separate computers. MIDI messages flow from the DAW/Sequencer computer to the softsynth computer through MIDI interfaces, and digital audio flows back from the softsynth computer to the DAW/Sequencer computer through audio interfaces

Connecting multiple computers using MIDI and audio interfaces can be cumbersome, and there are some products available that allow you to send and receive MIDI and audio over Ethernet cables. For example, the Vienna Ensemble Pro sampler software allows you to run the program on multiple slave computers connected to the master computer by Ethernet cables and a router/switch. A DAW/Sequencer running on the master computer communicates with the slave computers using a special plug-in and Vienna Ensemble Pro's server software. This eliminates the need for audio and MIDI interfaces on the slave computers.

Latency

One important factor for all software synths is **latency**. Latency in the context of softsynths refers to how long it takes from the time you press a key on an external controller to the time you hear the sound. For live performance situations or for recording softsynth tracks, this latency must be kept low—it is very difficult to perform properly when the sound is delayed by a perceivable amount. Any delay of more than about 10–15 ms is likely to be perceivable, depending on the timbre.

MIDI input latency is quite small, so the main source of latency here is the **output buffer** that is set in your DAW/Sequencer (see Figure 3.24). Software that plays back audio doesn't send individual samples directly to the DAC, because if a sample is delayed coming from a softsynth, it will produce an unpleasant pop or a dropout in the audio. Instead, some number of samples are first stored in an output buffer and then sent to the DAC. Now if a sample is delayed coming from the softsynth, there are other samples

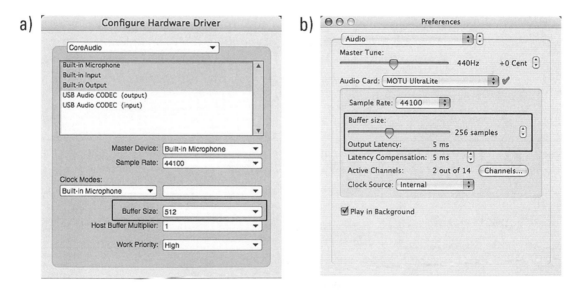

Figure 3.24   Audio configuration windows in a) Digital Performer 6 (courtesy of MOTU); and b) Reason 4 (courtesy of Propellerhead Software). The rectangles highlight the buffer settings

ahead of it in the buffer, so the DAC always gets a steady stream of samples. The size of this output buffer determines the delay.

When you're recording softsynth tracks, this buffer has to be small enough that you don't perceive the latency, or at least it doesn't bother you. The drawback to small buffer sizes is that your computer has to work harder and thus has less power to devote to audio processing plug-ins and other tasks. As a result, you may want to record softsynth tracks using a small output buffer (low latency) and then raise the buffer size (higher latency) when you're done. When you're just playing back a sequence of audio and instrument tracks, a small delay between pressing "play" and hearing the audio doesn't sound wrong, so the delay caused by the increased buffer size during playback won't be a problem.

Polyphony and Multitimbral Capacity

Two key concerns with synthesizers and samplers are how many simultaneous notes can be played and how many simultaneous timbres can sound. These two measurements, **polyphony** and **multitimbral capacity** respectively, determine what you can accomplish with a computer and a given hardware or software instrument. Hardware instruments are effectively special-purpose computers with a certain amount of processing power, and software instruments utilize the host computer's CPU for sound generation.

There is no fixed standard for all hardware instruments, though there are some published standards that can serve as guideposts. The General MIDI standard discussed later in Chapter 9 requires at least 24 voices of polyphony and the newer General MIDI 2 standard requires at least 32 voices of polyphony. However, most modern hardware synthesizers have the capacity to produce 64, 128, or more voices simultaneously. This appears at first to allow for as many as 128 notes at once, but "voices" and "notes" are not identical. Depending on the synthesizer and the patch each note may require two or more voices of polyphony. In practice, you have to learn to listen for notes that cut off unnaturally, notes that play late, or even notes that don't play at all to tell if you've exceeded your synth's polyphony.

Software instruments don't necessarily have a fixed polyphony, since their polyphony is based on the available CPU power, though you can often set the maximum polyphony from the instrument's graphical interface. Demanding software setups can quickly tax a CPU, particularly if the computer is a laptop or a modestly powered desktop. Such situations have led some to run their software instruments on a separate computer or multiple computers as discussed above. In another form of distributed computing, the Logic Pro DAW/Sequencer has a special Node application that can be installed on a separate computer that can allow you to offload some of the synthesis and effects processing to that computer.

The General MIDI 1 and 2 standards require compatible synths to be at least sixteen-part multitimbral (sixteen simultaneous timbres). Most hardware synthesizers adhere to this standard and don't exceed it, largely because this is sufficient to allow one timbre on each of the sixteen MIDI channels that can be addressed across one cable connected to the MIDI In Port. There are a few synthesizers that have more than one In Port, which allows them to have more simultaneous timbres, and there are a few specialized synthesizers that allow for only one or a few simultaneous timbres.

While software synthesizers do not have to adhere to the same numeric limitations in terms of number of simultaneous timbres, most multitimbral softsynths still use the number 16 as their basis to coordinate with the number of possible MIDI channels. Many software instruments, particularly samplers, allow for some multiple of sixteen channels by defining multiple virtual MIDI In ports. Others may require that a separate instance of the software instrument be loaded. Multiple instances of a software instrument typically use more processing resources than a single instance.

Now that we've covered the basics of MIDI hardware, MIDI messages, MIDI sequencing, and the relationship between DAW/Sequencers and software instruments, we turn our attention to the generation of sound through synthesis and sampling. Throughout this discussion I will emphasize the relationship between MIDI messages and the synthesis and sampling elements that they control.

CHAPTER 4

Synthesis, Sampling, and MIDI Control

In the last chapter, we looked at MIDI hardware, messages, and sequencing, and the relationship between DAW/Sequencers and software instruments. In this chapter we will focus on the basic components of software instruments with special attention to how MIDI messages are used to control them. We will stick to the basics in this chapter by developing a simple model and then expand on that model in subsequent chapters. We should first note that there are two basic ways for hardware and software instruments to produce sound: synthesis and sampling.

Synthesis refers to any method of sound production in which the timbre is created "from the ground up" through various configurations of simple materials such as basic waveforms. The techniques by which these simple materials are combined to create new timbres are referred to as **synthesis algorithms**. There are a wide variety of synthesis algorithms, including additive, subtractive, amplitude modulation, frequency modulation, waveshaping, wave terrain synthesis, physical modeling, and granular synthesis. New algorithms or variants on existing algorithms pop up regularly, leading to an enormous array of synthesis possibilities.

The idea of mastering so many synthesis techniques can be daunting, but not all of these techniques are in widespread use in commercial hardware and software instruments. A solid understanding of a handful of diverse synthesis techniques can help you to understand and master new techniques and new variants of old techniques when you encounter them.

Sampling involves playing back pre-recorded sound files (samples) using MIDI note messages to start them and stop them. These pre-recorded sound files can range from sound effects, to individual instrument notes, to entire musical passages (loops). A loop used in a sampler differs from one placed in an audio track in that the sampler loop can be triggered by a MIDI controller and held (made to loop continuously), re-triggered, or transposed by playing different keys on the controller. When sampling is used to imitate the performance of acoustic instruments, the samples will be a combination of individual instrument notes and groups of notes such as trills and glissandi.

Unsurprisingly, an instrument that generates audio primarily by sampling is referred to as a sampler and an instrument that generates audio primarily by synthesis is referred to as a synthesizer. However, these categories are not always kept strictly apart: many synthesizers use more than just basic waveforms as the basis for their sounds. Hybrid sampling/synthesis is quite common and represents a powerful combination for generating rich, complex timbres. In addition, the meaning of the term "sampler" has changed in recent years.

A **sampler** originally referred to a hardware keyboard or module that could record sound from a microphone and play it back under MIDI control. With the migration of samplers to software, there is little need for them to act as sound recorders because there are already so many programs available for recording sound. The term sampler has instead come to mean a piece of software that can load different sets of samples and allow you to create such sets from individual samples. A sample-based instrument in which the samples are unchangeable can be referred to as a **sample player** or a **ROMpler** (for ROM-based sampler).

Once a sound has been generated through synthesis or sampling, it can be modified with filters, amplifiers, envelopes, LFOs (low frequency oscillators), and effects. We'll consider effects later when discussing processing techniques that are common to recorded, imported, and synthesized/sampled audio. Filters, amplifiers, envelopes, and LFOs, on the other hand, are integral components of synthesized sound and will be discussed in this and the next couple of chapters.

To lay the groundwork for more complex sound generation techniques, we'll first look at the basic techniques for synthesis and sampling and then expand on them in subsequent chapters. Along with these basic techniques, we'll see how MIDI messages are used to trigger and control the elements of software and hardware instruments. Much of the discussion that follows assumes that the synthesizer or sampler is software, but the concepts are still valid in the case of hardware instruments.

A BASIC SYNTHESIS MODEL

Our basic synthesis model has three components: an oscillator, a low pass filter, and an amplifier (see Figure 4.1). This model mimics the synthesis techniques found in the original analog synthesizers of the 1960s. Though a vast majority of modern synthesizers are digital—there are only a few genuine analog synths still being made—this analog model is widely utilized in software synths and is useful for understanding more complex techniques that do not have an analog origin.

The Oscillator

The **oscillator** generates a basic timbre and pitch by repeating a cycle of some waveform the appropriate number of times per second for the desired fundamental frequency. This is referred to variously as fixed-waveform synthesis, table-lookup synthesis, or wavetable

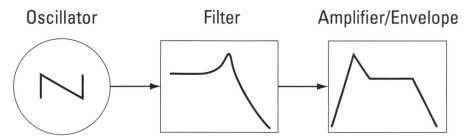

Oscillator   Filter   Amplifier/Envelope

Figure 4.1 A basic synthesis model based on analog synthesis

synthesis. The waveform can be one of the standard waveforms (sine, triangle, sawtooth, etc.) or any other shape that represents a single cycle of a waveform (see Figure 4.2). The waveform can even consist of multiple cycles, though the rate of repetition will no longer be the fundamental frequency. The basic oscillator, then, has two controllable parameters: the waveform (timbre) and the frequency (pitch), of which only the frequency is usually changed from note to note.

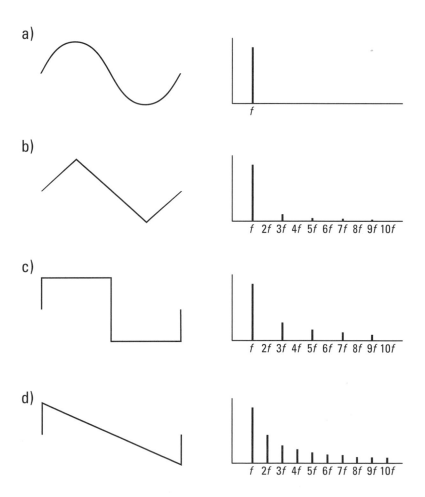

Figure 4.2 Basic waveforms and their spectra: a) sine wave; b) triangle wave; c) square wave; d) sawtooth wave

The Low Pass Filter

The **Low Pass Filter** modifies the timbre of the oscillator by reducing the amplitude of frequencies above a settable **cutoff frequency**. In broad terms, the lower the cutoff frequency the "darker" the timbre, and the higher the cutoff frequency the "brighter" the timbre (see Figure 4.3).

The extent of this darkness-brightness continuum is limited by the spectrum of the waveform coming from the oscillator. If the oscillator's waveform is a simple sine wave, then there is nothing for the low pass filter to change until it diminishes the fundamental itself, so there would be no "darker" or "brighter." Even if the waveform is more complex, like a sawtooth wave, if the cutoff frequency is below the fundamental, there will be little or no sound. If the cutoff frequency is above the highest partial, the filter will have no effect at all because the entire spectrum will be passed through unchanged.

In addition to the cutoff frequency, a low pass filter in a synthesizer usually has a **resonance** setting that results in a peak in the spectrum at the cutoff frequency. With resonance, the cutoff frequency of the filter becomes audible, particularly when it is

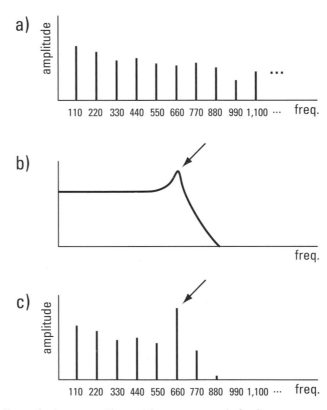

Figure 4.3 The effect of a low pass filter with resonance: a) the input spectrum to the filter; b) a resonant low pass filter with a cutoff frequency of approximately 660 Hz; c) the output spectrum from the filter. The arrow indicates the resonance peak in the filter and in the output spectrum

changed, or swept, during the course of a note or over multiple notes. The basic filter, then, has three controllable parameters: the filter type (low pass here), the cutoff frequency, and the resonance amount, of which only the filter cutoff is usually changed during the course of a note or from note to note, though the resonance can be changed as well.

The Amplifier and Amplitude Envelope

The **amplifier** modifies the overall volume of the sound. A simple amplifier has just one controllable parameter: the overall amplitude (loudness). However, the amplifier is also responsible for the articulation of a note through the use of an amplitude envelope that modifies the overall amplitude dynamically over the course of a note.

A basic amplitude envelope model is the four-stage ADSR (Attack, Decay, Sustain, Release) envelope (see Figure 4.4). An **ADSR envelope** for amplitude operates as follows:

- During the Attack stage, the amplitude rises from zero (no sound) to some peak amplitude over the amount of time set by the attack parameter (manipulated with a knob or slider in a softsynth).
- During the Decay stage, the amplitude falls from the peak amplitude to the sustain amplitude over the amount of time set by the decay parameter, which is sometimes referred to as the "initial" decay to avoid confusion with the end of the note.
- During the Sustain stage, the amplitude remains at the sustain level until the note is turned off. The sustain setting is not an amount of time as the attack, decay, and release settings are, but rather a percentage of the peak amplitude.
- During the Release stage, the amplitude falls from the sustain amplitude to zero (no sound) over the amount of time set by the release parameter.

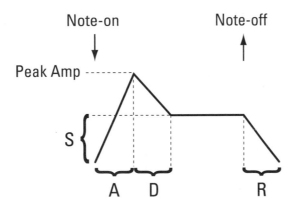

Figure 4.4 ADSR envelope showing gating by note-on and note-off messages and peak amplitude determined by the note-on velocity

The ADSR can be used to simulate both bowed/blown (sustained) or struck/plucked (non-sustained) articulations. Bowed or blown articulations are achieved by having attack and decay times that are not too long, a non-zero sustain level, and a zero or short release time (see Figure 4.5a). The attack and decay times need to be short enough so that you perceive the note reaching the peak amplitude and then falling away to the sustain level, and the release should be zero or short to give the sense that no more energy is being put into the instrument causing the amplitude to go to zero. Clearly, long attack and decay times and long release times are perfectly permissible in a synthetic sound, but such an envelope will cease to give the impression of being a "bowed or blown" articulation.

A struck or plucked articulation can be simulated with a short attack, a moderate to long decay, a zero sustain value, and any release time. The short attack simulates the quick rise in amplitude that plucking or striking would cause, the decay time determines how long the note "rings," the zero sustain level will cause the peak amplitude to fall to zero over the course of the decay, and the release time is irrelevant because the amplitude is already at zero (see Figure 4.5b). Alternately, you could set the release time to be moderate to long and just play short notes. In that case, the amplitude will rise to the peak value and then immediately proceed to the release segment because the note has been released. The decay time and sustain level would be irrelevant because the envelope would skip right over them. In practice, you might set the decay time and release time to be the same and the sustain time to be zero so it doesn't matter whether you play short or long notes.

You could also get different struck/plucked articulations from the envelope by setting the decay time to be moderate to long and the release time to be fairly short (dampened pluck). If you play and hold a note, the decay time will determine how long the note rings (long). If you play and quickly release a note, then the release time will determine how long the note rings (short).

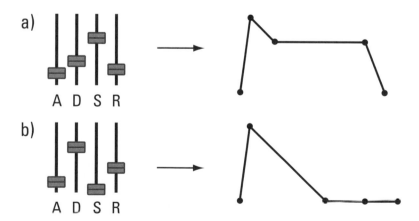

Figure 4.5 ADSR slider settings and their resultant envelopes: a) bowed/blown envelope; b) struck/plucked envelope

The ADSR envelope is a classic and useful envelope type, but an envelope can be made up of any number of segments. The common aspect to each stage of an envelope is that the amplitude changes from one level to another over some span of time, which includes the possibility of a "hold" similar to the sustain segment where the start and end amplitudes are the same.

The amplifier/envelope component of the basic synthesis model has a peak amplitude parameter, parameters for each stage of the envelope (A, D, S, and R), and requires a signal for the note to start and stop, also referred to as a **gate** signal. Of these parameters, the peak amplitude and the timing of the start and stop indicators are most likely to change from note to note.

Notice that these three simple synthesizer components account for the primary attributes of sound: pitch (frequency) from the oscillator, loudness (amplitude) from the amplifier, timbre (waveform) from the oscillator and filter, and articulation (amplitude envelope) from the amplifier. Once connected together, these three components are capable of generating a simple note, but they need to be supplied with information that specifies each note's attributes and indicates when a note should stop and start.

The parameters needed for each note played by this basic synthesizer are:

- start and stop indicators (amplifier);
- fundamental frequency (oscillator);
- cutoff frequency (filter);
- peak amplitude (amplifier).

The other parameters, such as the waveform, filter type, filter resonance, and envelope values (A, D, S, and R), are often the same for each note, though it may be desirable to change them from note to note in some circumstances.

The necessary parameters for each note are supplied to the synth by MIDI messages, either generated live by a controller or stored and played back from a MIDI track in a DAW/Sequencer. We will next look at how the data encoded in MIDI messages are mapped to these synth parameters.

MIDI MESSAGES AND SYNTHESIZER CONTROL

The last chapter provided an overview of messages available in MIDI. The messages most relevant for controlling synths are note messages and expressive messages.

Note-on, Note-off, and Gating

At the simplest level, MIDI note messages supply the synth with the commands to start (note-on) and stop (note-off) notes, as well as the fundamental frequency derived from the key number, and the peak amplitude derived from the velocity. Starting and stopping notes on a synth is sometimes referred to as gating: the on-message opens the gate and the off-message closes the gate.

The note-on/note-off gate may be applied to many components of a full-blown synth, but in our simplified model the gate applies only to the amplitude envelope of the amplifier. The note-on message starts the attack, causing the amplitude to rise to the peak level and then decay to the sustain level. The amplitude then stays at the sustain level until the note-off message is received, at which point the amplitude falls to zero (no sound) over the release time.

The sustain segments of the envelopes shown in Figures 4.4 and 4.5 above are more properly imagined as single points at which the envelopes stay (sustain) until the note-off message triggers the release stage (see Figure 4.6a). It is important to note that this shape does not indicate a plucked/struck envelope, but rather a bowed/blown envelope in which the sustain "segment" is represented as a single point. If this envelope were to simulate a plucked or struck envelope, the sustain point would be at zero amplitude as shown in Figure 4.6b. I will continue to show envelopes throughout this chapter with sustain "segments" for convenience, but it is worth keeping in mind that in most cases these are really sustain *points*.

Key Number and Keyboard Tracking

The key number of the MIDI note-on message is converted into a frequency by the synth (see the "Technically Speaking . . . key number conversion" sidebar). This frequency is then used by the oscillator to repeat the chosen waveform at that frequency. It is worth noting that the key number can be manipulated in any number of ways before it is converted into a frequency. For example, simply adding or subtracting a whole number can transpose the pitch up or down by that number of semi-tones or

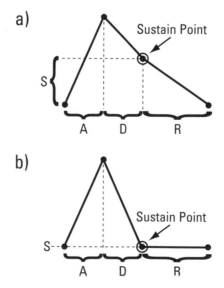

Figure 4.6 ADSR envelope with sustain shown as a point rather than a segment: a) bowed/blown envelope; b) struck/plucked envelope

by one or more octaves if the number is a multiple of twelve. This process is usually used to generate equal-tempered pitches, but a key number can, in theory, be mapped to any frequency, resulting in everything from Just Intonation to exotic artificial tunings. Oscillator frequencies can also be detuned from equal temperament by some number of cents (See "Technically Speaking . . . semitones and cents" in Chapter 1).

Another way that the frequency derived from the key number can be modified before being applied to the oscillator is through **keyboard tracking**, also called key tracking or key scaling. In typical use, an increase of one key number yields an increase in oscillator frequency equivalent to one semitone. This generally corresponds to a keyboard tracking value of 100 percent. However, a synth oscillator may allow you to

TECHNICALLY SPEAKING . . . KEY NUMBER CONVERSION

Technically speaking . . . MIDI key numbers can be converted into frequencies by using the fact that key number 69, the A above middle C, has a frequency of 440 Hz, and the fact that frequencies are related exponentially to pitches. We used this last fact in Chapter 1 to determine that, in equal temperament, every increase of a semitone in pitch is a factor of the $2^{(1/12)}$ ($\approx$ 1.0595) times the frequency of the previous semitone (See "Technically Speaking . . . equal-tempered ratios" in Chapter 1).

Those two facts are combined in the following formula:

$$Freq = 440 \times 2^{(KeyNumber-69)/12}$$

If the key number is 70 (B♭), then the formula becomes $Freq = 440 \times 2^{(1/12)}$. This is what we would expect: go up by a semitone and the frequency is multiplied by the factor of $2^{(1/12)}$. If the key number is 68, then the formula becomes $Freq = 440 \times 2^{(-1/12)}$. Negative exponents indicate division, so again this is what we would expect: go down by a semitone and the frequency is divided by a factor of $2^{(1/12)}$.

To reverse this formula and figure out the key number from a given frequency, we would take the logarithm, base 2, of both sides of the equation and, using a few rules of logarithms, come up with this:

$$KeyNumber = 69 + 12 \times \log_2 (Freq/440)$$

Converting the logarithm to base 10, as it's found on most calculators, we get:

$$KeyNumber = 69 + 39.86 \times \log_{10} (Freq/440)$$

Since the conversion factor from logarithm base 2 to base 10 is approximated here, you would round to the nearest whole number to get the key number. Of course, you would only expect whole number key numbers if the frequency (Freq) in question is in equal temperament relative to 440 Hz.

Technically Speaking

set the keyboard tracking to a lower value, such that an increase of one key number represents a smaller interval, such as a quarter-tone (half of a semitone). In addition to allowing for smaller-than-semitone intervals melodically, this can yield interesting, clangorous timbral effects if there are multiple oscillators set to different keyboard tracking values. Some oscillators only allow tracking to be turned on or off allowing for either regular use (on) or the generation of drones (off).

Keyboard tracking can also be used by the filter to adjust the cutoff frequency on a note-by-note basis. The actual cutoff frequency would then be determined by the cutoff frequency slider or knob on the synth *and* the frequency derived from the key number. This allows the results of the filtering process to remain uniform across the keyboard range. If the cutoff frequency does not change with the key number, then more partials are passed through for notes with lower frequency fundamentals than for notes with higher frequency fundamentals.

For example, if the cutoff frequency of the low pass filter was fixed at 440 Hz, a note with a fundamental of 110 Hz (key number 45) would have four partials pass through essentially unchanged: the 110 Hz fundamental plus the 220 Hz, 330 Hz, and 440 Hz partials (see Figure 4.7a). However, a note with a fundamental of 220 Hz (key number 57), just one octave higher, would only have two partials pass through

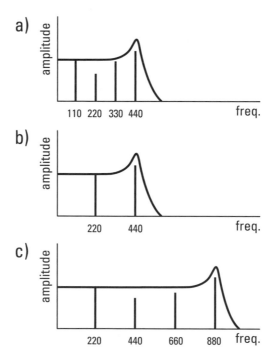

Figure 4.7   The effect of a low pass filter with keyboard tracking on and off: a) with a note fundamental of 110 Hz, a low pass filter cutoff of 440 Hz results in four partials, b) with a note fundamental of 220 Hz, no keyboard tracking on filter results in only two partials, and c) with a note fundamental of 220 Hz, keyboard tracking on filter results in four partials like a)

unchanged: the 220 Hz fundamental plus the 440 Hz second partial (see Figure 4.7b). As a result, notes would get more and more dull as they got higher and higher.

On the other hand, if the filter keyboard tracking value was set to 100 percent, the filter cutoff would be a multiple of the fundamental, instead of a fixed value, with the cutoff slider or knob determining the multiple. As a result, the 110 Hz note and the 440 Hz note would both have four partials pass through unchanged—a factor of four times the fundamental—and thus have a similar timbre (see Figure 4.7c).

This keyboard tracking value of 100 percent for the filter may not be desirable, as many acoustic instruments have fewer partials in their spectra at higher fundamentals. Synthetic tones that don't follow this practice may sound too bright in the upper registers. As a result, in situations where the filter keyboard tracking is variable, some value lower than 100 percent, such as 50 percent or 75 percent, may be desirable. As with many aspects of synthesizer sound design, this parameter is best chosen through careful experimentation with an attentive ear.

In some synths, the maximum keyboard tracking value allows *more* partials through for higher fundamentals than lower fundamentals. In that case, the "100 percent" value discussed above, in which the same number of partials is passed for all fundamentals, would be realized with a smaller keyboard tracking value.

The changing of a synth parameter by a MIDI message or other control source, such as an envelope or LFO, is often referred to as **modulation**. When using keyboard tracking on a filter, you can say that the key number is modulating the filter cutoff frequency. Creative modulation is at the heart of synthesizer sound design.

Velocity, Loudness, and Brightness

The velocity value in a note-on message reflects how much energy you put into depressing the key and is most directly mapped to the peak amplitude of the amplitude envelope. As a result, notes that are struck harder are louder than those struck more softly.

In acoustic instruments, putting more energy into the system typically results in both a louder *and* a brighter sound. To mimic that effect, the velocity may be used to set the peak amplitude of the amplitude envelope *and* modulate the cutoff frequency of the filter. If the filter is also set to keyboard track, then the key number, the velocity, and the cutoff slider on the synth would all influence the cutoff frequency of the filter.

More energy at the start of a note in an acoustic instrument may also result in a faster response from the elements of the physical system such as reeds, drum heads, or vocal folds. To simulate this, the velocity can be used to modulate the attack time of the amplitude envelope, with higher velocities resulting in shorter attack times. When an increase in a modulation value—velocity in this case—results in a *decrease* in the target parameter—attack time—it is often referred to as **inverted modulation** (see the "Technically Speaking . . . scale and offset" sidebar on page 84).

The note-off message also has a velocity value; in this case the release velocity. In theory, the release velocity could be used to modulate the duration of the release segment of the amplitude envelope. A quick release of a key, resulting in a high release velocity value, could be made to shorten the release segment, while a gentle release, resulting in a low release velocity, could lengthen the release segment. However, as mentioned in the previous chapter, release velocity is seldom used for this purpose and many controllers don't send note-off messages at all. Instead, they send note-*on* messages with a velocity of zero, which is defined in the MIDI specification as being equivalent to a note-off message. The rationale behind this is discussed in Chapter 9: MIDI in Detail.

At this point, with just two messages, note-on and note-off, we've attained a remarkable degree of control over our three-component synth. The following is a list of the mappings discussed above between the information in note-on and note-off messages and the commonly controlled parameters of our basic synth model:

- note-on → trigger attack phase of amplitude envelope (amplifier/envelope);
- note-off → trigger release phase of amplitude envelope (amplifier/envelope);
- note-on key number → fundamental frequency (oscillator);
- note-on key number → cutoff frequency modulation (filter) through keyboard tracking;
- note-on velocity → peak amplitude of envelope (amplifier/envelope);
- note-on velocity → cutoff frequency modulation (filter);
- note-on velocity → attack time modulation (amplifier/envelope).

It's important to note that not every synth or every synth patch will have all of these mappings active. The first three mappings above are nearly universal and the mapping between velocity and peak amplitude is common, but these mappings will vary from synth to synth and from patch to patch. Some synths may not even allow some of these mappings whereas others allow almost any mapping imaginable. This aspect will be discussed in the next chapter under "modulation routings." Though I use the word "control" frequently in this text, MIDI messages are merely transmitted information, and the receiving synth or sampler may be programmed to ignore any or all of the information.

With just our simple three-component synthesizer—oscillator, filter, amplifier/envelope—and two simple MIDI messages—note-on and note-off—we already have a sound generator capable of playing notes of variable pitch, loudness, timbre, and articulation. The other commonly used MIDI messages—the expressive messages—provide for additional control over synthesis parameters.

Expressive Messages and Synthesis Parameters

Expressive MIDI messages were created to allow you to change synth or sampling parameters over the course of a note or over the course of many notes. Otherwise, you would only be able to influence a synth note at the beginning of the note with the information in the note-on message and at the end of the note with the information in the note-off message. The three types of expressive MIDI message are pitch bend, pressure, and control change.

Mapping Pitch Bend Messages

Pitch bend messages are naturally applied to the pitch of the oscillator. As discussed in the last chapter, pitch bend messages range from −8,192 (bend all the way down) to +8,191 (bend all the way up), with 0 representing no pitch bend. The amount of modification to the oscillator frequency is determined by the value in the pitch bend message and the pitch bend range, or sensitivity, set in the synth patch. The most typical default pitch bend range is +/− two semitones.

In that case, the highest pitch bend value of +8,191 would result in a bend upward of two semitones, and the lowest pitch bend value of −8,192 would result in a bend downward of two semitones. Pitch bend values of +4,096 and −4,096 would result in bends of one semitone up and one semitone down, respectively. Any other pitch bend values would result in bends in between equal-tempered semitones.

Pitch bend messages, like the other expressive messages, are not actually connected in any way to note messages. As a result, you can bend the pitch during one note or over the course of several notes. You can even send pitch bend messages when no notes are playing at all—you won't hear anything as a result, but it demonstrates the independence of MIDI messages.

Mapping Pressure Messages

In our basic synthesis model, the most likely target for channel pressure messages is the cutoff frequency of the low pass filter. This would allow you to first play a note and then use aftertouch (pressure) to cause the sound to brighten and darken as the note sounds. The raising and lowering of the cutoff frequency of a low pass filter is sometimes referred to as "opening" and "closing" the filter. The initial cutoff frequency setting on the filter would have to be relatively low so that it has room to change when it receives channel pressure messages.

The amount of cutoff frequency modulation created by aftertouch values is set as part of the synth patch itself. Just as pitch bend values can cause a different amount of pitch change depending on the setting of the patch's pitch bend range, the aftertouch message can cause a different amount of cutoff frequency modulation. Each synth has a different way of setting the magnitude of the effect, but it is usually a knob, slider, or number field with values ranging from 0 to 1.0, 0 to 127, or 0 to 100 percent.

The starting point for the modulation, here set by the cutoff frequency slider/knob, and the magnitude of the change, here set by a slider, knob, or number field in the synth, are the two factors that determine how much an expressive message affects its target synth parameter. The starting point for the change can be thought of as an *offset* and the setting for the magnitude of the change can be though of as a *scaling* of the pressure value (see "Technically Speaking . . . scale and offset" on page 84). These two factors will show up again and again as we talk about various types of modulation.

So far, the cutoff frequency of the low pass filter has been a possible destination for the note-on key number through keyboard tracking, the note-on velocity value to allow

TECHNICALLY SPEAKING . . . SCALE AND OFFSET

Technically speaking . . . scale and offset are important concepts for understanding how MIDI messages modulate synth parameters. The values encoded in MIDI messages, such as the pressure value of the channel pressure message and the control value of control change messages, range from 0 to 127. These numbers by themselves have no particular meaning. If the channel pressure message (aftertouch) is mapped to the cutoff frequency of the filter, a pressure value of 64 will seldom mean a change of 64 Hz in the cutoff frequency. Instead, the value of 64 represents half of the total possible change afforded by the 0–127 range. The actual change in the cutoff frequency given in Hz is determined by a **scaling factor** applied by the synthesizer to this 0–127 range.

For example, if the scaling factor is 10, the range of pressure values (0–127) will result in a range of cutoff frequency change of 0–1,270 Hz. If the scaling factor is 100, the range of the cutoff frequency change due to the pressure value change will be 0–12,700 Hz. The scaling factor can also be *negative*, resulting in **inverted modulation**, such that a positive change in the modulation value would yield a negative change in the synth parameter. For example, if the scaling factor is –10, then the range of pressure values (0–127) will result in a range of cutoff frequency value change of 0 to –1,270.

In practice, you don't usually set the absolute scaling factor, but rather a fraction of the maximum scaling factor given as a percentage from 0 percent to 100 percent, as a normalized range from 0.0 to 1.0, or a range of values from 0 to 127, similar to MIDI message data. The actual number associated with the maximum scaling factor is set by the computer programmers who created the synth and is not usually accessible to the user. However, there are a few synths that are highly programmable by the user, such as Native Instruments' Reaktor or Cycling 74's Max/MSP, in which you can access such detail.

We've assumed so far that the scale factor is *linear*, or a simple multiplication of the scale factor and the MIDI message value. It's possible for the scaling to be a more complicated function such as a logarithmic or exponential function or some arbitrary function. For example, the frequency change in an oscillator or filter cutoff due to keyboard tracking is an exponential function of the note-on key number (see "Technically Speaking . . . key number conversion" earlier in the chapter). For the most part, it's fine for us to think of these scale factors as linear for now to ease the process of understanding.

The other important concept here is *offset*. The offset value represents the value of a synth parameter before the modulation is added to it. Sticking with our example of the pressure value mapped to the cutoff frequency, the offset would be the value of the cutoff frequency slider or knob before you began modulating it with pressure values. In general, the range of the synth parameter would be:

$$\textit{offset to offset} + (\textit{scale\_factor} \times \textit{max\_control\_value}),$$

and the actual synth parameter value at a given time would be:

$$synth\_parameter\_value = offset + (scale\_factor \times control\_value)$$

where the max control value is 127 for most MIDI messages (0–127 range) and the control value could be the pressure value, or the control value in a control change message, or any other MIDI information that's being used for a similar purpose.

To make this concrete, if the cutoff frequency is initially set to 2,000 Hz (the offset) and the scaling factor for the pressure values is 10, the range of cutoff frequencies would be:

$$2{,}000 \text{ Hz to } 2{,}000 \text{ Hz} + (10 \times 127) = 2{,}000 \text{ Hz to } 3{,}270 \text{ Hz}$$

If the pressure value at a given moment is 64, then the cutoff frequency would be:

$$cutoff\_frequency = 2{,}000 \text{ Hz} + (10 \times 64) = 2{,}640 \text{ Hz}$$

If keyboard tracking is used for the filter, the offset won't be a fixed value, but rather a multiple of the fundamental frequency.

It is important to note that the offset value is not always given in absolute values and the scaling factor seldom is. As a result, both the offset and the scale values are usually set by ear rather than by entering concrete numbers as we did in the example above. Nevertheless, it is important to understand the concepts of offset and scale in order to make these intuitive adjustments.

louder sounds to be brighter, and now the channel pressure value to allow you to control the brightness of the sound while the note is playing. In a given synth patch, these would probably not all be used, but each is a legitimate use of the data from MIDI messages.

Mapping Control Change Messages

Control change messages contain a control number as well as a control value, so there are really 128 different control change messages. Only a handful of them are used regularly, but they provide many possibilities for mapping CCs to synth parameters.

The most likely target in our basic synthesis model for CC1 (mod wheel) is the cutoff frequency of the low pass filter. This would allow you to modulate the brightness/darkness of the note continuously over the course of one or several notes. The cutoff frequency has been named as the possible modulation target for so many messages thus far because it represents such a clear and expressive change to the timbre, and because our current synthesis model is rather limited. As we expand the synthesis model and introduce other synthesis and sampling techniques, we'll find other useful targets for CC1 and other controller messages. CC1 is actually most often used to control vibrato, which will be discussed in the next chapter.

Other control numbers that could also be mapped to the cutoff frequency of the low pass filter include CC2, which is defined as **Breath controller**, and CC74, whose default definition is **Sound controller #5: Brightness**. CC74, in particular, was defined for this purpose.

The MIDI specification suggests that for CC74, control values below 64 cause the sound to progressively darken, and values above 64 cause the sound to progressively brighten (See "Technically Speaking . . . scale and offset"on page 84). As a result, CC74 changes the cutoff frequency relative to the initial cutoff frequency set by the knob, slider, or number field, rather than providing an absolute change in that synth parameter. CC1 and CC2, on the other hand, provide a change in the synth parameter in only one direction. As with most of the MIDI messages that we'll discuss in this section, CC74's effect on timbre is determined by how a particular synth and synth patch is programmed. If a synth is not programmed to use CC74, then the control values sent along with CC74 will have no effect on the timbre.

There are several other "Sound Controllers" that can be used to alter the synth parameters in the basic synth model, including CC71, CC72, CC73, and CC75. The default definition for CC71 is **Sound controller #2: Timbre/Harmonic Intensity**. This has many possible meanings depending on the particular synthesis method used by the synthesizer, but in our basic model the most logical mapping is to the filter resonance. According to the General MIDI 2 specification, CC71, like CC74, provides a change in the resonance *relative* to the setting provided by the knob, slider, or number field; values above 64 increase the resonance value and values below 64 decrease the resonance value. The original MIDI specification describes CC71's value as an absolute rather than relative value.

CC72, CC73, and CC75 affect the **release time**, **attack time**, and **decay time** of a synth's envelopes respectively as **Sound controllers #3**, **#4**, and **#6**. These are also relative controllers with values above 64 causing the specified envelope segment to get longer, and values below 64 causing the envelope segment to get shorter. These are designated as "performance controllers," meaning that they change the synth parameters during performance, but don't change the synth patch permanently. There is only one envelope in our basic synth model, but in the next chapter we'll see that envelopes can be used to modulate many different synth parameters. By default, these controllers should affect all of a synth's envelopes, but it is up to the manufacturer to determine that. Not every synth implements these controllers, and each manufacturer can determine the way in which they're implemented.

Despite the apparent utility of the sound controllers, there is no requirement that a synthesizer implement them. Even the General MIDI 2 standard, which provides full definitions for them, only "recommends" their implementation in General MIDI 2 compatible devices. See Chapter 9: MIDI in Detail for more information on sound controllers and control change messages in general.

Another useful control change message is CC64, the Damper Pedal (Sustain) controller. When CC64 is on, note-off messages are "deferred" until CC64 is turned off. Since the amplitude envelope in the basic synth model is gated by the note-on and note-off messages, deferring the note-off means that the envelope will stay in the sustain portion of the envelope until CC64 is turned off, which is what you would expect from a sustain pedal.

There are several commonly used control change messages that affect the synth *after* the sound has been produced by the synthesis components in the basic synth model or affect the instrument track in the DAW/Sequencer, including CC7, CC11, and CC10. As a result, while these controllers are important and useful, they are not mapped specifically to one of the parameters of the basic synth model.

Expressive messages—pitch bend, aftertouch, and control change—have significantly expanded our possible mapping between information contained in MIDI messages and synthesis parameters. The following is a summary of those mappings:

- pitch bend values → bend fundamental frequency up or down (oscillator);
- aftertouch value → brighten sound by increasing cutoff frequency (filter);
- Control Change 1 (CC1) → brighten sound by increasing cutoff frequency (filter);
- CC2 → brighten sound by increasing cutoff frequency (filter);
- CC74 → brighten/darken sound by increasing/decreasing cutoff frequency (filter);
- CC71 → increase or decrease resonance (filter);
- CC72 → increase or decrease envelope release time (amplifier);
- CC73 → increase or decrease envelope attack time (amplifier);
- CC75 → increase or decrease envelope decay time (amplifier).

Now that we've explored a basic synthesis model and the ways in which MIDI messages can be mapped to synth parameters, we will discuss the other fundamental way for hardware and software instruments to produce sound: sampling.

SAMPLING

In the basic synthesis model discussed above, the sound source was a simple fixed-waveform oscillator, which was then processed by a filter and an amplifier controlled by an amplitude envelope. This model can also serve as a basic model for a sample-based instrument by replacing the oscillator with a collection of samples that are played back under MIDI control. Initially, we will imagine that the cutoff frequency of the filter is so high that it won't have any effect on the timbre and there is no amplitude envelope so the samples' natural envelopes will be heard. Later we'll see that filters and amplitude envelopes can be useful for samples as well.

Sampling is one of the most commonly used techniques for electronically generating sounds. This is particularly true when timbres imitative of acoustic instruments are desired, but many software and hardware instruments generate even "synth-y" timbres through the use of samples. A number of companies even offer sample collections of vintage synthesizers.

The term "sample" has three distinct meanings in music technology:

1. a single amplitude measurement of an analog waveform expressed in some number of bits. This is the sample definition used in Chapter 2: Digital Audio;
2. a recording of a single instrument note that can be played using MIDI note messages. These single instrument samples are usually part of a large group of such samples that form a **sample library**;
3. a distinct chunk of music, such as a two- or four-bar beat that serves as the basis for another tune. This is the definition used in hip-hop and dance music.

There are many samples that cross categories or lie in between them. For example, a sample of a James Brown shout is neither an instrument sample (definition 2) nor a distinct chunk of music (definition 3). Nevertheless, it is probably best classed in definition 3 due to the way it would likely be used as a reference to an older, revered style in a hip-hop tune.

On the other hand, a harmonic glissando on strings is certainly no individual instrument note (definition 2) and is a recognizable chunk of music (definition 3). Nevertheless, it is probably best classed in definition 2 due to the fact that it is likely to be used as part of a sequence that imitates an acoustic instrument. The discussion below will concentrate on definition 2 samples with the understanding that many types of samples could be collected together and used as a library in a software sampler.

Samples for a particular instrument are organized into a **sample patch**, which consists of the samples for that instrument along with configuration information that makes the samples playable and modifiable using MIDI messages. A group of sample patches form a **sample library**. A sample library can be anything from a full set of orchestral instruments to a collection of various types of guitars to various types of percussive sounds made with garden tools.

To understand how a sampler and sample libraries work, we will go through the process of building a sample patch starting with the recordings. A basic sample patch can be constructed using multisampling, looping, and keymapping.

Multisampling, Looping, and Keymapping

The process of constructing a sample patch starts with recording. In the case of instrumental samples, this would involve bringing a performer into a recording studio and having them play notes that span the range of the instrument. The act of recording instrumental samples across the range of the instrument is referred to as **multisampling**. Notes can be recorded every few semitones across the range of the instrument or every semitone. The latter is referred to as **chromatic sampling**.

Right from the start, we have to make a decision concerning the length of each note. Clearly the performer being recorded can't be expected to play an arbitrarily long note. However, it's impossible to predict how someone might wish to use the final sample patch in their music—they may want a trumpet note held for two seconds, two minutes, or two hours. To address this problem, each recorded sample can be **looped** so that when it is triggered by a MIDI note-on message, the sampler will play back the attack and decay portions of the note's envelope and then repeat a specified part of the sustain portion of the envelope. When the sampler receives the corresponding note-off message it will leave the loop and play the release portion of the note's envelope (see Figure 4.8).

Looping involves using sample editing software to specify the beginning and ending points for the loop—an act that is as much art as science. The goal is to match the amplitudes of the beginning and end points, which should be placed on a zero crossing— the point where the waveform crosses from positive to negative or vice versa (see Figure 4.9). That way the repetition of the loop is as smooth as possible. Otherwise, there may be a discontinuity in the amplitude resulting in a pop.

When the looped sample is imported into the sampler, you specify the loop mode, which determines how the loop is played. Different samplers allow for various loop modes. In the most basic mode, the loop is played forward from beginning to end, at which point the sampler skips back to the beginning of the loop, possibly crossfading between the end of the loop and the beginning of the loop. Loops can also be played forward and then backward. This may seem odd, but playing the middle of a note backward doesn't sound dramatically different than playing it forward, and there's no chance of an amplitude discontinuity.

Once the samples are recorded, edited, and looped, they are imported into a sampler and each is mapped to a MIDI key number or a range of key numbers. If the patch is not chromatically sampled, then the same sample will be assigned to several keys, referred

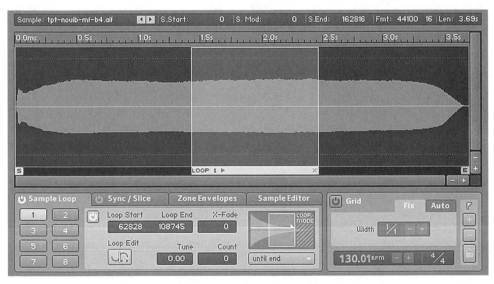

Figure 4.8 A looped sample (courtesy of Native Instruments GmbH, Germany). The start and end times of the loop are expressed precisely as the number of audio samples from the start of the sound file

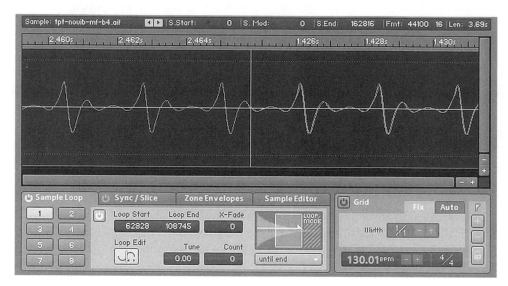

Figure 4.9 The loop point shown in Kontakt's loop editor (courtesy of Native Instruments GmbH, Germany). The beginning of the loop is to the right of the center line and the end of the loop is to the left of the center line

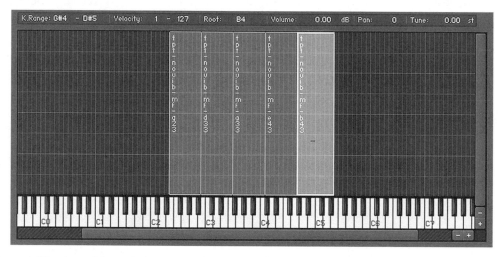

Figure 4.10 A multisampled trumpet (courtesy of Native Instruments GmbH, Germany). Five trumpet samples covering the full range of the instrument with key zones of seven semitones. One key zone is highlighted showing that it is being played

to as a **key zone** or **key range**. One of the keys in that zone will be designated as the **root key** and will play the sample back without alteration. Any key above the root key in the key zone will transpose the sample up and any key below the root key in the key zone will transpose the sample down. Figure 4.10 shows a trumpet sample patch with relatively wide key zones.

The drawback to a wide key zone is that a sequence of MIDI notes that crosses the key zone boundary will be going from a sample that is transposed up several semitones

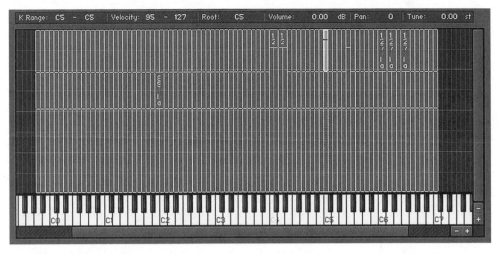

Figure 4.11   A chromatically sampled piano with three velocity zones (courtesy of Native Instruments GmbH, Germany). One of the key/velocity zones is highlighted, showing that it is being played

to one that is transposed down several semitones. A smaller key zone will improve those transitions. If the sample patch is chromatically sampled (a key zone of one semitone), then there will be no transposing of notes. However, more samples mean more expense for the sample library creator and more memory for the computer hosting the samples. In addition, any inconsistencies in timbre or articulation from note to note in the recording will be apparent. More expensive sample libraries tend to use chromatic sampling more, particularly for piano samples (see Figure 4.11).

Multisampling, looping, and keymapping provide a MIDI-controllable sample patch that can play notes across the full range of the sampled instrument. However, there are several refinements that can improve the sample patch including velocity switching, round-robin, and key switching.

Loudness, Brightness, and Velocity Switching

So far, our sampled instrument can be played across its full range, but every note will have the same volume. One simple solution is to map the velocity of the MIDI note-on message to the level of the amplifier. However, as noted above, putting more energy into an acoustic instrument usually results in a timbre that is both louder *and* brighter.

The same solution to this problem discussed above for the synthesis model can be used here as well: mapping the velocity of the note-on message to the cutoff frequency of the low pass filter. In this case the resonance should be set to zero so that it doesn't "color" the sound. In this way, a higher velocity will yield an increase in brightness. To use this strategy, it would be necessary to sample the instrument being played at the maximum desired volume, because the low pass filter can only remove partials, not add them. In addition, the filter would likely be set to some percentage of keyboard tracking so that the effect of playing at the same velocity at different places on the keyboard would be similar.

Another way of creating the loudness-brightness linkage in a sample patch would be to record each sample at several different dynamic levels. The velocity of the note-on message would then be used to select which dynamic level sample to use. This technique is referred to as **velocity switching**.

The advantage of velocity switching over a velocity-controlled low pass filter is that it can take into account other timbral changes that happen as a note is played louder, such as changes in the attack time, changes in the amount of noise associated with the attack, changes in the decay time, and changes in the way the partials in the spectrum behave over time. The disadvantage is that it requires more samples to be recorded, edited, mapped, and stored in memory. Fortunately, computer memory is a fairly inexpensive commodity now.

Velocity switching involves **velocity zones**, sometimes called **velocity layers**, just as multisampling involves key zones. To smooth the change from one sample to another at the velocity switch point, samples on either side of the switch point can be crossfaded with one another. Figure 4.12 shows the multisampled trumpet from Figure 4.10, now with three velocity zones instead of the initial one. The chromatically sampled piano in Figure 4.11 also has three velocity zones. Three velocity zones are shown in these examples for simplicity, but it is a relatively modest number—higher end sample libraries tend to have more velocity zones for certain instruments such as pianos.

Velocity switching can also be used for alternate instrumental gestures or articulations. For example, you could have a bass patch in which most of the velocity zones trigger louder and louder samples, but the highest velocity zone triggers a slap bass sample. That sample patch then becomes more useful for live performance and sequencing because you don't have to use a different sample patch or a different track

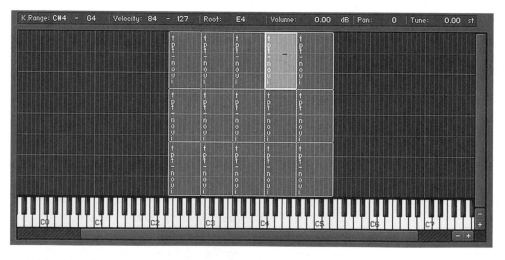

Figure 4.12   A multisampled, velocity-switched trumpet with three velocity zones (courtesy of Native Instruments GmbH, Germany). One of the key/velocity zones is highlighted showing that it is being played

for that alternate gesture. This works well for a single alternate gesture or articulation, but to create a sample patch that can play multiple articulations, you would use key switching.

Alternate Articulations and Key Switching

In order for a sampled instrument to plausibly mimic an acoustic instrument, it must be able to execute that instrument's various articulations. Some articulations could be mimicked using elements of the basic synthesis model. For example, a staccato articulation could be realized by applying a staccato amplitude envelope to a regular sample. Similarly, an accented articulation could be realized using an amplitude envelope with a fast attack, fast decay, and sustain level of 50–75 percent of the peak so that the attack is noticeably louder than the sustain. That amplitude envelope could be used in conjunction with a velocity-controlled filter so that the attack is both louder and brighter.

However, as discussed with velocity switching above, there are facets to those articulations that cannot be fully captured with a filter and an amplitude envelope. In addition, there are some articulations that are so different that only more samples will do the job.

One common strategy is to create a separate multisampled, looped, keymapped, velocity switched set of samples for each articulation and use a MIDI message to switch between them. If the switch message is a MIDI note message that is outside the range of the instrument, the sample patch is said to be **key switched**. Any number of MIDI messages could also be used for this purpose, such as a control change message in which the control value is used to select the articulation. This can be thought of as creating "articulation zones" by analogy with key zones and velocity zones. Key switching allows you to use a single track of a sequencer for one instrument and still have access to all of the various articulations for that instrument. This is a more natural setup for a composer/arranger who is used to thinking of the various articulations of an instrument as simply a part of that single instrument.

Stringed instruments are prime candidates for key switching because there are so many different articulations, including arco (bowed), staccato/marcato, pizzicato (plucked), sul tasto (bowed over the fingerboard), and sul ponticello (bowed near the bridge). In addition, there are gestures such as tremolos, half-step trills, and whole-step trills that are commonly used in orchestral mock-ups. Wind instruments also have legato, staccato, and trills, with brass instruments also needing various kinds of mutes. Longer and more complex instrumental gestures such as glissandi can also be used as just another "articulation layer" for a key switched instrument.

Round Robin

Another possible problem with sampled sounds is repetition. When an instrumentalist repeats a note, the note is slightly different each time. As listeners, we have come to expect this from acoustically produced sounds. However, samples are, by definition, the same each time they are played, resulting in disconcertingly perfect repetition. This is particularly true of drum sounds, but many timbres are susceptible to the issue.

One solution is to record multiple samples for each key zone and each velocity zone and cycle through them in a **round robin**. The slight variations between the samples mimic the natural variations found in an acoustic performance. As with many of the sampling techniques discussed here, the solution to a sampling problem is often to use more samples.

Sample Patches

Our sample patch now consists of a set of multisampled, looped, keymapped, velocity switched, key switched, and round robin-ed samples ready to be played by MIDI messages. In addition, the output of the sample playback process can be processed by filters, amplitude envelopes, and various audio effects, and sample playback can be modulated by envelopes and LFOs as discussed in the next chapter. The configurations of these elements are also part of the sample patch. Figure 4.13 shows some of the envelope and filter settings for a sample patch.

The next several chapters will focus primarily on synthesis, but it is important to keep in mind that most of these synthesis techniques can be applied to samples as well. The results of these techniques on samples may be unpredictable at times, but samples allow you to bring valuable real world complexity into an electronic context.

To this point, the motivation for the various sampling techniques has been the realistic imitation of acoustic instruments, especially orchestral instruments. This is, of course, the bread and butter for composers/arrangers working in TV and film. However, a sample patch can contain any type of sample imaginable including recordings of

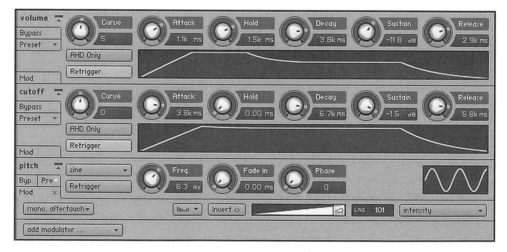

Figure 4.13   The modulation window in Kontakt showing some synthesizer elements assigned to modify sample playback including a volume envelope, a filter envelope, and an LFO assigned to pitch (vibrato) (courtesy of Native Instruments GmbH, Germany)

synthesized sounds, percussive effects, sound effects, and vocal utterances, as well as longer samples such as multiple measures of a drum groove or melodic and harmonic phrases. Sampling is a very powerful and flexible way of generating sound using a computer.

MIDI Mappings for Sampling Techniques

Some of the possible mappings between MIDI messages and sampling techniques are summarized below. In addition, all of the mappings discussed above with regard to synthesis are valid here. These mappings for synthesis and sampling will expand greatly in the next chapter when we take up modulation with envelopes and LFOs.

These are the primary sample mappings:

- note-on key number → play back sample from particular key zone;
- note-on velocity → play back sample from particular velocity zone;
- note-on velocity → make sample louder or softer within velocity zone (amplifier);
- note-on key number → out-of-range key selects articulation.

The following mappings can serve as an alternative to velocity switching:

- note-on velocity → cutoff frequency (filter);
- note-on key number → cutoff frequency (filter) through keyboard tracking.

In the next chapter we'll expand the basic synthesis and sampling models to include envelopes and LFOs as tools for producing dynamic sound. In addition, we will explore modulation routings in greater detail.

CHAPTER 5

Modulation and Dynamic Sound

One of the primary characteristics of natural musical sounds is that they are constantly in motion—they are dynamic. The pitch, loudness, and timbre of an acoustically produced sound are never truly steady. In fact, one of the characteristics of a "synthetic" sound is its machine-like regularity. In most cases, even when you're using unusual, synthesized timbres, you will want to imbue them with some of the constant motion found in acoustically produced sounds. There may, of course, be instances when you want to evoke antiseptic perfection in your music, but for all other circumstances dynamic change is an important characteristic of a synthesized timbre.

One way of creating dynamic sound involves modifying, or **modulating**, synthesis parameters over the course of a note or across many notes. The basic synthesis and sampling models presented in the last chapter provided only a few parameters to modulate. As we continue to expand those models in this chapter and introduce other synthesis techniques in later chapters, there will be more and more controllable parameters that can be modulated. The three basic ways to accomplish this modulation are through direct control, envelopes, and LFOs.

MODULATION BY DIRECT CONTROL

We encountered modulation by **direct control** in the last chapter when we discussed how MIDI note messages and expressive messages can be used to modify synthesis parameters. For example, we saw how the velocity value in a note-on message can be used to modulate the cutoff frequency of a low pass filter.

Expressive messages were designed for the very purpose of directly controlling synthesis parameters. For example, the pitch bend message is used to directly modify the pitch played by the oscillator either on the occasional note or over many notes. Aftertouch or control change messages, particularly CC1 or CC74, can be used to directly modify the cutoff frequency of a low pass filter. This can also be done on a note-by-note basis so that single notes can be made brighter or darker or over the course of many notes so that a whole musical phrase can be made brighter or darker.

Modulation by direct control emphasizes the distinction between MIDI messages and the synth parameters that they control. MIDI messages originate from a controller or from a MIDI track in a DAW/Sequencer and are sent to a hardware or software instrument. The mapping between the data in those MIDI messages and an instrument's synthesis parameters is generally determined on a patch-by-patch basis. Except for a few standard mappings, such as the key number of the note-on message determining the frequency of the oscillator, most of these mappings are set by modulation routings that are specific to each patch. Thus each patch can have its own expressive characteristics and MIDI messages may cause different changes in the sound depending on the modulation routings in each patch.

In modulation by direct control and the other techniques discussed in this chapter, the concepts of scale and offset are important. A **scaling factor** determines how *much* the modulation wheel (CC1) changes the filter cutoff frequency or how much the pitch bender changes the pitch. If the scaling factor is negative, or inverted, then a positive change in a modulator, such as CC1, would result in a negative change in a synth parameter, such as the cutoff frequency. **Offset** determines the starting point for the modulation, such as the initial setting for the cutoff frequency before you start using the modulation (mod) wheel, or the initial pitch before you start using the pitch bend wheel. This was discussed in the last chapter in the "Technically Speaking . . . scale and offset" sidebar.

Figure 5.1 shows the 0–127 range of the mod wheel message (CC1) that is modified in the synth through scaling by an "amount" slider, knob, or number field and offset by the cutoff frequency slider or knob. In practice, the degree of scaling is usually specified in the synth as 0–100 percent, 0–1.0, or 0–127, with the actual range of scaling values being determined by the computer programmers who created the synth. The offset determined by the cutoff frequency slider or knob may be given in absolute Hertz values or as an abstract range such as 0–100 percent, 0–1.0, or 0–127. If the filter utilizes keyboard tracking then the offset as set by the cutoff frequency slider or knob will be some multiple of the fundamental frequency as determined from the key number and the key tracking percentage.

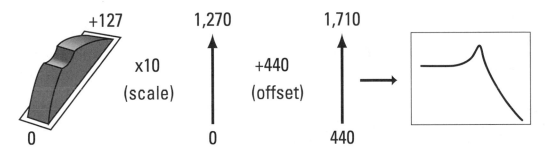

Figure 5.1 Mod wheel range scaled by 10, offset by 440 Hz, and applied to the cutoff frequency of a low pass resonant filter

As mentioned in the last chapter, expressive MIDI messages are not directly connected to note messages; they can be sent when no notes are playing, during just a few notes in a passage, or constantly over many notes. If you want to modulate a synthesis parameter in a regular way on every note, then an envelope is a better tool.

MODULATION WITH ENVELOPES

Envelopes are not a new concept in this book: an amplitude envelope is a fundamental part of the basic synthesis model presented in the last chapter. However, envelopes can be mapped to other synthesizer elements besides the amplifier. To generalize the use of envelopes, it is useful to re-conceive of the amplifier/envelope as an amplifier component with one parameter—peak amplitude—that is modulated by an envelope. In this light, an envelope can be seen as a separate modulation source that can be applied to a variety of synthesis parameters.

Filter Envelopes

A **filter envelope** is a common application of a modulation envelope; so common, in fact, that most synths have a dedicated filter envelope along with their dedicated amplitude envelope. A filter envelope is applied to the cutoff frequency of the low pass filter and is gated with note-on/note-off messages just like the amplitude envelope.

One of the primary differences between amplitude envelopes and filter envelopes is that amplitude envelopes start at zero amplitude (no sound), whereas filter envelopes start at a frequency determined by the cutoff frequency knob/slider. In addition, the peak value of the envelope, which represents the greatest amount of change from the cutoff frequency knob/slider, is determined by a modulation "amount" value that is set by a knob, slider, or number field. The modulation provided by the filter envelope is *offset* by the filter's cutoff frequency control and *scaled* by the envelope's amount control (See "Technically Speaking . . . scale and offset" in the last chapter). In an amplitude envelope, the offset is zero and the peak amplitude is often scaled by the note-on velocity.

An ADSR filter envelope would operate as follows, in which all of the envelope values are *added* to the initial offset value set by the filter cutoff knob/slider (see Figure 5.2):

- During the Attack stage, the cutoff frequency rises from the offset determined by the cutoff frequency slider/knob to some peak amount of change determined by the amount setting over the time set by the attack parameter.
- During the Decay stage, the cutoff frequency falls from the peak amount of change to the sustain value (a percentage of the peak set by the sustain parameter) over the time set by the decay parameter.
- During the Sustain stage, the cutoff frequency remains at the sustain value until the note is turned off.

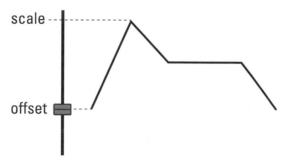

Figure 5.2   Filter envelope showing offset by slider position and scale

- During the Release stage, the cutoff frequency falls from the sustain value to the original offset value over the time set by the release parameter.

We assumed above that the offset (starting point) and scale (setting of the peak change) of the filter envelope were set by knobs or sliders on the synth, but other MIDI information can influence those parameters. For example, we saw in the last chapter that the offset of the filter can be modified by keyboard tracking, in which the filter cutoff frequency changes depending on the key number of the note-on message. The amount of change created by the envelope can also be scaled by the velocity value so that notes that are softly struck have fairly little cutoff frequency modulation due to the envelope, and notes that are struck quite hard have a large amount of cutoff frequency modulation due to the envelope.

It is common for the filter envelope to have a shape similar to that of the amplitude envelope so that the sound brightens as it gets louder and darkens as it gets softer, though with perhaps a lower sustain value to accentuate the effect. For sounds that are meant to sustain longer, the attack value of the filter envelope might be set a little longer so that the sound grows in brightness slowly after the primary attack of the note. In these situations an envelope with more stages might be useful so that the brightness can fluctuate over the course of the sustained note, though this effect could also be accomplished by directly controlling the cutoff frequency of the filter using CC1 or CC74.

The filter resonance becomes a dramatic part of the timbre when a filter envelope is used. The filter resonance accentuates the change in the cutoff frequency making it an audible feature of the timbre. This is also true when the filter is "swept" using direct control through CC1 or CC74. The filter envelope essentially creates an automated sweep on each note.

The difference between direct control by CC1 or CC74 and the filter envelope is that the filter envelope is executed on every note, gated by the note-on/note-off messages, whereas direct control can be applied occasionally to a note or can be applied over the course of many notes. The choice of which to use when designing a patch depends on whether you consider the cutoff frequency change to be an essential part of every note or just an occasional modification. Both direct and envelope modulation could be used at the same time so that the envelope executes its attack and decay and the CC1/CC74 messages alter the cutoff frequency during the sustained part of the note.

Pitch Envelopes

A **pitch envelope** is applied to the frequency of the oscillator and, like all of the other envelopes, is usually gated by the note-on and note-off messages. Unlike the amplitude and filter envelopes, there is seldom a dedicated pitch envelope. Instead, a general-purpose envelope with a settable destination, called something like the "mod" envelope, is used for this purpose.

Like a filter envelope, a pitch envelope is *offset* from zero, here by the key number of the note-on message. Also like the filter envelope, the pitch envelope is *scaled* by an "amount" slider, knob, or number field. The function of a pitch envelope is similar to that of the pitch bend message in that both are offset by the key number of the note-on message and both are scaled, the pitch bend message by a factor derived from the pitch bend range (sensitivity) and a pitch envelope by the amount knob, slider, or number field. A pitch envelope, then, can be seen as an automated pitch bend on every note.

A simple ADSR pitch envelope operates as follows, in which all of the envelope values are *added* to the initial offset value set by the note-on key number (see Figure 5.3):

- During the Attack stage, the pitch rises from the note-on key number to some peak amount of pitch change determined by the amount setting over the time set by the attack parameter.
- During the Decay stage, the pitch falls from the peak pitch change to the sustain level pitch change (a percentage of the peak set by the sustain parameter) over the time set by the decay parameter.
- During the Sustain stage, the pitch remains at the sustain value until the note is turned off.
- During the Release stage, the pitch falls from the sustain value to the original pitch set by the key number over the time set by the release parameter.

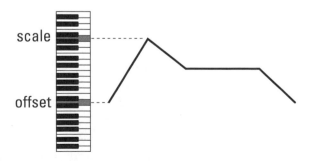

Figure 5.3   Pitch envelope showing offset by key number and scale

In the above discussion, we assumed that the initial offset pitch was simply the note-on key number, but that offset pitch can be modified by transposition and detuning in the oscillator or the keyboard tracking setting of the oscillator. Similarly, we assumed that the scaling of the envelope was set by an amount knob/slider/field, but that can also be modified by other sources such as the note-on velocity. In the latter case, the pitch envelope will have a greater effect when the velocity is higher.

It is common for a pitch envelope to have little to no attack, a short decay, and a zero sustain level (see Figure 5.4). This causes the pitch to start immediately at a higher level than the key number offset and fall very quickly back to the key number (no sustain level), giving the sound just a quick bit of change at the beginning. This is one of many strategies for creating a somewhat more complex timbre during the attack phase, or transient, of a note. Pitch envelopes with non-zero attack times and sustain values can be useful for creating special effects such as sirens and laser guns.

The difference between a pitch envelope and direct control by the pitch bend wheel is similar to the difference between a filter envelope and direct control by CC1 or CC74. With a pitch envelope, the pitch change occurs in the same way on every note. With direct pitch bend control, the pitch change can be different on every note or change over the course of many notes. The choice of which to use when designing a patch depends on whether you consider the pitch change to be an essential part of every note or just an occasional modification. Both direct and envelope modulation could be used at the same time so that the envelope executes its attack and decay and the pitch bend messages alter the pitch during the sustained part of the note.

Mod Envelopes

Many synths have dedicated amplitude and filter envelopes and then provide one or more undesignated "mod" envelopes to control other parameters; the pitch envelope discussed above is one example of a mod envelope application. A mod envelope has all the standard features of the envelopes discussed above and can be routed to various synth parameters. With the basic synthesis model presented in the last chapter, the amplitude envelope, filter envelope, and a mod envelope assigned to pitch cover most of the available synth parameters. However, as you'll see later in this chapter, a mod envelope can also be applied to other modulators such as an LFO, and when we discuss more synthesis methods in the next two chapters, a whole new world of synth parameters, all ripe for the modulating, will open up.

Figure 5.4 Pitch envelope with no attack, a short decay, and zero sustain level that creates a sudden swoop down at the beginning of each note

Envelope Variations

Thus far our envelopes have all been ADSR envelopes with straight line segments that are gated by note-on and note-off messages. However, there are a number of variations on this model that can be found in some synths.

A straight-line ADSR is very useful and effective in most circumstances, but envelopes with more (or fewer) stages and/or curved lines can also be valuable. The additional stages of an envelope may share labels with the simple ADSR so that a more complex envelope could be $A_1A_2D_1D_2S_1S_2R_1R_2$. In this case, the multiple As, Ds, and Rs allow you to have a more complex shape and the multiple Ss allow the sustain level to increase or decrease before the note-off message arrives.

Alternately, new types of segments could be incorporated, such as "delay" (D or Del) for an amount of delay after the note-on before the envelope starts, or "hold" (H) for an amount of time the value stays static (see Figure 5.5). The initial delay segment is most likely to be found on a general modulation envelope than on an amplitude envelope. Some envelopes may actually have fewer stages, such as a simple attack-decay envelope as an amplitude envelope for creating only struck or plucked articulations or as an envelope dedicated to an LFO (more on LFOs later in the chapter). Some softsynths have a changeable number of segments so that different patches can use the envelope that is most useful.

Different line segment shapes allow the parameter being modulated to change at a rate other than the steady rate indicated by a straight line. To understand the value of non-linear segments, you should note that we are perceptually wired to hear not just the change in some property but also the change in that change. If you think of traveling in a car, when you are doing a steady 65 mph on the highway it feels as if you're not moving at all. Your position is changing rather rapidly, but because the change is constant (i.e., your velocity is constant), you stop noticing it. However, if you stop or speed up suddenly, you perceive that you are in motion because now the change in your position is changing (i.e., you are accelerating or decelerating).

Straight line segments can be thought of as going at a constant velocity: after a short while you stop paying attention to the change. **Curved line segments** can be thought of as accelerating or decelerating: you notice that the change is changing (see Figure 5.5). Sometimes the difference is subtle and it doesn't matter much whether you use straight lines or curved lines and sometimes it can make the difference between a

Figure 5.5   Complex envelope with delay and hold segments as well as curved segments

boring note attack and one that catches your attention. As with all of the elements in these chapters, experimentation is the best way to discover these effects.

All along, we've been assuming that an envelope "rises" above some offset and "falls" back to it. However, in certain circumstances an **inverted envelope** may be desirable, where the synth parameter falls *below* the offset during the attack phase, partway back *up* to the offset during the decay, and then all the way back *up* to the offset during the release phase (see Figure 5.6). For example, a filter envelope with a quick attack, a moderate decay, and no sustain, applied to a low pass filter, could be inverted to create a sudden darkening of the timbre right after the attack that returns to the offset level of brightness during the decay segment—a "bwah" sound at the beginning of every note. In this instance, the offset would have to be high enough to accommodate the scale of the inverted envelope. In the next chapter, we'll see different types of filters besides the low pass filter of the basic synth model where an inverted filter envelope could also be used.

When we were introduced to envelopes in the previous chapter, we were also introduced to the concept of a **gate**—a signal that turns something on and then turns it off. For most envelopes, particularly amplitude envelopes, it is quite sensible to gate them with the note-on and note-off messages, though some variations in envelope gating will be discussed below. **Triggering** is related to gating, but is subtly different. Gating is accomplished by a signal that turns an envelope on and then turns it off, such as note-on/note-off messages. Triggering, on the other hand, is accomplished by just a single signal that turns an envelope on and lets it run its course. We'll see below how gating and triggering interact.

In normal synth playing where several notes might be sounding at one time—either as a chord or in a polyphonic texture—a synth's envelopes would be gated for each new note. In other words, if you play and hold one note, the amp, filter, and mod envelopes are all started by the note-on message. If you add a second note, it will have its own amp, filter, and mod envelopes started by its note-on while the envelopes for the other note are independently executing their shapes. This is normal **polyphonic** behavior for envelopes.

For many classic analog-type sounds, particularly leads and basses, the synth is played in monophonic mode, meaning that only one note will play at a time. Naturally, when a single note is pressed and released the envelopes will be gated as described above. However, if you play another note before you release the first—as you would when playing legato on a keyboard—then the old note will stop and the new note will play. In that case, there are a couple of possibilities for the behavior of the envelopes. They

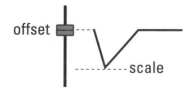

Figure 5.6 Inverted filter envelope with a short attack, moderate decay, and no sustain

can either all start again as they do in polyphonic playing when a new note starts—this is referred to **retriggering** (see Figure 5.7a)—or the oscillator can change to the new pitch while the envelopes stay in their sustain segments—this is referred to as **legato** mode (see Figure 5.7b). In legato mode, the envelopes aren't retriggered unless a note is released before the note-on of the next note.

In addition to different gating/triggering modes, it is sometimes desirable to have a completely different way to gate or trigger an envelope than the note-on/note-off messages. For example, if you have a mod envelope assigned to pitch that creates a quick glissando down to the key number as described previously (see Figure 5.4), it creates a bit of desirable complexity at the beginning of a note when it's gated by note-on and note-off messages. However, if you want that downward glissando to happen in other places during the note, you need to gate that envelope with some other signal.

One possibility would be to use a signal from an oscillator playing a square or pulse wave. The start of the square or pulse could act as the gate-on signal and the point where the square or pulse drops below a certain point could be the gate-off. This would generally happen far too quickly in a typical oscillator, but as we'll see below, there are special "low frequency" oscillators that can handle the task. This type of modulation was commonly available in analog synthesizers, but in modern software synthesizers you are often limited by the synth's design as to how you can route the modulators. Synthesizers that more faithfully replicate analog synth behaviors and synth programming applications—such as Reaktor and Max/MSP—usually provide the most flexibility in this regard.

Another way to achieve this repeated envelope modulation is to use an envelope that can be **looped**, which is available in some synths. Once the envelope has been gated on by the note-on message, the envelope follows its shape, usually excluding the release segment, and then repeats that shape over and over until the note is released. The duration of each loop is the sum of the segments that are looping. For most envelopes, these duration values are given in seconds, milliseconds (ms), or in some abstract value, such as 0–100 percent, 0.0–1.0, or 0–127. A synth that allows a looped envelope may also allow the durations to be synchronized to the tempo of the sequence.

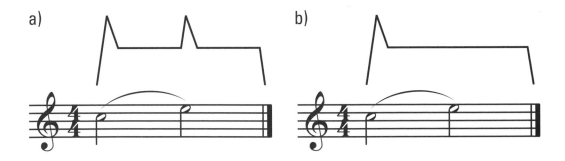

Figure 5.7   a) Monophonic legato playing with envelope retriggering and b) monophonic legato playing in legato mode

In that case, the durations for each segment are given in musical units such as 1/8 for an eighth note, 1/4 for a quarter note, and 1/2 or 2/4 for a half note. A "t" appended to the duration often indicates a triplet value and a "d" or "." indicates a dotted value.

As we've seen, envelopes allow you to modulate a synthesis parameter in a particular pattern over the course of the note, but if you want that parameter to change up and down in a regular fashion, then an LFO would be a better tool.

MODULATION WITH LFOS

LFO stands for **low frequency oscillator**, where the "low frequency" part indicates a frequency below 20 Hz, and hence below the range in which we hear frequencies as pitches. As a result, if we were to listen to a low frequency oscillator directly we would hear nothing—or at least nothing musically useful. However, when we use an LFO to modify a synthesis parameter such as pitch, cutoff frequency, or amplitude, the effect of the LFO is quite audible (see Table 5.1 on page 109).

An LFO has three basic parameters: **shape** (waveform), **rate** (frequency), and **depth** (amplitude). The names associated with regular oscillators are included in parentheses for reference, but it is useful to use the terms shape, rate, and depth in order to keep clear the function of an LFO as a modulator rather than a sound source. We'll see later that the depth parameter has several names and is manipulated at different places on the synth interface depending on the specific synth.

When an LFO modulates a synth parameter, that parameter changes periodically, unlike modulation by envelope where the parameter change follows a specific path only once during the course of the note (unless the envelope is looped or retriggered). The speed of the change is set by the LFO rate, the amount of the change by the LFO depth, and the way that the parameter changes by the LFO shape. The perceived effect of the LFO depends which specific synth parameter is modulated. Almost any synth parameter can be a target for LFO modulation, but in our basic synth model, the likely targets are the pitch of the oscillator, the cutoff frequency of the filter, and the overall amplitude of the amplifier.

Pitch LFO

When an LFO modulates the pitch of an oscillator, the pitch periodically rises above and falls below the frequency determined by the key number—in other words, **vibrato**. A natural vibrato requires a fairly smooth shape, such as a sine wave or a triangle wave. Other waveforms are also useful for LFO modulation, but their effects can't really be described as vibrato. A natural vibrato rate varies from instrument to instrument, but about 5–10 Hz is a reasonable range. In some synths, the rate of the LFO can be modified by keyboard tracking so that the rate increases as the pitch of the note increases.

The LFO depth in vibrato is the amount of change in Hz or cents above and below the frequency given by the note-on key number. If the vibrato depth is too large, it will sound unnatural and potentially comical. In a synth this value is set by a knob, slider, or number field and is usually given in abstract values such as 0–100 percent, 0.0–1.0, or 0–127. You might recognize this as the familiar *scaling factor* (see "Technically Speaking . . . scale and offset" in the previous chapter) and the frequency given by the key number of the note-on message as the *offset*. As with other parameters discussed in this chapter, the rate and depth are usually set by ear.

An LFO mapped to oscillator pitch is not limited just to smooth waveforms or natural vibrato rates and depths. Most LFOs can assume a variety of shapes including sine, triangle, sawtooth, square, stepped random, and smooth random. As we've already discussed, **sine** and **triangle waveforms** generate smooth changes in pitch suitable for traditional vibrato (see Figures 5.8, 5.9a, and 5.9b). A sawtooth wave when slowed down to low frequencies becomes either a **ramp up** or a **ramp down** (see Figures 5.9c and 5.9d). When a sawtooth wave is used in a regular oscillator, the ramp up or down aspect isn't audible. However, when the rate is slow enough to hear the ramp, it becomes important whether it's a linear ascent followed by a sudden drop or a sudden jump up followed by a linear descent. The depth determines the height of the sudden drop or jump up. This generates special effects type sounds such as sirens and laser guns.

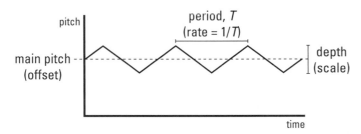

Figure 5.8 Vibrato resulting from a triangle wave LFO applied to the pitch of an oscillator

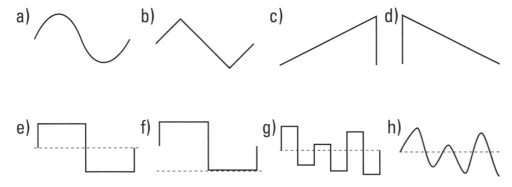

Figure 5.9 A variety of LFO waveforms: a) sine; b) triangle; c) ramp up; d) ramp down; e) bipolar square; f) unipolar square; g) stepped random (multiple periods); h) smooth random (multiple periods)

A **square wave** in an LFO effectively becomes a trill because there is no transition between up and down states. The depth determines the musical interval and the rate determines the speed of the trill. Square waves in normal oscillators go above and below the zero line like all other waveforms—these are referred to as **bipolar waveforms** (see Figure 5.9e). However, some LFOs provide a square wave that only goes above zero—a **unipolar waveform** (see Figure 5.9f). This is handy for a trill because then the trill would go up from the key number (offset) and back down to it, as you would expect from a trill, rather than going above and below the key number.

The **stepped random waveform** is similar to a square wave in that it acts as a series of steps (see Figure 5.9g). However, where each step of the square wave is the same, as determined by the depth, the size of the steps of the stepped random waveform are randomly chosen between zero and the depth setting in both the positive and negative direction (above and below the key number of the note-on message). When applied to pitch, this generates a random series of pitches at a time interval determined by the rate (inverse of the rate)—a sound reminiscent of computers in old sci-fi movies.

The stepped random waveform is similar to the output of **sample-and-hold** modules that were found on many analog synths. Sample-and-hold modules measured the amplitude of an incoming signal at regular time intervals and held that amplitude until the next time interval, at which point another measurement was made. If the incoming signal was noise, the result would be similar to the stepped random waveform here.

The **smooth random waveform** is related to the stepped random waveform, except that it uses a sort of "sample-and-glide" process instead (see Figure 5.9h). There are still a series of random amplitude values in the smooth random waveform, but the LFO glides from one to the other during the time interval (inverse of the rate) rather than stepping from one to the other at the end of the time interval like the stepped random. As with the stepped random waveform, the amplitude values for the smooth random waveform range from zero to the depth setting both above and below the key number. Applying this signal to the pitch of the oscillator generates a ghostly effect. Varying the rate on both the stepped random and smooth random waveforms increases the speed of the irregularity in the result.

Besides the choice of waveform, the other primary type of variation on an LFO is the choice of an absolute rate or one that is synchronized (locked) to your DAW/ Sequencer's tempo. Effects such as vibrato are independent of the tempo of the music, but other LFO effects such as trills or random pitch steps could benefit from being locked to the tempo. The non-synchronized rate is given either as an abstract value (0–100 percent, 0.0–1.0, 0–127) or in Hz, but the **tempo-synchronized** "rate" is usually given as the *period* (the inverse of a real rate) during which the LFO completes one cycle (see Figure 5.10). For example, if you set the waveform of the LFO to a ramp up (a type of sawtooth) and want the pitch to rise over the course of two beats and then drop back down and start over, you would set the LFO period as a half-note, perhaps shown as 1/2 or 2/4. Other note values might be given as 1/16, 1/8, or 1/4, with the addition of a "t" indicating a triplet value and a "d" or "." indicating a dotted value.

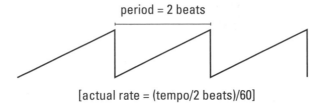

period = 2 beats

[actual rate = (tempo/2 beats)/60]

Figure 5.10   A tempo-synchronized LFO waveform with a two-beat (half-note) period

Filter Cutoff LFO

When an LFO modulates the cutoff frequency of a low pass filter, the sound periodically grows brighter and darker. If you simulate this opening and closing of the filter by opening and closing your mouth as you say "ah," you'll discover why this is referred to as **wah-wah**. To create this effect, the waveform would be something smooth like a sine or triangle wave. The rate of the LFO determines the speed of the wah-wah and the depth determines how extreme the effect is.

The other LFO shapes described above can also be used, though they are less distinctive when modulating the cutoff frequency than they are when modulating the pitch. On a thick-textured timbre, the smooth random waveform can be used with a moderate rate and depth to produce a texture with some lively variation. Faster rates and greater depths with smooth or stepped random waveforms result in a jittery sound.

In certain genres of music, such as electronic dance music, tempo synchronization of a filter LFO with triangle or ramp waveform is used to achieve the characteristic effect of the filter opening and closing over the span of multiple beats or measures.

Amplitude LFO

When an LFO modulates the overall amplitude, the sound periodically grows louder and softer—an effect referred to as **tremolo**. With a smooth LFO waveform and relatively low values for rate and depth, the effect is a pleasing undulation of the sound. Using a stepped waveform such as a square wave, a moderate rate, and a relatively large value for depth, you can achieve an effect where the sound shuts down suddenly and turns back on just as suddenly creating an uneasy sensation of the sound breaking up. This sensation is accentuated if you vary the rate from moderate up to maximum and back.

Tremolo is characteristic of the sound of a vibraphone. A vibraphone has tubular resonators that hang below the metal bars. At the top of these resonators are small discs connected to a motor that causes them to rotate, periodically opening and closing the resonator. This effect can be simulated by using an LFO modulating the overall amplitude. Because there is a timbral effect from closing off the resonators, amplitude modulation by an LFO can be combined with cutoff frequency modulation by an LFO (wah-wah), and perhaps some pitch modulation by an LFO (vibrato), to better match

Table 5.1   Some examples of LFO modulation

Mapping	LFO → pitch (oscillator)
Effect	Vibrato (with smooth waveform and appropriate rate and depth settings)
Mapping	LFO → cutoff frequency (filter)
Effect	Wah-wah (with smooth waveform and appropriate rate and depth settings)
Mapping	LFO → overall amplitude (amplifier)
Effect	Tremolo (with smooth waveform and appropriate rate and depth settings)

the effect of the spinning discs. This would be a combined tremolo, wah-wah, and vibrato effect.

LFO Variations

So far we've seen a few variants on the basic LFO, including a variety of waveforms and the option of synchronizing the rate with the tempo in which the "rate" is a musical duration instead of an absolute rate given in Hz. In addition, there are a few other facets to an LFO that bear mentioning, including delay, polyphony, and key sync.

The **LFO delay** parameter, when available, simply allows you to set an amount of time after the start of the note at which the LFO modulation will begin. This allows you to have short notes with no LFO modulation and longer notes with LFO modulation. An envelope could also be used to fade in the LFO modulation as described later in the chapter. If the LFO is generating vibrato, then the delay will allow short notes to sound without vibrato, while longer notes will have a delayed vibrato. A fade-in envelope allows the start of the vibrato to be more subtle.

If an LFO is **polyphonic**, then each note played on a synth will have its own separate LFO and those modulations will not be synchronized in terms of how they rise and fall. If the LFO is monophonic, then the LFO modulation for every note will rise and fall at the same time. For example, if a polyphonic LFO is being used to create vibrato, then the vibrato on notes played at separate times will be independent (see Figure 5.11a). If that LFO is instead **monophonic**, all of the notes played will have the same synchronized vibrato (see Figure 5.11b). Many synths have one or more polyphonic LFOs and one or more monophonic LFOs. Polyphonic LFOs can provide a sense of independence for each note, whereas monophonic LFOs make the modulation for all the notes follow the same path.

A tempo-synchronized **monophonic LFO** would be desirable when it is modulating the cutoff frequency of a low pass filter such that it opens and closes across the span of several beats or measures. Being monophonic would guarantee that the tempo-synchronized effect would be heard clearly no matter when the notes were actually played in those measures.

The **key sync**, or trigger, parameter determines whether the LFO starts its cycle from zero on each note—key sync "on"—or whether the LFO can be in the middle

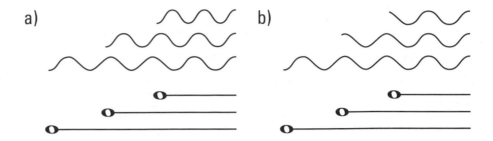

Figure 5.11 Three separate notes with modulation by a) a polyphonic LFO yielding independent modulation and b) a monophonic LFO yielding synchronized modulation

of its cycle when a note starts—key sync "off." For modulation effects such as vibrato, having key sync turned on is valuable because the pitch of each note will be in tune when the note is first struck before the modulation starts. For other modulation effects, such as wah-wah, it is less critical that the LFO starts at zero and it might be desirable to have a bit of unpredictability at the beginning of the note, particularly if the timbre has an atmospheric quality.

MODULATION ROUTING

Modulation routing refers to the mapping of modulation sources, such as control change messages, velocity values, envelopes, and LFOs, to synthesis parameters, such as pitch, filter cutoff frequency, and amplitude. The flexibility in modulation routing varies drastically from synth to synth, with the simple ones providing only a few possibilities and the complex ones allowing almost any modulation routing imaginable. In the most flexible arrangement, you would have a variety of envelopes and LFOs, and could map them, along with expressive MIDI messages and data from note messages, to almost any synth parameter with a changeable amount of modulation (scaling). Many synths with more complex modulation capabilities provide a unified interface for modulation, often referred to as a **modulation matrix**. Synthesis programming applications such as Reaktor and Max/MSP allow you to create as many envelopes and LFOs as needed and devise any routing scheme desired.

In this section, I will present a number of modulation routing examples based on direct modulation, modulation with envelopes, and modulation with LFOs mapped to the synth parameters of the basic synth model (oscillator, filter, amplifier). There are many more routings that could be included here, so you should take these as a sampling of the possibilities rather than a comprehensive list. When more synthesis techniques are taken up in the next two chapters, the number of synth parameters that can be targets for modulation will expand greatly.

In the modulation examples discussed above, there was usually one modulation source—direct control, envelope, or LFO—mapped to one modulation target (synth

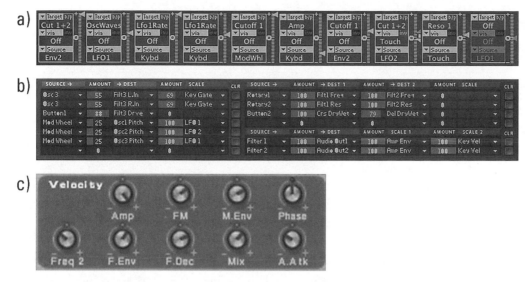

Figure 5.12 Modulation routing: a) ES 2 synth modulation matrix in Logic Pro 9; b) Reason's Thor synth modulation matrix; and c) velocity mapping in Reason's SubTractor

parameter). A modulation matrix often allows you to have one modulator mapped to multiple targets and multiple modulators mapped to one target.

One Source to Multiple Targets

An example of one modulation source mapped to multiple targets was given in the vibraphone simulation discussion above. To simulate the effect of the spinning discs in the vibraphone resonators, I suggested that an LFO be simultaneously mapped to amplitude (tremolo), filter cutoff (wah-wah), and pitch (vibrato). Separate modulation amounts for the targets would allow you to balance the results of the three effects.

Another multiple sources to single target example would be the mod wheel (CC1) mapped to both the cutoff frequency and the resonance of a filter. In that case, moving the mod wheel both brightens the sound and increases the audibility of the cutoff frequency itself by increasing the resonance. Alternatively, the velocity of the note-on message could be mapped to both the filter cutoff and resonance so that the effect is applied automatically to every note. Examples of single modulator to multiple targets effects are summarized in Table 5.2.

Multiple Sources to One Target

One simple example of multiple modulators for one target is the mapping of both CC1 (mod wheel) and aftertouch to control the cutoff frequency of the low pass filter. You would not typically manipulate the mod wheel and send aftertouch messages simultaneously, so this mapping is primarily about having multiple options for achieving the desired modulation.

Table 5.2   Examples of single modulator to multiple targets routings

Mapping	LFO → pitch, cutoff, and amplitude
Effect	This simulates the vibraphone effect
Mapping	CC1 → filter cutoff *and* filter resonance
Effect	Changing the mod wheel brightens the sound and increases the resonance peak
Mapping	velocity → filter cutoff *and* filter resonance
Effect	Brightness and resonance peak modulation is applied automatically to each note

Another example is the mapping of both an envelope and the mod wheel (CC1) to the filter cutoff frequency. In this example, the envelope executes its shape for every note creating an automated filter sweep. Having the mod wheel also control the cutoff frequency allows you to open the filter back up after the envelope has closed it down to the sustain level, providing the opportunity for more variation on longer notes. If the initial cutoff frequency (the offset) is relatively low, then CC1 can be used to alter the starting point for the envelope across a group of notes, again allowing for more variation in the sound.

A third example is the mapping of both an envelope and an LFO to the pitch of the oscillator. As described above, a typical application for a pitch envelope has a zero attack time, a short decay time, no sustain, and no release, providing for a quick gliss down to the pitch indicated by the key number of the note-on message. This acts a sharp accent at the beginning of the note. The LFO, on the other hand, creates vibrato. They are both modulations of pitch, but they create perceptions that are nearly independent of one another. Since the pitch bend message is typically routed to the oscillator by default, it represents a third modulation source mapped to this one target. Examples of multiple modulators to single target routings are summarized in Table 5.3.

Thus far, most of the discussion has centered on mapping modulation sources directly to the modulation targets (synth parameters). However, it is often desirable to have one modulation source affect *another* modulation source, which is in turn mapped to a modulation target (synth parameter). It is common to use information from a MIDI message to control an envelope or LFO, which then modulates a synth parameter, or

Table 5.3   Examples of multiple modulators to single target routings

Mapping	CC1 *and* aftertouch → filter cutoff frequency
Effect	Performer has the option of using either one to brighten or darken the sound
Mapping	envelope *and* CC1 → filter cutoff frequency
Effect	Envelope creates an automatic sweep, but you then have the option of using the mod wheel to open the filter up again
Mapping	envelope *and* LFO (*and* pitch bend) → pitch of oscillator
Effect	Envelope creates a quick gliss down and LFO generates vibrato. Pitch bend also allows you to bend the pitch on occasional notes or across multiple notes.

to have an envelope control an LFO parameter, which then modulates a synth parameter. When modulators can affect other modulators, the number of possibilities becomes astronomical, so I will mention just a few common scenarios below.

Variable-Strength Envelopes

One of the most common applications of a chain of modulators is to allow a MIDI message value to determine the strength, or amount, of the modulation caused by an envelope. Since most envelopes are gated by note-on/note-off messages, the strength of their modulation needs to be contained in the note-on message, and the most likely candidate is the velocity value. Fortunately, this is a logical choice in that we expect notes that are struck with more energy (higher velocity) to be louder, brighter, and more dynamic.

We've already encountered the standard mapping of note-on velocity to amplitude envelope to amplifier that allows the velocity to affect the peak amplitude. A similar mapping of velocity to filter envelope to cutoff frequency would allow louder notes to be brighter, simulating the timbral effect of playing louder on an acoustic instrument. The pitch envelope described earlier in this chapter with zero attack time, a short decay time, and no sustain level or release time can also be modulated by the note-on velocity to provide a more extreme gliss-down effect at the beginning of the note for louder notes. The variable-strength envelope effects are summarized in Table 5.4.

Variable-Length Envelope Segments

Another application of a modulation chain involving envelopes is to modify a segment of the envelope based on information in the note-on messages. For example, the velocity could be made to affect the envelope attack time so that the harder a note is struck the faster its attack. This is an example of an **inverted modulation** where a higher velocity value causes a shorter attack time value. This can be indicated in modulation routings through the use of a negative strength, or amount, value or by clicking a specific "invert" button. This same inverse relationship between velocity and envelope attack time can be applied to the filter envelope so that the filter opens up faster on louder notes.

Table 5.4   Examples of variable-strength envelope effects

Mapping	Note-on velocity → envelope amount → amplifier amplitude
Effect	Harder-struck notes are louder
Mapping	Note-on velocity → envelope amount → filter cutoff frequency
Effect	Harder-struck notes become brighter
Mapping	Note-on velocity → envelope amount → oscillator pitch
Effect	Harder-struck notes have a more extreme gliss-down to pitch

Table 5.5   Examples of variable-length envelope segments

Mapping	Note-on velocity → (inv) envelope attack time → amplifier amplitude
Effect	Harder-struck notes get to full volume more quickly
Mapping	Note-on velocity → (inv) envelope attack time → filter cutoff frequency
Effect	Harder-struck notes get to full brightness more quickly
Mapping	Key number → (inv) envelope decay/release time → amplifier amplitude
Effect	Higher pitches have shorter decays/releases of plucked or struck envelopes

The key number of the note-on message can also be used to modify envelope segments. For example, to emulate the behavior of a piano in which higher notes decay more quickly, you can use keyboard tracking mapped to either the decay or the release of an envelope configured as a plucked or struck envelope (see the discussion under "The Amplifier and Amplitude Envelope" in the previous chapter). This would also be an inverted modulation because the higher the key number, the lower the decay or release time value would be. The variable envelope segment effects are summarized in Table 5.5.

Variable-Strength/Rate LFOs

In the previous discussion of the use of LFOs to create vibrato, wah-wah, and tremolo, there was little capacity to control those effects aside from the use of LFO delay. Vibrato in particular is often applied only to sustained notes and then usually gradually. To be able to apply vibrato to some notes and not others in a passage, you can use an expressive message such as a channel pressure message or a control change message for this purpose. In fact, though we've seen CC1 mapped to other parameters previously, the most common use of CC1 is to control vibrato. In addition to applying it to only selected notes, variable-strength vibrato can be used to "fade-in" vibrato during long notes. I refer to this as the "Broadway vibrato" in tribute to its common use in musical theater singing. Variable control of both wah-wah and tremolo depth is also desirable in many circumstances to allow short notes to be relatively simple and long notes to have more complexity.

Table 5.6   Examples of variable-strength/rate LFOs

Mapping	CC1 or pressure value → LFO depth (amount) → pitch/cutoff/amp
Effect	The vibrato, wah-wah, or tremolo can be applied variably
Mapping	CC1 or pressure value → LFO rate → pitch/cutoff/amp
Effect	The LFO rate can be variably controlled
Mapping	CC1 or pressure value → LFO depth *and* rate → pitch/cutoff/amp
Effect	Both depth and rate can be controlled simultaneously

The same strategy for controlling LFO depth can also be used to control the LFO rate: CC1 or aftertouch can be mapped to the LFO rate, which is in turn mapped to the pitch, cutoff frequency, or amplitude. This wouldn't create the typical vibrato, wah-wah, or tremolo, but rather a more dynamic and decidedly synthetic effect. CC1 could simultaneously be mapped to the LFO rate and the LFO depth allowing one move of a wheel/joystick to transform the timbre from simple to chaotic. The variable-strength LFO effects are summarized in Table 5.6.

Enveloped LFO

Just as expressive MIDI messages can be used to variably control the LFO depth, an envelope can be used to control the LFO depth in an automated fashion on every note; some synths even have a dedicated LFO envelope for this purpose. An envelope with a long attack time causes the LFO to fade in on held notes, but has little effect on short notes. This is essentially a gradual version of the LFO delay mentioned under "LFO Variations" above. If the LFO is modulating pitch (vibrato), then this is similar to the Broadway vibrato effect described above when the vibrato was controlled by CC1 or aftertouch. The effect is also useful if the LFO is mapped to cutoff frequency or amplitude in that it gives held notes some motion so that they don't seem stale or overly synthetic.

If the envelope has a zero attack time and a moderate decay, then the LFO's effect is present automatically and fades out if the notes are held. This creates a simplifying effect on held notes and gives them a sense of suspended motion. The enveloped LFO effects are summarized in Table 5.7.

LFO-Gated Envelopes

As mentioned in the "Envelope Variations" section above, it is possible to use something besides note-on/note-off messages to gate an envelope such as a filter or pitch envelope. If you route an LFO with a square/pulse waveform to the gate of an envelope, which in turn modulates a parameter such as pitch, the rate of the LFO will determine how quickly the gate is turned on and off and therefore how often the pitch is modulated.

Table 5.7   Examples of enveloped LFOs

Mapping	Envelope → LFO depth (amount) → pitch/cutoff/amp
Effect	Vibrato, wah-wah, and tremolo can be faded in or out on long notes

---

Table 5.8   Examples of LFO-gated envelope effects

Mapping	LFO → envelope (gate) → pitch/cutoff/amp
Effect	Envelope modulation is triggered (gated) multiple times during a note at a rate determined by the LFO rate

If the LFO rate is set to synchronize with the tempo, this modulation routing creates an envelope that is gated in tempo with the sequence. This requires a synth with a flexible modulation routing that is not available in all synths. In addition, if the synth has a loop-able "mod" envelope with tempo synchronization, then this modulation routing is unnecessary. The LFO-gated envelope effects are summarized in Table 5.8.

As you can see from the above discussion, there is a close relationship between MIDI messages and the synth parameters that they control. A software synthesizer, its settings, and modulation routings represent the *potential* for sound. The MIDI messages sent from a MIDI controller or played back from a MIDI track in a DAW/Sequencer provide the essential musical information to convert that potential into actual sound.

In the next chapter, we will delve more deeply into oscillators and filters and discover new parameters that can be targets for modulation.

CHAPTER 6

Oscillators and Filters

Over the course of the previous two chapters, we established basic synthesis and sampling models, explored how the parameters of those models can be controlled by MIDI messages, expanded those models to include modulators such as envelopes and LFOs, and discussed modulation routings. Despite the fact that our basic synthesis model has become much more sophisticated over the last two chapters, the basis for sound production in the synthesis model has remained a single oscillator repeating a single-cycle waveform processed by a resonant low pass filter.

In this chapter, we'll explore some more possibilities with single oscillators, the possibilities available with multiple oscillators, and several different filter types. With each expansion of our synthesis resources, we'll find additional synth parameters to modulate. With these additional resources, we will expand our ability to produce rich, expressive timbres to realize our musical goals.

OSCILLATORS

The oscillator in our basic synthesis model uses single-cycle waveforms such as sine, triangle, sawtooth, and square. These single-cycle waveforms don't have to conform to these few shapes; they can be almost any shape, representing a wide variety of timbres. By themselves, single-cycle waveforms are useful but can grow stale through repeated use because of their unchanging timbre. In addition to the filters, envelopes, and LFOs that we encountered in previous chapters, there are several useful variants on the simple oscillator that can help to make the synthesized sound more dynamic.

Pulse Width Modulation

A pulse wave is a variant of the standard square wave that provides a useful modulation target. A square wave can be thought of as being "up" for 50 percent of the time and "down" for 50 percent of the time, with very little, if any, transition in between the two states (see Figure 6.1a). A pulse waveform also spends part of each cycle all the way up and part of it all the way down. However, it differs from a square wave in that the amount of time that it spends up versus down is variable (see Figure 6.1b). The amount of time spent up is referred to as the **pulse width**, or the **duty cycle**. A duty cycle of 50 percent corresponds to a square wave.

Pulse waveforms are useful because the timbre can be modified while a note is playing by varying the pulse width, a process referred to as **pulse width modulation**, or **PWM** (see Figure 6.1c). You can change the duty cycle of a pulse wave through direct control by an expressive MIDI message, with an LFO, or with a mod envelope. Direct control using aftertouch or a CC message would allow you to change the pulse width over the course of one note or several notes. An LFO would cause the pulse width to change periodically, perhaps with the mod wheel (CC1) controlling the depth of the modulation. An envelope would cause a patterned change in the pulse during each note, perhaps with velocity modulating the envelope amount. Changing the duty cycle over the course of a note or many notes through PWM can breathe life into the synthetic waveform. The pulse width modulation routings discussed are summarized in Table 6.1.

Noise

Another useful waveform has no real waveform at all: noise. When we think of music, we often think of pitch, but there are many aspects to the sound of music that are noisy. These include the burst of breath at the beginning of a flute sound and the "thunk" of the hammers at the beginning of a piano sound, as well as the traditionally noisy

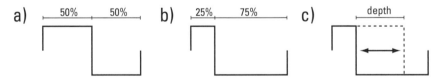

Figure 6.1 a) square wave, duty cycle = 50 percent, b) pulse wave example, duty cycle = 25 percent, and c) pulse width modulation with a 50 percent modulation depth

Table 6.1   Pulse width modulation routings

Mapping	CC or aftertouch → pulse width (oscillator)
Effect	The pulse width is changed directly over the course of a note or several notes
Mapping	CC or aftertouch → LFO (depth) → pulse width (oscillator)
Effect	The pulse width oscillates with a variable depth controlled by CC1
Mapping	Velocity → mod envelope (amount) → pulse width (oscillator)
Effect	The pulse width changes in a pattern over the course of a note with the strength of the envelope controlled by note-on velocity

percussion sounds of cymbals and snare drums, for example. To make synthetic sounds more realistic, it is often useful to incorporate noise.

Because noise has no repeating pattern, and thus no fixed spectrum, it is best characterized by its frequency distribution. There are several common frequency distributions that are given colors as names, with white and pink being the most commonly encountered. **White noise** has equal energy per frequency band, so it would, for example, have the same amount of energy between 100 Hz and 200 Hz as between 1,000 Hz and 1,100 Hz. **Pink noise**, on the other hand, has equal energy per octave, and so would have the same amount of energy between 100 Hz and 200 Hz (an octave) as between 1,000 Hz and 2,000 Hz (also an octave). In this example, white noise would have ten times the amount of energy, between 1,000 Hz and 2,000, Hz as pink noise would. As a result, white noise sounds much brighter and harsher than pink noise.

In most musical situations, noise is a transient event, occurring at the beginning of the note and then dying away relatively quickly. Even when the sound is meant to be almost all noise, such as that of a snare drum, it doesn't usually sustain. A patch using noise, then, would likely utilize a struck or plucked envelope rather than a bowed or blown sustained envelope. When utilizing noise, the filter is also a useful component. The low pass filter that's part of the basic model can change the "color" of noise depending on the setting of the cutoff frequency.

A pure noise generator doesn't have many parameters to modulate, except perhaps a parameter to change the color. The filter, on the other hand, could be modulated through keyboard tracking to cause the cutoff frequency to follow notes from a keyboard or a sequence. If the resonance is set high enough, the filter can impose a sense of pitch on the noise. In addition, the filter envelope could cause the cutoff frequency to quickly sweep down to the keyboard-tracked value creating a swooping, whistling quality in the resultant sound. The strength of the envelope could also be modulated by the velocity in the note-on message.

Between the struck or plucked envelope shape and the filter settings, a noise source can be made into a versatile percussive effect. There are many more modulation routings that could be used, including mapping the velocity to the attack time of the amplitude envelope (inverse mapping) and routing CC1, CC74, or aftertouch to the cutoff

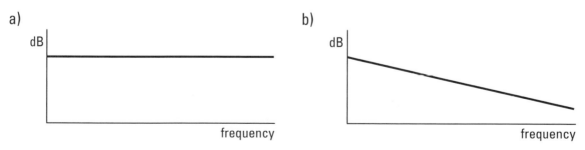

Figure 6.2 Noise color frequency distributions: a) white noise—equal energy per frequency band; b) pink noise—equal energy per octave

Table 6.2   Modulation routings for a noise source

Mapping	Key number → filter cutoff frequency (keyboard tracking)
Effect	With a high enough resonance setting, the filter imparts a sense of pitch to the noise
Mapping	Velocity → filter envelope (amount) → filter cutoff frequency
Effect	Variable strength filter envelope causes a swooping effect down to the keyboard tracked value (with a high enough resonance setting)
Mapping	Velocity → amplitude envelope attack (inverse) → amplifier
Effect	Notes with higher velocities have sharper, more percussive attacks
Mapping	CC or aftertouch → filter cutoff frequency
Effect	The "base" frequency for the keyboard tracking can be changed over the course of many notes

frequency of the filter. The modulation routings detailed in this chapter should be seen as a few selected possibilities rather than a comprehensive list. The modulation routings discussed for a noise source are summarized in Table 6.2.

Multiple Oscillators: Mixing and Detuning

Though the basic synthesis model has just one oscillator, it is common in analog-style software synthesizers to have at least two, plus, perhaps, a noise generator. This allows for more complex timbres as the oscillators are mixed and detuned. More multiple oscillator interactions, including oscillator sync, ring modulation, and frequency modulation, will be discussed later in the chapter.

Mixing oscillators allows you to start with a more complex waveform before the filter and amplifier stages, but not all combinations work well. For example, a sawtooth wave combined with another sawtooth wave often results in a weaker sound rather than a stronger one, because if the oscillators are somewhat out of phase with one another, the waveforms' partials may partly cancel each other out, resulting in a paler sound than just a single sawtooth. A combination of a sawtooth plus a square wave is also not a particularly compelling improvement over just a sawtooth wave, in part due to the phase issue and in part due to the fact that they share many of the same partials, so not much new is added.

Combining a standard waveform, such as a sawtooth wave with a waveform that contains partials that the sawtooth doesn't have or partials that are relatively weak in the sawtooth, is one way of making useful waveform combinations. Each successive partial in triangle, square, and sawtooth waves has a lower amplitude than the one before it, so the energy decreases steadily as the partial number increases. If you were to combine one of these waveforms with a non-standard waveform that has more energy in its upper partials, you would be creating a new, unique timbre (see Figure 6.3).

If the mix between the waveforms can be modulated, then you can use a control change message or aftertouch to change which waveform is emphasized at a given time,

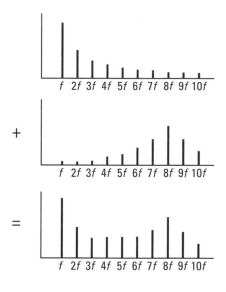

Figure 6.3 Waveform mixing shown through spectra: the spectrum of sawtooth wave is combined with the spectrum of another waveform to create a more complex result

perhaps increasing or decreasing the waveform with energy in its upper partials to change the timbre over the course of a note or many notes. If you want that change on every note, you could use a mod envelope to alter the mix over the course of the note. As a simple example, you could have oscillator one use a sawtooth wave and oscillator two use a triangle wave. A mod envelope with similar settings to the amplitude envelope could cause the attack and decay of the note to emphasize the sawtooth and the sustain and release of the note to emphasize the triangle, thus achieving the linkage between loudness and brightness characteristic of acoustically produced timbres.

Many synths have a noise source that is part of the oscillator section. As mentioned above in the discussion of noise, many acoustically produced timbres have at least some noise component. A noise source mixed with an oscillator or oscillators utilizing more traditional waveforms can allow you to create a percussive or breathy attack. To limit the noise to just the attack of a note requires the noise source to have its own simple AR envelope, or just "R" envelope, so that an instantaneous attack is followed by a controllable release. An adjustable "color" to the noise would also be valuable for greater control over the intensity of the noise. As with noise alone, noise mixed with other waveforms can be filtered using a high resonance value to create a bright, percussive attack. The mixing modulation routings discussed are summarized in Table 6.3.

Table 6.3   Modulation routings for mixing oscillators

Mapping	CC or aftertouch → oscillator mix
Effect	Timbre can be made to change over the course of a note or multiple notes
Mapping	Mod envelope → oscillator mix
Effect	Waveform emphasis changes over the course of the note

Another way to make waveform combinations work is to transpose or detune them from each other. Most oscillators allow you to transpose them up or down by octaves, semitones, and cents. A sawtooth wave **transposed** one octave lower than a square wave is a far more interesting timbre than those two waveforms sounding in the same octave. For a synth patch meant to sound in the bass register, it is common for at least one oscillator to be transposed down at least one octave so that you can play bass register notes on a 61-key controller. An occasional variation on octave transposition notation is for an oscillator's register to be given in organ pipe lengths. In that notation, when middle C is played on a keyboard, the "eight foot" setting will result in an actual middle C, the "sixteen foot" setting will result in an octave below middle C, and the "four foot" setting will result in an octave above middle C.

Transposition by semitones is sometimes useful, but can be tricky because each note has some harmony associated with it. Transposition by a fourth (five semitones) or a fifth (seven semitones) avoids most, but not all, of the out-of-key problems that other transpositions can cause, but can sound hackneyed if overused. Transposition by one or two semitones can create thick clusters when played as chords.

The term **detuning** is used to indicate a difference in pitch of less than a semitone, and is often measured in **cents**, with 100 cents per semitone. One common practice is to detune one oscillator up five or ten cents and the other oscillator down five or ten cents. This results in a single clear pitch whose timbre has a live throbbing to it as the waveforms beat against one another. In this situation, two sawtooth waves in the same register work just fine together with no octave or semitone transposition, creating a fat, analog sound that is characteristic of analog bass patches. Detuning by a full quarter-tone (50 cents) can result in interestingly thick and possibly grating timbres, and you would probably use such detuning only for special effects and noise patches and not for bass, lead, harmony, or pad patches.

Another technique that creates a transposition/detuning relationship between oscillators is to turn off keyboard tracking on one oscillator while the other has it turned on. In that instance, the keyboard-tracked oscillator will change pitch in response to MIDI note messages as expected, but the other will sound the same drone pitch for each note. The frequency for the non-keyboard tracked oscillator is usually set by its tuning controls so that the drone will sound at a specific frequency.

Multiple Oscillators: Oscillator Sync

In addition to the mixing and detuning described above, there are several ways for one oscillator to modulate the output of another, including oscillator sync, ring modulation, and frequency modulation. **Oscillator sync** is a practice drawn from analog synthesis in which one oscillator (the master) is used to restart the cycle of another (the slave). Each time the master oscillator starts a new cycle of its waveform, the slave oscillator is forced to break off wherever it is in its cycle and start again, thus causing a dramatic change in its basic waveform (see Figure 6.4). Sawtooth waves and square waves are typical waveforms for this application, though other waveforms will work as well, with different timbral effects. Figure 6.4 shows a "hard" sync where the slave waveform resets immediately. Some synths allow you to specify a softer sync where the reset isn't quite so abrupt.

Oscillator sync is most effective when the pitch of the slave oscillator is higher than that of the master oscillator. If master and slave are at the same pitch, then they would naturally start their cycles together, so syncing them would not be very interesting. When the slave is at a higher pitch, it will go through more than one cycle, but probably not a whole number of cycles, before it is forced to start over. As a result, its waveform is more complex and thus timbrally richer than it would be if left unsynced. If the pitch of the slave changes over the course of the note, then the resultant waveform also changes, creating a dynamic timbre.

The pitch of the slave oscillator can be made different from the master through transposition and/or through modulation by direct control, an envelope, or an LFO. If the slave oscillator is transposed up from the master by some number of semitones, the result is a change in the timbre rather than harmonized oscillators. This simple change results in a more complex waveform, but the characteristic timbre of synced oscillators comes from dynamic change in the pitch of the slave oscillator.

The timbre of the slave oscillator can be changed directly by routing a control change message, such as CC1, to the pitch of the slave oscillator. The timbre changes as you raise the mod wheel. A mod envelope routed to the pitch of the slave oscillator allows for a regular change in timbre at the attack of every note. This envelope can in turn be modulated by the velocity, thereby varying the strength of its effect. The envelope and direct control can be used simultaneously so that the envelope creates a pitch sweep

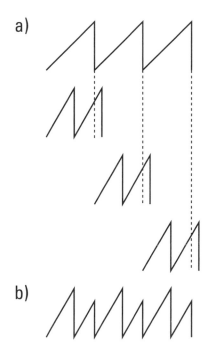

a)

b)

Figure 6.4 Oscillator sync with master and slave as sawtooth waves: a) each new cycle of the master waveform (top) causes the slave waveform to start its cycle again, even if it is not complete; b) the new synced waveform

Table 6.4   Oscillator sync modulation routings

Mapping	CC or aftertouch → slave oscillator pitch
Effect	Changing the CC or aftertouch value creates a change in the slave oscillator's waveform
Mapping	Velocity → mod envelope → slave oscillator pitch
Effect	The mod envelope causes a sweep in timbre on every note, the strength is controlled by the velocity
Mapping	CC or aftertouch → LFO depth → slave oscillator pitch
Effect	The waveform of the slave oscillator changes periodically (perhaps locked to the tempo) due to the LFO, the strength of the effect is controlled by a CC or aftertouch

in the slave oscillator, and thus a dynamic change in waveform, at the beginning of each note, and the mod wheel is used to modify the timbre during the sustain portion of the sound. An LFO applied to the pitch of the slave oscillator, possibly under the control of the mod wheel or aftertouch, creates a periodic sweep in the timbre. Locking the LFO period to the tempo of the music locks the change in timbre to the tempo as well. The oscillator sync modulation routings are summarized in Table 6.4.

Multiple Oscillators: Amplitude and Ring Modulation

Two common types of oscillator-to-oscillator modulation are amplitude modulation (AM) and ring modulation (RM). Although they are sometimes used as synonyms for one another, ring modulation is actually a special case of amplitude modulation, and there are some significant differences in their results. Ring modulation is more common than amplitude modulation in softsynths, but in order to understand ring modulation, it is useful to start with the more general case of amplitude modulation. In addition to their use in synthesizers, these techniques can be used as effects for processing audio; we will revisit them when we discuss effects processing later in the book.

We already encountered a form of **amplitude modulation** (**AM**) in the last chapter when we used an LFO to modulate the overall amplitude of the amplifier in the basic synthesis model. When the rate of the modulation is relatively slow, the effect can be described as **tremolo**. However, when the rate of the modulation increases above 20 Hz (i.e., the modulator is no longer a *low* frequency oscillator), the result is very different. We'll encounter a similar phenomenon when we discuss frequency modulation later in the chapter.

In amplitude modulation, the modulator is still called the **modulator**, or modulating oscillator, but the target for the modulation is now referred to as the **carrier**. Since AM in sound synthesis is the same technique found in AM radio transmission—though used for quite a different purpose—some of the terminology derives from radio engineering. The modulator creates a periodic change in the amplitude of the carrier oscillator, above and below the original amplitude, at a rate referred to as the **modulating frequency**. The magnitude of this periodic change is referred to as the amount or depth, and is related to a parameter known as the **modulation index**. The shape of the change in amplitude is determined by the waveform of the oscillator. The rate, depth, and waveform parameters should be familiar from the discussion of LFOs in the last chapter.

When the modulator and carrier are both sine waves, the resultant waveform and spectrum are as shown in Figure 6.5a and 6.5b respectively. In the spectrum (Figure 6.5b), the frequency of the modulating oscillator (denoted by f_m) is reflected on either side of the carrier frequency (denoted by f_c). The frequency components $f_c - f_m$ and $f_c + f_m$ are referred to as **sidebands**, and their amplitudes are determined by the modulation index, which is in turn related to the amplitude of the modulating oscillator. The sidebands effectively "steal" amplitude from the carrier, so as the modulation index goes up, the amplitudes of the sidebands increase and the amplitude of the carrier decreases.

If f_c and f_m are related by a relatively simple ratio (denoted as $f_c{:}f_m$), then the carrier and the two sidebands form a portion of an overtone series and the resultant timbre will be **harmonic**. If the $f_c{:}f_m$ ratio is not simple, then the resultant timbre will be **inharmonic**.

For example, if f_c was 220 Hz and f_m was 110 Hz, then $f_c - f_m$ would be 110 Hz, f_c would be 220 Hz, and $f_c + f_m$ would be 330 Hz. The result, shown in Figure 6.6a, would be a portion of the overtone series with 110 Hz as its fundamental. On the other hand, if f_c was 220 Hz and f_m was 65 Hz, then $f_c - f_m$ would be 155, f_c would be 220, and $f_c + f_m$ would be 285. The result, shown in Figure 6.6b, would not form a portion of an overtone series, and would thus be inharmonic.

However, unlike the above examples, most oscillators can and do take on waveforms other than sine waves. From Fourier's Theorem we know that any periodic waveform, which includes all of the standard waveforms, can be thought of as a sum of sine waves that are harmonically related (see Chapter 1). For example, a sawtooth wave can be thought of as a sine wave with a frequency of f, plus a sine wave with a frequency of $2f$, plus a sine wave with a frequency of $3f$, and so on. To create a sawtooth wave, the amplitude for the first partial would be 1, the amplitude for the second partial would be 1/2, the amplitude for the third partial would be 1/3, and so on. If a sawtooth wave is used as the modulator, then each of the sawtooth wave's frequencies would act like a separate modulating frequency and each would be mirrored around the carrier frequency, f_c, in the resultant spectrum.

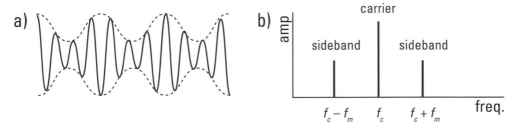

Figure 6.5 Amplitude modulation: a) waveform view (solid line = carrier, dashed line = modulator); b) spectrum view

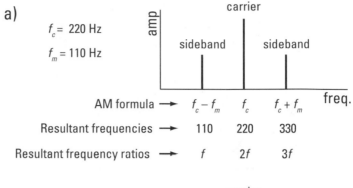

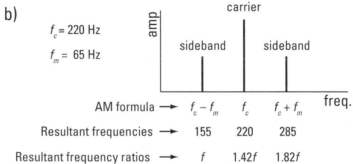

Figure 6.6 Amplitude modulation examples: a) f_c:f_m ratio results in harmonic spectrum; b) f_c:f_m ratio results in inharmonic spectrum

If we consider a relatively simple case of a modulator with three frequency components—labeled f_{m1}, f_{m2}, and f_{m3}—and a sine wave carrier with a frequency of f_c, the resultant spectrum would have seven components: f_c, $f_c + f_{m1}$, $f_c - f_{m1}$, $f_c + f_{m2}$, $f_c - f_{m2}$, $f_c + f_{m3}$, and $f_c - f_{m3}$ (see Figure 6.7). If the modulator is harmonic, then the equal spacing of the modulator partials will result in amplitude modulation sidebands that are equally spaced as shown in Figure 6.7, though the spectrum may still be inharmonic if the carrier and sidebands don't form a harmonic series. A non-harmonic modulator will result in unevenly spaced sidebands.

If the carrier also has multiple frequency components, each of those will be surrounded by plus and minus each of the modulating frequency components. For example, a three-frequency-component modulator and a two-frequency-component carrier would result in fourteen partials—seven for each frequency component in the carrier. As you can see, the partials pile up fast.

If the fundamental of the carrier and the fundamental of the modulator form a simple ratio, as discussed above in the sine waves example, then the mirrored components in the resultant AM spectrum would also be simply related to each other, resulting in a harmonic spectrum. If the fundamental of the carrier and the fundamental of the modulator are not simply related, the resultant spectrum would be inharmonic, and possibly quite dense.

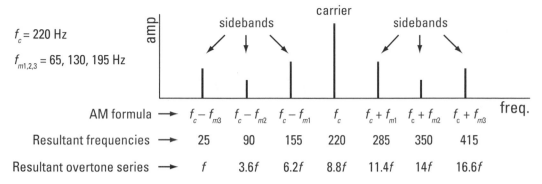

f_c = 220 Hz

$f_{m1,2,3}$ = 65, 130, 195 Hz

AM formula →	$f_c - f_{m3}$	$f_c - f_{m2}$	$f_c - f_{m1}$	f_c	$f_c + f_{m1}$	$f_c + f_{m2}$	$f_c + f_{m3}$
Resultant frequencies →	25	90	155	220	285	350	415
Resultant overtone series →	f	$3.6f$	$6.2f$	$8.8f$	$11.4f$	$14f$	$16.6f$

Figure 6.7 Amplitude modulation with a three-component modulator. Notice that even though the modulator is harmonic, the non-simple $f_c{:}f_m$ ratio results in an inharmonic spectrum

Ring modulation is a version of amplitude modulation in which the resultant spectrum *doesn't* contain the carrier frequency, but still contains the modulator frequencies mirrored around the absent carrier frequency (see Figure 6.8a). The amplitude of the sidebands is dependent on the amount of modulation (the modulation index). If the modulator is more complex than a sine wave, its partials will also be mirrored around the absent carrier. This effectively frequency shifts all of the modulator's partials by the carrier frequency as well as creating a mirror of those partials below the carrier frequency (see Figure 6.8b).

Harmonically related partials that have been frequency shifted by a constant frequency become inharmonic. If you take two frequencies, f and $2f$, and add a constant frequency C to them, you get the new frequencies $f + C$ and $2f + C$, which are no longer related by a whole number factor: $2(f + C) = 2f + 2C \neq (2f) + C$. This effect is more obvious when the modulator is a recognizable audio source, such as speech or music. Ring modulation as an audio effect will be discussed later in the chapter on effects.

Ring modulation can create everything from richer harmonic timbres to glassy inharmonic timbres to chaotic noisy timbres. Which of these effects you get is dependent on the waveforms used by the carrier and modulator, the relationship between their fundamentals, and the amount of modulation. Often it is possible to hear not just the result of the ring or amplitude modulation, but also the output of the modulating oscillator and other oscillators that are active, allowing the ring modulated timbre to be just one part of the overall timbre.

Ring modulation and amplitude modulation have several parameters that can be modulated by direct control, envelopes, and LFOs. The amount of amplitude/ring modulation (the modulation index) has a clear effect on the timbre. When controlled by a mod envelope, the modulation can be more intense at the attack of each note and less intense during the sustain. If a CC sent by a slider, knob, or wheel on your controller or aftertouch is also mapped to the amount of modulation, then you can raise the intensity of the modulation during the sustain on longer notes after the mod envelope has reached its sustain stage. An LFO could be used to create a varying amount of modulation, perhaps under the control of a CC or aftertouch.

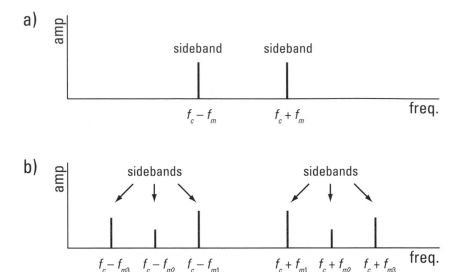

Figure 6.8 Ring modulation spectra: a) modulator and carrier are sine waves; b) modulator has three components and carrier is sine wave—notice the frequency shifting effect on the modulator partials

The frequencies of the carrier and modulator are the other primary parameters in amplitude/ring modulation and can be altered through direct modulation, envelopes, and LFOs. Pitch bend would normally change the pitch of both oscillators, so a slider, knob, or wheel sending a CC or aftertouch would have to be mapped to the pitch of the carrier or modulator in order to change them independently. If the mod envelope is used like a regular pitch envelope—no attack, short decay, no sustain—then this effect would be similar to having a noise element during the attack of the note. Changing the pitch relationships between carrier and modulator in these ways can be a fairly drastic modulation, because after only a little bit of detuning, the amplitude/ring modulation spectrum quickly becomes inharmonic.

In addition to modulating the carrier and modulator frequencies, you could also use the octave, semitones, and cents tunings to create a fixed frequency relationship between the oscillators. Clearly an octave relationship will generate harmonically related partials, but so will other intervals from the overtone series such as an octave and a fifth, two octaves and a third, or two octaves and a minor seventh. In amplitude/ring modulation, the intervals between the oscillators are subsumed within the overall spectrum, so you don't hear the oscillators as playing a musical interval. It is important to keep in mind that the octave and semitone controls on a synth are likely to be in equal temperament, so you will need to use the fine-tuning control to adjust the equal tempered intervals to the pure ratios found in the overtone series. You can do this by ear by listening for the beating between the frequency components to stop. On the other hand, a small amount of deviation from the ideal ratios can create a lively pulsing, much like detuned oscillators that are mixed together.

Table 6.5   Amplitude/ring modulation routings

Mapping	CC or aftertouch → amount of ring/amplitude modulation
Effect	Changes the intensity of the modulation during a note or over several notes
Mapping	Mod envelope → amount of ring/amplitude modulation
Effect	Changes the intensity of the modulation in the same way on each note
Mapping	Mod wheel → LFO → amount of ring/amplitude modulation
Effect	Changes the intensity of the modulation periodically, depth controlled by mod wheel
Mapping	CC or aftertouch → Carrier or Modulator pitch
Effect	Changes spectrum from harmonic to inharmonic (assuming the fundamentals of the modulator and carrier are in a simple ratio to begin with) over one or several notes
Mapping	Mod envelope → carrier or modulator pitch
Effect	Changes the spectrum from harmonic to inharmonic in the same way on each note. With no attack, a short decay, and no sustain, this gives a bit of complexity during the note's attack
Mapping	Mod wheel → LFO → carrier or modulator pitch
Effect	Changes the spectrum from harmonic to inharmonic periodically, controlled by the mod wheel
Mapping	CC or aftertouch → pulse width of pulse waveform (carrier or modulator)
Effect	Changes the strengths of the partials in the resultant spectrum over one or many notes
Mapping	Mod envelope → pulse width of pulse waveform (carrier or modulator)
Effect	Changes the strengths of the partials in the resultant spectrum the same way on each note
Mapping	Mod wheel → LFO → pulse width of pulse waveform (carrier or modulator)
Effect	Changes the strengths of the partials in the resultant spectrum periodically, controlled by the mod wheel

Another type of modulation would be to alter the waveform of the carrier or modulator. For example, if the modulator is a pulse wave, its spectrum can be modulated through PWM by direct control, an envelope, or an LFO. A pulse wave carrier can be treated in a similar manner. The modulation routings for AM and RM are summarized in Table 6.5.

Multiple Oscillators: Frequency Modulation

Frequency modulation (**FM**) is another technique that can be found on a number of softsynths. Though FM is a full-blown synthesis technique in its own right, it is available in many synths whose sound production is based on just a few oscillators in order to enrich the output of those oscillators. In this context, the technique has a similar function to oscillator sync and amplitude/ring modulation. We'll consider FM as a standalone synthesis technique in the next chapter.

Frequency modulation is similar to amplitude modulation, except that the modulating oscillator is altering the *frequency* of the carrier oscillator rather than the amplitude. We already encountered frequency modulation in the last chapter when we used an LFO to modulate the pitch of an oscillator. When the rate of the modulation is relatively slow, the effect can be described as vibrato. However, when the rate of the modulation increases above 20 Hz (i.e., the modulator is no longer a *low* frequency oscillator), the result is very different.

The terminology from amplitude modulation carries over to frequency modulation. In FM, there is also a modulating oscillator utilizing some waveform at some frequency, a carrier oscillator utilizing some waveform at some frequency, a modulation index that indicates how much modulation is taking place, and sidebands that are part of the resultant spectrum.

We'll assume for the moment that both the modulator and carrier are sine waves— a configuration referred to as **simple FM**. With that assumption, the difference between FM and AM is that, where increasing the modulation index in AM increases the amplitudes of the two sidebands, increasing the modulation index in FM actually generates *more* sidebands. The spectrum of FM, even when just using two sine waves, can be quite rich in partials, and the number of partials, which influences the brightness of the overall sound, is controlled by the modulation index.

The spectrum of simple FM is shown in Figure 6.9. As you can see, like AM there is a frequency component at the carrier frequency, and the modulating frequency is mirrored around this (see Figure 6.5b for the AM spectrum). However, the single modulating frequency generates additional frequency components spaced at $2f_m$ above and below the carrier, $3f_m$ above and below the carrier, and so on, up to the number of partials that a given modulation index (modulation amount) generates.

Like AM, the ratio of the carrier frequency to the modulating frequency, $f_c{:}f_m$, determines the specific qualities of the spectrum. If $f_c{:}f_m$ is a simple whole number ratio, then the spectrum will be harmonic. If $f_c{:}f_m$ is not simple, then the spectrum will be inharmonic. For example, if f_c was 440 Hz, f_m was 110 Hz ($f_c{:}f_m$ = 4:1), and the modulation index was sufficient to create three sidebands above and below the carrier, the spectrum would be as shown in Figure 6.10a. As you can see, these partials form an overtone series (f, $2f$, $3f$, $4f$, etc.) on the fundamental of 110 Hz.

On the other hand, if f_c was 440 Hz, f_m was 130 Hz ($f_c{:}f_m$ = 3.38:1), and the modulation index was sufficient to create three sidebands above and below the carrier, the spectrum would be as shown in Figure 6.10b. As you can see, these partials do *not*

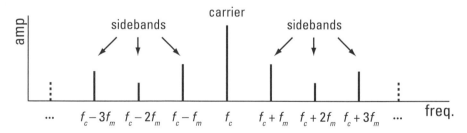

Figure 6.9 The simple FM spectrum. The dashed lines and ellipses indicate that the number of sidebands could be larger depending on the modulation index

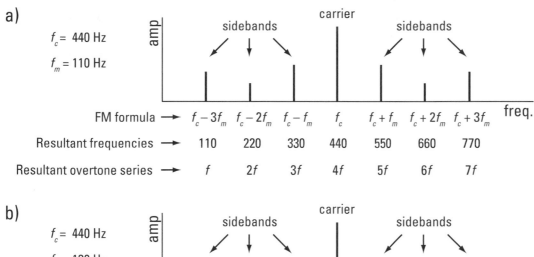

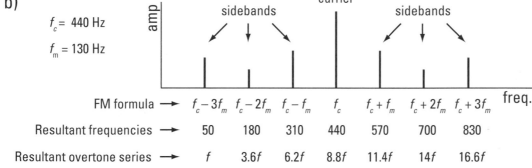

Figure 6.10   FM spectra with different f_c:f_m ratios: a) a harmonic spectrum formed by an f_c:f_m of 4:1; b) an inharmonic spectrum formed by an f_c:f_m of 3.38:1

form an overtone series. Instead the ratios are f, $3.6f$, $6.2f$, $8.8f$, and so on, and the timbre is thus inharmonic. An inharmonic simple FM timbre can sound glassy and otherworldly if the sidebands are far enough apart or noisy and dense if the sidebands are close together, as determined by the modulating frequency. One of the strengths of FM is the wide range of timbres from harmonic to inharmonic that can be produced. It's important to remember that in these examples, we are only using two oscillators and they are both producing sine waves.

If the modulating oscillator has just one more partial—two total—then that partial would be mirrored around each of the frequencies in Figure 6.9. It would be as if each of the frequencies in Figure 6.9 acted as a carrier frequency to the new second partial in the modulator. The number and amplitudes of all of the sidebands would be determined by the amount of modulation (modulation index) and the amplitudes of both partials in the modulator and the one partial in the carrier. If the waveforms for both the carrier and modulator are something other than sine waves, you can see that even with just two oscillators the spectrum could become quite dense very quickly. If the fundamentals of the modulator and carrier are simply related and their waveforms are harmonic, then the sidebands generated by their harmonic partials will be as well, and a harmonic spectrum will result. Otherwise, the result will be inharmonic and possibly dense and rough as well, due to the beating of closely spaced inharmonic partials.

Modulation routings and possibilities for AM are the same as for FM, so they won't be repeated here. However, the results can be quite different because altering the modulation amount creates more partials, not just higher amplitude for the partials. Often it is possible to hear not just the result of the frequency modulation but also the output of the modulating oscillator and other oscillators that are active, allowing the frequency modulated timbre to be just one part of the overall timbre.

So far, we've been considering FM as a possible interaction between two oscillators in a relatively simple synth. However, as mentioned above, FM can be implemented not just as an option for timbral enrichment, but also as the primary technique for sound generation in a synth. FM as a standalone synthesis technique will be discussed in the next chapter.

FILTERS

The basic synthesis model is, at its heart, a form of **subtractive synthesis**. The waveform output from the oscillator(s) is passed through a filter that reduces or removes—subtracts—a certain range of frequencies. Instruments based on sampling will usually have filters as well. A sample patch designed to be imitative of an acoustic instrument will use such processing sparingly, but a sample patch designed to produce non-imitative timbres may use filters just as extensively as any synthesizer patch.

Just as the oscillator section of a typical synth is richer than just a single oscillator and a single waveform, the filter section in a synth or sampler can be richer than just a single filter and single filter type. In addition to the low pass filter with resonance that we've been discussing, there are several other filter types available in most synths, including high pass with resonance, band pass, and notch. There are also some specialty filters available in some instruments such as comb filters and formant filters. Filters are also used in the EQ, or equalization, process that will be discussed in the chapter on effects later in the book. In that chapter we will explore peaking and shelving filters as well.

The basic function of a filter is to boost or attenuate (reduce) the amplitude of the incoming audio signal for a given range of frequencies. A filter can thus be thought of as a frequency-dependent amplifier with some amount of gain change (positive or negative) associated with a range, or ranges, of frequencies. The aspect of a filter that we're most interested in, then, is the filter's **amplitude-versus-frequency response**. This is often shortened to "frequency response" and is also variously referred to as the "amplitude response" or the "magnitude response." A filter also has a phase response that indicates how the phases of various frequencies of the input signal will be changed by the filtering process. The phase response is an important technical issue, but we'll focus on just the frequency response (amplitude-versus-frequency response) here because that more directly concerns our musical use of filters.

A graph of the frequency response of a filter shows us what effect the filter has on the spectrum of the incoming audio signal. There are several standard frequency response shapes including low pass, high pass, band pass, and band reject (notch). Each of these filters has one or more parameters that determine how the filter affects the spectrum of the incoming audio signal. This "parametric" control is what gives parametric EQ its name, as we'll see later in the book.

Low Pass and High Pass Filters

The frequency response for a **low pass filter**, LPF for short, is shown in Figure 6.11a. At its simplest, an LPF has only one changeable parameter: the **cutoff frequency**. The flat part of the frequency response, referred to as the pass band, represents no gain change at those frequencies (0 dB of gain) and the line sloping down represents a greater and greater reduction in gain (negative dB) as you go up in that range of frequencies. The fact that the line doesn't just drop immediately to zero (−∞ dB of gain) shows that the frequencies above the cutoff frequency aren't just turned off, but are rather "rolled off" above the cutoff. A sudden drop to nothing—a so-called "brick-wall" filter—may be ideal in some situations, but it's not useful in practice because it would cause unusual timbral effects. In addition, in a synth we want interesting sounding filters, not necessarily ideal ones.

The cutoff frequency for this simple low pass filter is defined as the point at which the gain has been reduced by 3 dB—this is the **half-power point** (see "Technically Speaking . . . the half-power point"). In a simple LPF there is a relatively flat **pass band** followed by a curving down with the cutoff frequency lying at the −3 dB point on this curve.

In many synths and EQs, the **slope** of an LPF can be selected to change the sharpness of the rolloff above the cutoff frequency. These slopes are usually given as some number of dB per octave. A 6 dB per octave slope will reduce the affected frequencies steadily by 6 dB for every doubling of frequency (octave) beyond the cutoff frequency. In resonant low pass filters 12 dB/octave, 18 dB/octave, and 24 dB/octave slopes are common (see Figure 6.11b). The higher the number, the "sharper" the gain reduction is above the cutoff frequency.

In addition to cutoff frequency and slope, an LPF in a synth usually has a **resonance** parameter as mentioned in Chapter 4: Synthesis, Sampling, and MIDI Control. The

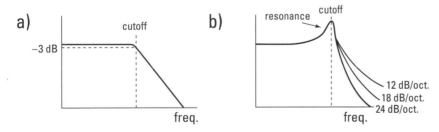

Figure 6.11 Low pass filters: a) simple LPF; b) resonant LPF with a variable slope of 12, 18, or 24 dB per octave

TECHNICALLY SPEAKING . . . THE HALF-POWER POINT

Technically speaking . . . the half-power point is the frequency at which the gain has been reduced by 3 dB. To see why this represents a halving of the power, you may recall from the discussion of decibels in Chapter 1 that the decibel formula for intensity or power is:

$$\text{Gain in dB} = 10 \log_{10} (P/P_0)$$

where P is the power level of the point we're measuring and P_0 is the power level that we're comparing that point to. If the power P is half of the reference power P_0, the resultant gain is:

$$10 \log_{10} (0.5P_0/P_0) = 10 \log_{10} (0.5) = -3 \text{ dB}$$

Since power is proportional to amplitude squared, the –3 dB half-power point represents an amplitude factor of 0.707 (the square root of 0.5). You can verify this by substituting the square of the amplitude for the power in the decibel formula:

$$\text{Gain in dB} = 10 \log_{10} (P/P_0) = 10 \log_{10} (A/A_0)^2$$

When the amplitude is reduced by a factor of 0.707 relative to the reference amplitude A_0:

$$\text{Gain in dB} = 10 \log_{10} (0.707A_0/A_0)^2 = 10 \log_{10} (0.707)^2$$

$$\text{Gain in dB} = 10 \log_{10} (0.5) = -3 \text{ dB}$$

resonance parameter provides a boost (positive gain) around the cutoff frequency (see Figure 6.11b). This makes a changing cutoff frequency more audible. The resonance parameter is sometimes referred to as "Q," with a higher Q representing a larger, narrower boost at the cutoff. We'll go into more detail concerning Q when discussing band pass and band reject (notch) filters.

A **high pass filter**, or HPF, is the mirror image of a low pass filter. In an HPF, frequencies above the cutoff frequency are passed without change while frequencies below the cutoff frequency are rolled off according to the slope (see Figure 6.12a). An HPF may also have a resonance parameter that provides a boost in the spectrum around the cutoff frequency and a variable slope (see Figure 6.12b). One of the functions of the LPF in a synth is to provide the variable brightness found in natural systems based on factors such as peak amplitude (as controlled by the velocity). The HPF doesn't have such a function and is instead useful largely in creating interesting synthetic timbres. For example, raising the cutoff frequency can have the effect of removing the "body" of a sound leaving only the upper partials ringing, giving the timbre a kind of ghostly shimmer.

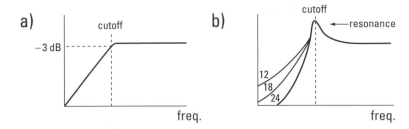

Figure 6.12 High pass filters: a) simple HPF; b) resonant HPF with a variable slope of 12, 18, or 24 dB per octave

Band Pass and Notch Filters

A **band pass filter**, or BPF, allows only a certain band of frequencies to pass while reducing or eliminating the frequencies outside of that band. You can use a BPF in a synth to emphasize just one or a few partials of the waveform or sweep up or down to hear each of the partials in the input spectrum in succession. This is similar to the effect of sweeping an LPF or HPF with a high resonance value, but a BPF rejects more of the partials outside the pass band.

The center of the band of frequencies is determined by **the center frequency** parameter, and the width of the band is determined by the **bandwidth** parameter (see Figure 6.13a). The edges of the band of frequencies are the frequencies above and below the center frequency where the power has been reduced by 3 dB (the half-power points), or, equivalently, where the amplitude has been reduced by a factor of 0.707 (see "Technically Speaking . . . the half-power point"). The bandwidth parameter could be given as some number of Hertz (50 Hz, 100 Hz, etc.), but it is usually given as a musical interval or a Q value, where Q is sometimes said to be the "Quality" factor. In multi-mode filters that can be set to different filter types, the Q is sometimes referred to as the "resonance" to match the language used by the LPFs and HPFs.

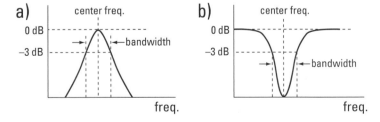

Figure 6.13 a) Band pass filter with bandwidth measured at the half-power points, b) band reject, or notch, filter with bandwidth measured at the half-power points

For a BPF, Q is proportional to the center frequency (CF) over the bandwidth (BW):

$$Q \propto CF/BW$$

One interpretation of this relationship is that Q is a measurement of the "sharpness" of the filter with a higher Q indicating a narrower bandwidth and a lower Q indicating a wider bandwidth. However, Q also has a valuable role making the bandwidth relate to our perception of frequency differences.

To understand this, consider the octave, which we perceive to be the same "size" whether it is played very low or very high. Despite our perception of octaves being the same in every register, the absolute size in Hertz of octaves increases as we play them in higher and higher registers. The interval between 110 Hz and 220 Hz is an octave, as is the interval between 220 Hz and 440 Hz, the interval between 440 Hz and 880 Hz, and the interval between 880 Hz and 1760 Hz. These are all perceived as octaves despite the fact that they are of very different absolute sizes: 110 Hz, 220 Hz, 440 Hz, and 880 Hz. We hear the 2:1 proportion as being the same, not the actual size in Hertz.

If we want a BPF to have the same perceptual effect regardless of its center frequency, the bandwidth has to grow and shrink as the center frequency increases and decreases (see Figure 6.14). By connecting the bandwidth and the center frequency together through Q, we can achieve this: as the center frequency increases, the bandwidth must also increase to keep Q at the same value (**constant Q**). This allows us to specify the relative narrowness of the band with the Q value and let the filter take care of adjusting the bandwidth as the center frequency changes. Q can be given as the actual CF/BW ratio, as an abstract number ranging from 0.0–1.0 or 0–127, or as a musical interval.

Using a musical interval for the bandwidth automatically takes into account the fact that we perceive proportions rather than absolute values as being equivalent. When BPFs are displayed graphically in software, the horizontal axis is usually shown logarithmically with each octave taking up the same amount of space. In that display, a constant Q filter would have the same visual shape regardless of its center frequency (see Figure 6.15).

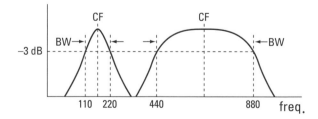

Figure 6.14 Band pass filters with bandwidths of equal perceptual size (an octave) with different center frequencies shown on a linear frequency scale. The bandwidth must increase as the center frequency increases to maintain the same perceptual size

BPFs are related to the peaking filters found in EQs. The primary difference is that BPFs *cut* frequencies outside of the band, while peaking filters have no effect on frequencies outside of the band (0 dB of gain outside of the band). In addition, peaking filters have a gain factor that allows you to variably boost frequencies within the band (positive dB of gain). Figure 6.16 shows a BPF (6.16a) compared to a peaking filter (6.16b). The bandwidth for the peaking filter is measured from the half-power points that are 3 dB down from the total gain. For higher values of Q, a BPF may have a positive gain at the center frequency rather than the 0 dB gain (no change) shown.

The inverse of the BPF is the band reject filter, or **notch filter** (see Figure 6.13b). A notch filter passes all frequencies except those within the band. A very narrow notch filter can be used to cut an individual partial of the oscillator waveform, or cut them in succession if it is swept up or down. A wider notch can be swept up and down to dynamically change the amplitude relationships between the overtones, thus subtly altering the timbre.

As with the BPF, the center of the band is controlled by the center frequency parameter and the bandwidth is specified by a Q value or by a musical interval. Ideally a notch filter would completely cut the frequency at the center of the band ($-\infty$ dB of gain). Notch filters may also have a variable negative gain, allowing you to determine the extent of the notching. This is particularly true of notch filters found in EQs where a peak and a notch can be the same filter with the peak or notch function chosen through the gain factor: + dB gain for peak and − dB gain for notch. Variable gain peak/notch filters often measure the bandwidth using points that represent 3 dB of change below the maximum positive gain or *above* the maximum negative gain as opposed to the notch filter shown in Figure 6.13b.

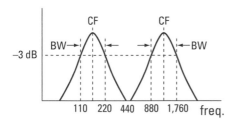

Figure 6.15 Band pass filters with bandwidths of equal perceptual size (an octave) with different center frequencies shown on a logarithmic frequency scale. The log scale allows them to appear the same despite the difference in their absolute bandwidths

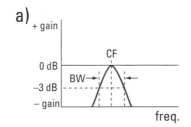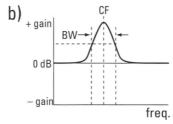

Figure 6.16 Comparison of (a) a BPF and (b) a peaking filter

Comb and Formant Filters

As the name suggests, the frequency response of a **comb filter** consists of a series of evenly spaced notches or evenly spaced peaks, depending on how the filter was designed (see Figure 6.17). The primary parameter for a comb filter controls how far apart the notches or peaks are spaced. This parameter will likely be given in abstract values, such as 0.0–1.0, 0–100, or 0–127, rather than in an absolute frequency difference between peaks. Some comb filters will also have a feedback parameter that increases the gain and sharpness of the peaks, giving the resultant sound a metallic tinge.

A comb filter is actually a very short delay that, when combined with the original signal, results in phase cancellation and reinforcement at regular frequency intervals. The frequency interval is determined by the delay time, with smaller delays yielding a wider spacing of the notches/peaks and longer delays yielding closer spacing of the notches/peaks. The delay time in a comb filter is quite short, ranging from a fraction of a millisecond to a few tens of milliseconds—much shorter than a delay time that would be heard as an echo. If a short delay time on the order of a few milliseconds is varied periodically and fed back into the input, the result is a flanging effect whose characteristic sound is the shifting comb peaks. Flanging and other effects will be discussed further in Chapter 8: Effects.

It may seem odd that a short delay results in filter, but it turns out that all of the filters we've discussed are the result of one or more extremely short delays—some as short as a single sample. Filter theory is a complex subject, but, fortunately, we don't need to know much more than we've discussed here in order to use them well. A few technical details concerning filter theory can be found in the sidebar "Technically speaking . . . a little filter theory" on page 140.

Though there are many other possible filter shapes, most can be thought of as a combination of the LPF, HPF, BPF, and notch filter. Synths that have more than one filter that can be applied simultaneously may configure those filters in parallel or in series. If the filters are applied in **parallel**, the same signal is sent to each filter and the results of each individual filter are added together at the end. When filters are applied in **series**, or cascaded, the signal is sent first to one filter, and then the output of that filter is sent to the next.

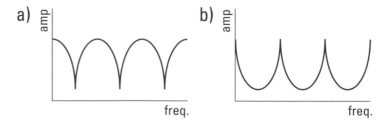

Figure 6.17   Two types of comb filter: a) evenly-spaced spectral notches; and b) evenly-spaced spectral peaks

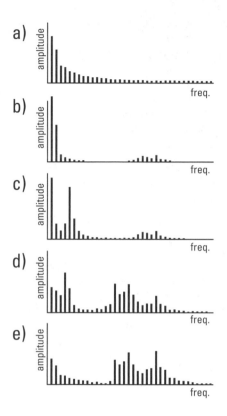

Figure 6.18 A sawtooth wave processed by the formant filter in Reason's Thor synthesizer: a) unchanged sawtooth; b) through e) various filter settings that yield progressively brighter vowel–like spectra

An example of a "combination" filter is a **formant filter**. A formant filter creates multiple peaks in a spectrum that are usually chosen to match the spectral peaks, or **formants**, found in spoken or sung vowel sounds. Most acoustic instruments have one or more characteristic formants created by the size and shape of their resonating chambers, such as those of guitar or violin. The resonating chambers for the human voice are our throat, mouth, and nasal cavities.

To change vowels, we change the shape of these cavities, which in turn changes the center frequency, bandwidth, and gain for several peaks in the output spectrum. Similar peaks can be imposed upon an input spectrum by a special formant filter or by multiple band pass filters (see Figure 6.18). The result is eerily similar to the human voice provided that the formant frequencies are chosen properly. Vowel formants are different for men and women and even for different voice types within each gender. Three to five formants are used to mimic the spectrum of vowel sounds. Tables of formant frequencies can be found in Dodge and Jerse (1997) and in Bennett and Rodet (1989).

Filter Modulation Routings

For LPFs and HPFs the changeable parameters are the cutoff frequency, slope, and resonance, and for BPFs and notch filters the changeable parameters are center frequency, bandwidth/Q, and possibly gain. Of these parameters, the cutoff frequencies and center

TECHNICALLY SPEAKING . . . A LITTLE FILTER THEORY

Technically speaking . . . a little filter theory can help us to better understand and utilize filters. Much of filter theory is beyond the scope of a book written for musicians and is the province of electrical engineers and digital signal processing programmers. However, it is useful to understand the basics of the filter equation.

The output of a filter is a combination of current and past inputs to the filter and past outputs of the filter. Filters that only use current and past inputs are referred to as **feedforward filters** and those that use past outputs, perhaps in addition to current and past inputs, are referred to as **feedback filters**.

A simple feedforward filter can be represented by the following "difference" equation:

$$y[n] = (x[n] + x[n-1])/2$$

The y in this equation stands for the output of the filter and x for the input. It is a feedforward filter because y depends only on values of x, current and past inputs, and not on previous values of y, past outputs. The n in the equation stands for the current sample (remember, digital audio is just a stream of samples). So, $x[n]$ is the current sample going into the filter and $y[n]$ is the current sample coming out of the filter.

The term $x[n-1]$ represents the input sample immediately before $x[n]$; $n-1$ represents an earlier time just as subtracting some number of minutes from the current time on the clock represents an earlier time. The term $x[n-1]$, then, is an $x[n]$ that has been delayed by one sample (see Figure 6.19a) and then added to the current input value. This delay is *very* short: at a sampling rate of 44,100 Hz, a single sample delay is approximately 0.023 ms, or 0.000023 seconds.

The above equation is the sum of the current input sample and the previous input sample divided by two, which is an *average* of the two most recent samples. The filter represented by this equation is referred to as a "moving average filter."

To understand what that filter actually does, we can think of what it would do to actual sample values. If the last two samples were close in amplitude value, then the average of them would be about the same. By analogy, if one person is 5′6″ and another is 5′7″, then their average height is about the same as each of their actual heights. Similar values are passed mostly unchanged. If the last two samples were very different in value, then the average of them would "even out" those differences. Again by analogy, the average height of a 5′6″ person and a 7′6″ person is 6′6″. Differences between values are evened out.

A signal whose amplitude is changing quickly—a higher frequency signal—will have larger differences between successive samples than a signal whose amplitude is changing more slowly. The more slowly changing signals are passed with little alteration and the quickly changing signals are evened out. In other words, this is a low pass filter.

I wrote the above equation as two samples added together and then divided by 2 to emphasize that it was an average. However, the equation would generally be written with the individual multiplier in front of each term:

$y[n] = 0.5x[n] + 0.5x[n-1]$, or more generally $y[n] = a_0x[n] + a_1x[n-1]$

The a_0 and a_1 are the **filter coefficients** for those terms. Changing the filter coefficients changes the frequency response of the filter.

A simple change to the previous equation results in this equation:

$y[n] = 0.5x[n] - 0.5x[n-1]$

Here the previous input sample is subtracted from the current input sample. Successive sample values that are very similar result in a small output, whereas sample values that are quite different result in a larger output value. In other words, this is a high pass filter.

A feedback filter would include past *outputs* of the filter as well as current and possibly past inputs. The following is an example of a feedback filter equation:

$y[n] = 0.5x[n] + 0.5y[n-1]$, or more generally $y[n] = a_0x[n] + b_1y[n-1]$

Here the term $y[n-1]$ represents the previous output of the filter and is thus a feedback term, and the feedback coefficient is represented by the letter "b" and a subscript (see Figure 6.19b). The coefficients here are both 0.5, but we could have chosen different coefficients to change some aspect of the frequency response. However, the coefficient for any feedback term must be less than one, otherwise the output will continue to grow and grow and eventually distort. This simple feedback filter turns out to be a low pass filter with a different frequency response than the simple feedforward one discussed above. As above, the term $y[n-1]$ can be interpreted as a one-sample delay, this time of the output.

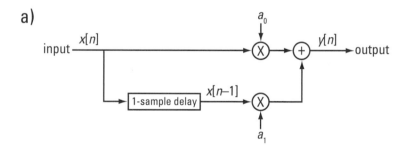

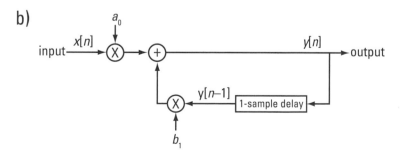

Figure 6.19   Filter diagrams: a) simple feedforward filter, b) simple one-pole feedback filter

Technically Speaking

In terms of the frequency response, each feedforward term contributes a **zero**, or a reduction in amplitude around some frequency, and each feedback term contributes a **pole**, or a peak in amplitude around some frequency. A resonant peak in a filter is the result of pole (a feedback term). The phrases "two-pole filter" and "four-pole filter" are used in the documentation for some synths—in general, the more poles a filter has, the steeper its rolloff, or slope, can be.

If you're interested in learning more about filter theory, Dodge and Jerse (1997) and Roads (1996) go into a fair bit of detail. If you have a substantial math background and really want to delve deeply into filter theory, Steiglitz (1996), Loy (2006, Vol. 2), or any textbook on digital signal processing are good resources.

frequencies are the most likely targets for modulation with resonance, Q, and gain (where available) also being possibilities. These modulation targets were discussed in conjunction with the resonant LPF that was part of the basic synthesis model. For mappings from various modulation sources to these parameters, see the previous two chapters.

For comb filters, the spacing between notches/peaks as controlled by the amount of delay time is a useful target for modulation along with the feedback amount. For consistent changes over the course of each note, the notch/peak spacing can be modulated by an envelope, the strength of which could be controlled by velocity. Modulation with an LFO would create periodic changes in the notch/peak spacing, resulting in flanging if the delay time is on the order of a few milliseconds. If you want the notch/peak spacing to change over the course of several notes, then a CC would be a useful modulation source. Similarly, the feedback can be controlled by velocity, CC/aftertouch, an envelope, or perhaps an LFO.

The parameters of a formant filter often include the gender and vowel. These in turn would determine the center frequency, bandwidth, and gain of the internal BPFs. To change smoothly from one vowel to another, some formant filters provide a two-dimensional pad with different vowels positioned at the corners and a moveable "puck" to morph between vowels. The position of this puck can be usefully modulated by velocity, a CC, aftertouch, an envelope, or an LFO.

In this chapter, we've expanded the basic synthesis model to include multiple oscillators and various types of oscillator-to-oscillator modulation, along with more complex filters that can also be used in sample-based instruments. In the next chapter, we will break from the two- or three-oscillator analog model and explore several different synthesis techniques. Each of these techniques has its own unique set of parameters that can be controlled by MIDI messages, LFOs, and envelopes to create dynamic synthesized sound.

CHAPTER 7

Synthesis Techniques

Over the last several chapters we've established a basic synthesis model, expanded it to include a variety of modulation sources, and explored oscillators and filters in some detail. In this chapter we will explore synthesis techniques that go beyond a few fixed waveform oscillators, including multiple wavetable, additive synthesis, frequency modulation synthesis, physical modeling synthesis, and granular synthesis/processing. The key elements of subtractive synthesis—filters—were covered in the last chapter, as were the essentials of amplitude modulation and ring modulation.

Each of the synthesis techniques discussed here provides its own unique parameters that can be modulated directly using information contained in various MIDI messages and with envelopes and LFOs. As with the basic analog synthesis model that we've been using, modulation is the key to creating rich, dynamic, and evolving timbres.

The synthesis techniques chosen for this chapter represent a wide range of practices, and most are used in commercial softsynths. Nevertheless, there are many more synthesis techniques than can be covered here, many of which are primarily of interest only to researchers and experimental composers. Software that can be programmed to utilize almost any synthesis technique will be discussed briefly at the end of the chapter.

MULTIPLE WAVETABLE SYNTHESIS

In the previous chapters, synth patches have been based on one or a few oscillators, each of which utilizes just one waveform at a time. To create a dynamic timbre using those fixed-waveform oscillators, it is necessary to use filters and/or multiple oscillator interactions such as oscillator sync, ring modulation, and frequency modulation, in conjunction with various modulation sources. For example, to create a linkage between loudness and brightness—a linkage typical of acoustic instruments—we can use a low pass filter modulated by a filter envelope similar in shape to the amplitude envelope. However, it is also possible to create such a dynamic timbre by directly changing an

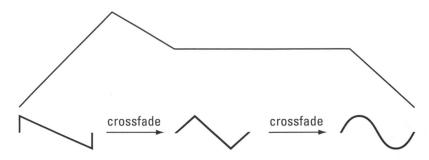

Figure 7.1 Simple multiple wavetable synthesis: a note represented by its ADSR envelope in which the waveform starts as a sawtooth, crossfades to a triangle, and finally crossfades to a sine wave

oscillator's waveform during the course of a note. This is referred to as **multiple wavetable synthesis**, or sometimes just wavetable synthesis.[1]

We saw a simple version of multiple wavetable synthesis in the last chapter when discussing mixing oscillators (see p. 121), where the mix parameter was modulated by an envelope such that a brighter waveform—such as a sawtooth wave—was dominant during the attack and decay phases and a darker waveform—such as a triangle wave— was dominant during the sustain and release phases. Figure 7.1 shows a slightly more complex version of this in which the waveform begins as a sawtooth wave during the attack, crossfades with a triangle wave during the decay, remains a triangle wave during the sustain, and then crossfades with a sine wave during the release.

Multiple wavetable synthesis takes this idea and expands it greatly by using a table of up to dozens of waveforms that are used during different portions of a note. One standard way to organize such a table of waveforms is to have the darkest sounding waveform first in the table and progressively brighter waveforms throughout the rest of the table. Each waveform is indexed by a position in the table of waveforms with low position numbers being darkest and higher position numbers being brightest. A modulation envelope whose amplitude is mapped to the position index can then be used to change quickly to the brightest waveforms during the attack, to intermediate waveforms during the decay, and to darker waveforms during the release (see Figure 7.2). The simplest way to change from one waveform to another is to crossfade—fade one out while the other fades in.

Though this is a useful arrangement, a table of waveforms needn't be this straightforward. There is no requirement that each waveform in a table of waveforms must have the same fundamental frequency, be in a darkest-to-brightest order, or even be remotely similar in timbre. For example, a table of waveforms might consist of different

---

1   There is a bit of confusion in the music technology literature over the term "wavetable." A number of the more technical sources (Dodge and Jerse 1997; Loy 2006, Vols 1 and 2; Roads 1996; Moore 1990) use the term "wavetable" or "wave table" to refer to a table of amplitude values used for fixed waveform synthesis. Other sources (Aikin 2004; Bristow-Johnson 1996) use the term wavetable to mean a table of different waveforms. To avoid confusion, I will refer to this type of synthesis as "multiple wavetable synthesis" after Roads (1996).

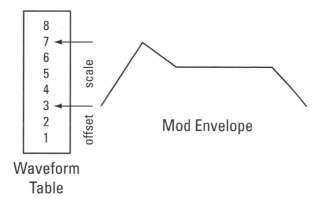

Figure 7.2 Multiple wavetable synthesis: a small table of waveforms, numbered 1–8, are indexed by a mod envelope. The offset and scale (amount or depth) of the modulation determine the starting index and maximum index that the mod envelope will reach

numbers of sine wave cycles. The first waveform in the table could have one cycle of a sine wave representing a fundamental, the second could have two cycles of a sine wave sounding an octave higher, the third could have three cycles of a sine wave sounding an octave and a fifth higher, and so on. Such a table of waveforms would thus consist of partials from the overtone series, and sweeping through the table would result in sweeping through the overtone series.

The primary modulation target in multiple wavetable synthesis is the position index. As mentioned above, a mod envelope could be used to sweep through the table of waveforms in a predictable way on every note. The velocity could be mapped so as to modulate the strength of this envelope, in which case the velocity would determine the maximum position in the table of waveforms reached by the envelope. Maximum velocity could mean that the envelope reaches all the way to the last waveform in the table. The initial position number set on the oscillator would be the offset for this envelope modulation and the velocity would scale the strength of the envelope.

A simultaneous mapping of a knob or slider on your controller to the position index would allow you to move through the table of waveforms on longer notes or over the course of many notes. An LFO controlled by the mod wheel could be used to create a periodic change in waveforms. In addition to a typical triangle wave for the LFO, some of the other patterns such as the smooth random pattern could be useful for creating a random path through the table of waveforms. If the waveforms in the table consisted of different members of the overtone series, the smooth random pattern would create a glassy, bubbling timbre.

It is worth noting that the output of a multiple wavetable oscillator can be treated like the output of any oscillator in that it can be mixed with other oscillators, transposed, detuned, used in amplitude/ring modulation, or used in frequency modulation.

The modulation routings for multiple wavetable synthesis are summarized in Table 7.1.

Table 7.1   Modulation routings for multiple wavetable synthesis

Mapping	Velocity → mod envelope amount → position index in table of waveforms
Effect	The mod envelope sweeps through the table of waveforms on each note; the velocity determines how far the envelope gets into the table
Mapping	CC → position index in table of waveforms
Effect	You can change the waveform selected from the table of waveforms over the course of one or many notes
Mapping	Mod wheel → LFO amount → position index in table of waveforms
Effect	The waveform selected from the table of waveforms can be changed periodically by the LFO under the control of the mod wheel. With a smooth random LFO shape chosen, the position index would slide around in the table of waveforms randomly with the amount of change of the position index controlled by the mod wheel

ADDITIVE SYNTHESIS

Additive synthesis creates a complex timbre by using one sine wave oscillator for each partial in the desired spectrum (see Figure 7.3). The advantage to additive synthesis is that you can explicitly specify the frequency, amplitude, and phase of each and every partial, allowing you to create *exactly* the timbre that you want. Many of the extensions of the basic synthesis model have focused on changing the synth's timbre over time through techniques such as dynamic oscillator mixing, detuning, ring modulation, frequency modulation, and filtering. With complete control of every partial, additive synthesis provides the ultimate platform for dynamic timbre. However, with all of this power comes several drawbacks.

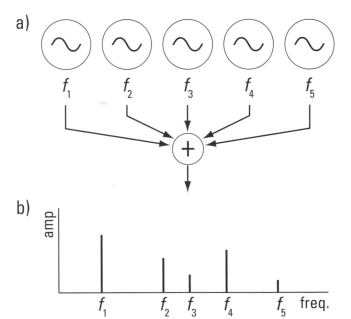

Figure 7.3 Additive synthesis: a) five sine wave oscillators with different frequencies are added together; b) the resultant spectrum can be harmonic or inharmonic (as shown)

One of the drawbacks is that you have to supply the frequency, amplitude, and phase for *every partial*. In addition, since amplitude and frequency can change continuously over the course of a note, each is a time-varying signal rather than a single number. This is an enormous amount of data to have to specify, making the theoretical promise of "any sound you can imagine" a practical nightmare.

A second drawback to additive synthesis is that it requires a separate oscillator for each partial of each note. If an additive timbre were to have 25 partials with significant amounts of energy, then a ten-note chord would require 250 simultaneous oscillators. In the days of analog synthesizers, each oscillator was a separate box and 250 oscillators would be incredibly expensive. In the modern virtual synthesizer era, those extra oscillators come at no monetary cost, but they do have a computational cost. Even with our fast computers, it requires a lot of computing power to calculate the output of all those oscillators with their time-varying parameters. Even though additive synthesis can theoretically give us any sound we desire, it is far less computationally expensive to simply use recorded samples of the sounds we actually desire.

As a result of these practical difficulties few hardware or software synthesizers implement pure additive synthesis. Some implement a limited form of additive synthesis in which you specify the partials and their amplitudes, and the synth creates a fixed waveform from those unique specifications. The actual act of synthesis is then computationally inexpensive, but the parameters for each partial can't be changed over the course of a note.

To overcome the data-intensive nature of additive synthesis, some synths use a form of **analysis-resynthesis** in which they first analyze an existing timbre, generating the time-varying frequencies and amplitudes for a specified number of partials. These analyzed parameters can then be modified in a variety of ways and resynthesized by a bank of oscillators. The result is a new timbre based on the complex qualities of an analyzed timbre. Figure 7.4 shows a block diagram of analysis-resynthesis. Synths that utilize analysis-resynthesis include Camel Audio's Alchemy and VirSyn's Cube. There are other methods of analysis-resynthesis not based on additive synthesis, including phase vocoding and linear-predictive coding. For a discussion of these other analysis-synthesis techniques see Roads (1996) or Dodge and Jerse (1997).

The synths that do implement genuine additive synthesis can be useful even without an initial analysis phase. For example, the partial frequencies can be changed over the course of a note or several notes such that the partials shift between harmonic and inharmonic relationships creating a sense of the timbre going in and out of "focus" (see Figure 7.5a). Another example involves synthesizing a single waveform, such as a sawtooth wave, and then gradually morphing into another, such as a triangle wave. The spectra for those waveforms are sufficiently well known to allow us to synthesize them directly (see Figure 7.5b). In addition to a few specialized additive synths, there are several applications such as Native Instruments' Reaktor and Cycling 74's Max/MSP that allow you to construct any type of instrument that you want, including an additive synthesis instrument. These synthesis programming applications will be discussed further at the end of the chapter.

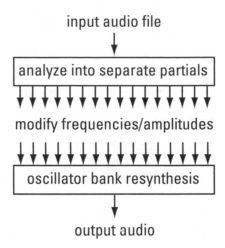

Figure 7.4 Additive analysis-resynthesis: the input audio file is analyzed into its separate partials (only sixteen in this illustration), the partial data is modified, and the partials are resynthesized using an oscillator bank

In terms of modulation, the parameters involved in pure additive synthesis would be too numerous to control directly with CCs. A synth would instead have to make available "meta parameters" such as brightness, degree of inharmonicity, or waveform morphing that could be controlled with CCs, envelopes, and LFOs. The synth would then use those meta parameters to modify the actual frequency, amplitude, and phase values of the individual sine wave oscillators. If this were a synth that you constructed in Reaktor or Max/MSP, you would be responsible for creating such meta parameters suitable for modulation.

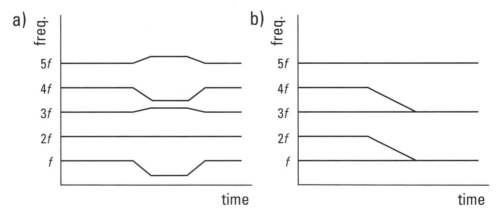

Figure 7.5 Additive synthesis examples shown as spectrograms: a) the spectrum morphs from harmonic to inharmonic and back to harmonic; b) the spectrum morphs from a sawtooth wave (all harmonics present) to a square or triangle wave (only odd harmonics)

FREQUENCY MODULATION

In the last chapter, we discussed frequency modulation as a technique available in a number of synths to allow one oscillator to modulate the frequency of another. This is most often used in an analog-modeling synth to increase the sonic possibilities available with just a few oscillators. However, FM with multiple oscillators in various configurations is a full-blown synthesis technique in its own right.

This form of FM was pioneered first by composer John Chowning at Stanford University and then by Yamaha through a licensing agreement with Stanford. The most prominent result was the Yamaha DX7, one of the first successful all-digital synthesizers. The use of FM as the synthesis technique in the DX7 and many subsequent Yamaha products resulted in a distinctive, rich timbre associated with much of the synthesized music of the 1980s.

As with many of the synthesis techniques in this chapter, FM was popular for some years in hardware synths and was then displaced by other approaches. Subsequently, it has been resurrected in software, most fully with Native Instruments' FM8 softsynth that emulates the architecture of the DX7 with some modifications.

FM: Refining Simple FM

When we discussed FM in the last chapter, we focused on the spectrum of one sine wave oscillator frequency modulating another sine wave oscillator at a modulating frequency above 20 Hz. This is referred to as simple FM and its spectrum is shown in Figure 7.6. This spectrum was discussed in the previous chapter and some specific examples given in Figure 6.10 on page 131.

In the example shown in Figure 7.6 (similar to Figure 6.10a), the carrier frequency, f_c, is 440 Hz and the modulating frequency, f_m, is 110 Hz. The resultant spectrum is an overtone series with a fundamental of 110 Hz. However, that fundamental is present only because the modulation index (related to the amplitude of the modulator) is high enough to produce three partials below the carrier frequency. This comes about because $f_c > f_m$ results in sidebands below f_c.

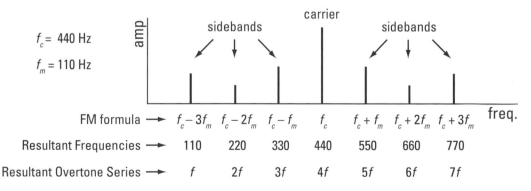

Figure 7.6   An example of the simple FM spectrum where $f_c > f_m$

To have a more predictable fundamental, we can instead restrict f_m to be greater than or equal to f_c (or $f_m \geq f_c$), so no sidebands will fall between f_c and 0 Hz. We can achieve a similar spectrum as that in Figure 7.6 by setting f_c to 110 Hz, f_m to 110 Hz, and setting the modulation index high enough to produce six partials above and below the carrier. That spectrum, shown in Figure 7.7a, also has a fundamental frequency of

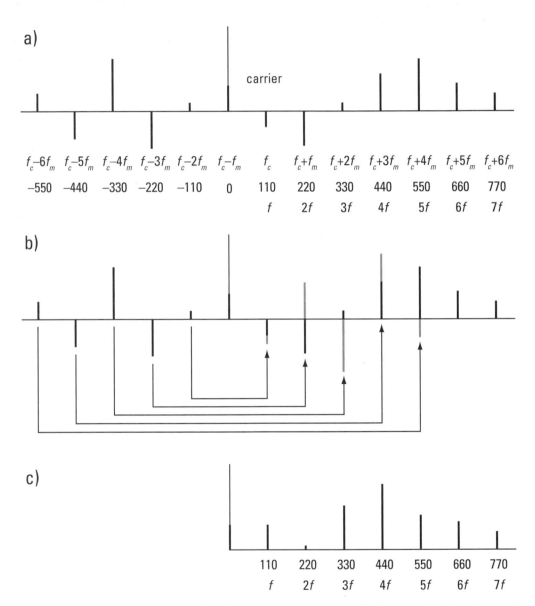

Figure 7.7   The FM spectrum for $f_c = f_m = 110$ Hz: a) six partials above and below the carrier, including negative frequencies (notice that some positive frequency partials have inverted phases—see "Technically Speaking . . . FM amplitudes" for more details); b) negative frequencies are phase inverted and added to/subtracted from the corresponding positive frequencies; c) the resultant spectrum showing all amplitudes as positive (compare to Figure 7.6)

110 Hz with six partials above the carrier, but there are also six partials below the carrier that are either at 0 Hz or have negative frequencies.

Negative frequencies may appear to be bizarre at first—they certainly don't make much intuitive sense—but they can simply be thought of as positive frequencies with an inverted phase. The amplitudes of those negative frequencies would then subtract from the amplitudes of the sidebands at the equivalent positive frequencies, resulting in a harmonic spectrum with somewhat different partial amplitudes than the example in Figure 7.6. Figure 7.7c shows the perceived result of the spectrum in Figure 7.7a once the negative frequencies have been "wrapped around" 0 Hz, had their phases inverted, and had their amplitudes added to the amplitudes of the corresponding positive frequencies (shown in Figure 7.7b). The 0 Hz partial only has an effect on the timbre in certain special circumstances.

Whether the amplitudes of the corresponding negative and positive frequencies add together or one subtracts from the other depends on whether they have the same phase or opposite phases once the negative frequency is wrapped around zero and inverted— a positive frequency may have an inverted phase, represented by a negative amplitude —and just what their relative amplitudes are. We have thus far avoided discussing the specific amplitudes for partials produced by frequency modulation. For some details on that subject, see the sidebar "Technically Speaking . . . FM amplitudes" on page 153.

Though we've focused on $f_c \leq f_m$ thus far, using $f_c > f_m$ is perfectly acceptable and can be useful in some circumstances. For example, $f_c > f_m$ could be useful if you want the partials in an inharmonic spectrum to be spaced more closely together than the overtone series. With harmonic spectra, $f_c > f_m$ can generate a timbre in which the fundamental appears *after* the partials if you control the modulation index with an envelope.

On the other hand, if we stick with the approach that $f_c \leq f_m$ wherever possible, then f_c will always be the fundamental (for harmonic timbres) and the modulation index will determine how many partials appear above that fundamental in the spectrum. This means that the instrument is playable by MIDI note messages where the key number determines the carrier frequency and thus the fundamental frequency, and the velocity can affect the modulation index and thus the brightness. The modulation index can also be controlled by an envelope whose strength is modulated by the velocity to shape the brightness over the course of each note.

FM: Modulation Index

So far the modulation index has been an abstract value that produces more sidebands as it increases and fewer as it decreases. In cases where FM is used as a technique to enrich the output of a synth with a few analog-style oscillators, that level of understanding is detailed enough, allowing you to predict what will happen generally when you turn up or down the knob controlling the "amount" of frequency modulation. However, in cases where the FM implementation is more extensive, it is useful to understand the effect of a specific modulation index value.

The modulation index is defined as the ratio of the peak deviation in carrier frequency to the modulating frequency. The peak deviation is how much the carrier frequency is modulated below f_c ($f_c - d$) and above f_c ($f_c + d$), and it is proportional to the amplitude of the modulator. If you think back to the application of an LFO to the frequency of an oscillator (vibrato), the LFO "depth"—which is the amplitude of the LFO—determines how much the pitch will change above and below the primary pitch. Using the letter d for the deviation, the modulation index, I, is given by:

$$I = d/f_m$$

The number of sidebands with significant energy on either side of the carrier is usually given by a rule of thumb as $I + 1$, though the actual relationship is more complicated (De Poli 1983; Moore 1990; Dodge and Jerse 1997). Using that rule of thumb, a modulation index of five will have six significant sidebands above the carrier frequency and six sidebands below the carrier frequency. In the case where $f_m \geq f_c$ and the spectrum is harmonic, this effectively means that the spectrum will contain $I + 1$ partials in addition to the fundamental, because the lower sidebands will wrap around 0 Hz and combine with the positive sidebands of the same frequency.

The modulation index also determines the amplitudes and phases of the sidebands and carrier frequency. See the sidebar "Technically Speaking . . . FM amplitudes" for more details.

FM: The f_c to f_m Ratio

The $f_c{:}f_m$ ratio—the carrier frequency to modulating frequency ratio—determines how the FM spectrum is structured. For the 1:1 ratio discussed above and shown in Figure 7.7c, all partials in the overtone series are present. If the ratio was instead 1:2, only the odd partials would be present. For a fundamental of 110 Hz, the partials would be 110, 330, 550, 770, etc. (see Figure 7.9a). This would produce a timbre similar to a square wave, which also lacks even partials. If the ratio was 1:3, only every third partial would be present: 110, 440, 770, 1,100, etc. (see Figure 7.9b).

When the $f_c{:}f_m$ ratio isn't a simple whole number ratio, the spectrum is *inharmonic*. For example, if the ratio was 1:1.41 (1.41 is approximately the square root of two), the partials above the carrier for a carrier frequency of 110 Hz would be approximately 265, 420, 575, etc. I call 100 Hz the carrier frequency here instead of the fundamental because there isn't necessarily a "fundamental" in an inharmonic spectrum. The partials below the carrier would be −45, −200, −355, etc. When the negative frequencies are folded around zero, the total spectrum becomes 45, 110, 200, 265, 355, 420, 575, etc. (see Figure 7.9c). Since 45 Hz is the lowest frequency, we can compare this inharmonic spectrum to a harmonic spectrum with 45 Hz as the fundamental and notice that these partials are "stretched" wider than the overtone series based on 45 Hz (45, 90, 135, 180, 225, 270, 315, etc.).

TECHNICALLY SPEAKING . . . FM AMPLITUDES

Technically speaking . . . simple FM involves one sine wave modulating the frequency of another sine wave. Mathematically, the output of the modulating oscillator can be expressed as:

Modulator output = $\sin(2\pi f_m t)$

where f_m is the modulating frequency and t is time. The amplitude of the modulator is multiplied by the index of modulation, I, and then added to the frequency of the carrier's sine wave. The output of the carrier, then, can be expressed as:

Carrier output = $\sin(2\pi f_c t + I \sin(2\pi f_m t))$

where f_c is the carrier frequency, I is the index of modulation, f_m is the modulating frequency, and t is time.

This equation can be expressed as a sum of sine waves whose frequencies are f_c, $f_c + f_m$, $f_c - f_m$, $f_c + 2f_m$, $f_c - 2f_m$, etc., and whose amplitudes are determined by a special set of functions known as Bessel functions of the first kind. These Bessel functions are indicated by the expression $J_n(I)$, where J represents Bessel functions of the first kind, n represents the *order* of the function, and I is the index of modulation from the FM equation.

The amplitude of the carrier frequency is determined by $J_0(I)$, the first sideband above and the first below the carrier by $J_1(I)$, the second sideband above and the second below by $J_2(I)$, and so on. In addition, the amplitudes of the odd-numbered sidebands *below* the carrier are the negative of the appropriate Bessel function. So the amplitude of the first sideband above the carrier is $J_1(I)$, but the first sideband below the carrier is $-J_1(I)$. These first four orders are graphed in Figure 7.8 as functions of I.

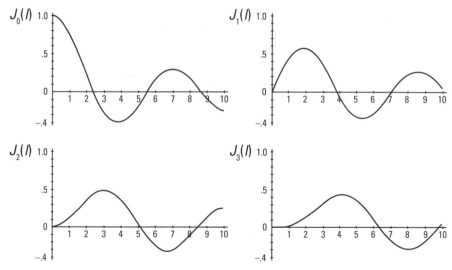

Figure 7.8   The first four orders of the Bessel functions of the first kind

As you can see, the amplitudes of the partials in the simple FM spectrum change in complex ways as the index of modulation increases and decreases. When the index is small, only the carrier frequency has a significant amplitude, but as the index increases, more and more partials have significant amplitudes. This behavior matches our rule of thumb that the higher the modulation index, the more partials present in the spectrum and the brighter the timbre.

When the Bessel functions cause negative amplitudes, these partials can be thought of as being 180 degrees out of phase with the positive amplitude partials. Another factor in the final spectrum is the "wrapping" of negative frequencies around zero with inverted phases. These will add to or subtract from any positive frequencies that they wrap around on top of (see Figure 7.7b).

The complex changes in the amplitudes of the partials caused by the Bessel functions are part of the characteristic "FM sound" that was so associated with the timbre of the DX7 and hence much synthesized music in the 1980s.

If the ratio were 1.41:1, the partials above a carrier frequency of 110 would be 188, 266, 344, 422, 500, etc., and those below the carrier would be 32, −46, −124, −202, −280, etc. When the negative frequencies are folded around zero, the total spectrum becomes 32, 46, 110, 124, 188, 202, 266, 280, 344, 422, 500, etc. (see Figure 7.9d). Notice that the partials are generally more narrowly spaced than the overtone series based on 32 Hz (32, 64, 96, 128, 160, 192, etc.), with a few "gaps" in the inharmonic spectrum.

If the synth is capable of changing $f_c{:}f_m$ ratios in real time, then you could use an envelope or a CC to modulate the ratio, resulting in timbres that shift from inharmonic to harmonic. For example, an envelope could modulate the $f_c{:}f_m$ ratio such that the attack of a note is inharmonic, the decay shifts from inharmonic to harmonic, and the sustain and release stay harmonic. If the decay segment of the envelope is longer than about a hundred milliseconds, there would be an audible "glissando" of partials during the $f_c{:}f_m$ change. Another possible modulation would be to use a CC to change the timbre from harmonic to inharmonic over the course of several notes resulting in an increasingly deranged phrase. Modulating the $f_c{:}f_m$ ratio can be tricky because smoothly changing the ratio quickly creates an inharmonic timbre, as opposed to a smooth transition from harmonic to inharmonic.

FM: Multiple Carriers

So far we've considered only simple FM in which one sine wave oscillator modulates a second sine wave oscillator. There are many other possible configurations including

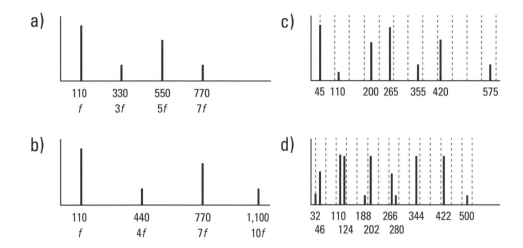

Figure 7.9   FM spectra with various $f_c{:}f_m$ ratios: a) 1:2 ratio, b) 1:3 ratio, c) 1:1.41 ratio, d) 1.41:1 ratio. For c) and d) the dashed vertical lines indicate harmonic partials of lowest frequency for comparison. The amplitudes of the partials are only approximate and are shown as positive

multiple parallel carriers, multiple simultaneous modulators, and feedback. The original DX7 implementation utilized up to six oscillators, referred to as operators, arranged in one of thirty-two separate configurations, or algorithms. Figure 7.10 shows several multiple oscillator configurations with simple block diagrams in which the bottom row always represents the carrier operator(s). We'll briefly consider two extensions to simple FM: more than one carrier and more than one modulator.

In the case of two carriers (see Figure 7.10b) the second carrier can be used to provide a formant, or peak in the spectrum, that can be found in the spectra of many instruments. Because the time-varying amplitudes of the partials in FM can be quite complex (see "Technically Speaking . . . FM amplitudes on page 153), it is difficult to guarantee that partials in a certain range will be emphasized. By using a second carrier with a frequency at the nearest partial to the desired formant frequency, a modulator with a modulating frequency equal to the spacing between the partials, and a modest modulation index, you can create a peak in the spectrum near the desired formant frequency (see Figure 7.11).

For the second carrier, the carrier frequency will necessarily be greater than the modulating frequency $(f_c > f_m)$, creating the characteristic spectrum with sidebands arrayed symmetrically around the fundamental as in Figure 7.6. The other carrier/ modulator pair provides the fundamental frequency and maintains the $f_c \leq f_m$ arrangement discussed above. Multiple carrier FM instruments have been used to successfully imitate the timbral qualities of trumpets (Morrill 1977) and voices (Chowning 1989).

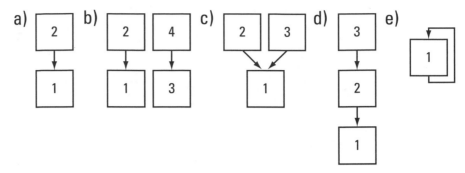

Figure 7.10 Block diagram for FM "operator" (oscillator) configurations: a) simple FM with modulator on top and carrier on bottom; b) multiple carrier FM as two simple FM pairs; c) multiple modulator FM with parallel modulators; d) multiple modulator FM with cascaded modulators; d) feedback FM with a single operator

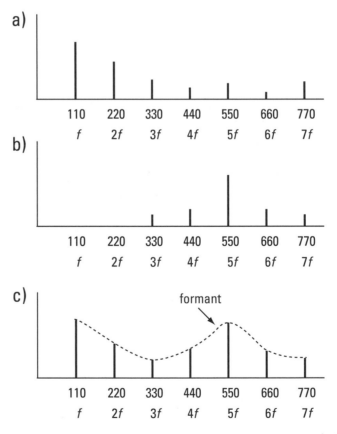

Figure 7.11 Double-carrier FM, each carrier with its own modulator: a) simple FM spectrum with $f_c \leq f_m$ providing the fundamental; b) simple FM spectrum with $f_c > f_m$ providing a formant; and c) the sum of the two spectra. The amplitudes of the partials are only approximate and are shown as positive

In this case, we assumed two carrier/modulator pairs. However, it is possible to use a single operator to modulate more than one carrier. In that case, the limitation is that you can't have independent envelopes or different f_c:f_m ratios. The case of two carriers can be easily extended to three carriers because the overall spectrum would be the sum of the spectra from each of the carriers just as it was with two carriers.

FM: Multiple Modulators

There are two basic configurations for multiple modulators: modulators in parallel (see Figure 7.10c) and modulators in series (cascaded; see Figure 7.10d). The spectrum produced from two modulators and one carrier includes sidebands around the carrier frequency from the frequencies of the modulators plus so-called "combination" sidebands. One way to think about combination sidebands is to first think of one modulator and one carrier producing the characteristic simple FM spectrum of a carrier plus sidebands, and then think of the second modulating frequency as creating sidebands around those sidebands.

The spectra resulting from two parallel modulators and two cascaded (series) modulators are similar with a few important differences. Most notably, there is more energy in the higher order combination sidebands in series modulation than in parallel modulation. For a detailed discussion of these differences, see Chowning and Bristow (1986).

For two modulators, the carrier frequency to modulating frequency ratio (f_c:f_m) of simple FM becomes the carrier to modulator to modulator ratios: f_c:f_{m1}:f_{m2}. When all the numbers in the f_c:f_{m1}:f_{m2} ratio are simple, the various sidebands will fall at the same frequencies, resulting in a bright, harmonic timbre. When the f_c:f_{m1}:f_{m2} ratio is not simple, the spectrum can become quite complex and dense.

One possible application of multiple modulators is to use the second modulator to enrich the spectrum during the attack of a note. In the DX7 implementation of FM, there were six "operators," each of which was a sine wave oscillator with its own amplitude and time-varying amplitude envelope. As a result, some operators could have envelopes that ramped up, ramped down, were plucked/struck, or bowed/blown. If we choose a plucked/struck envelope for operator 3 in Figure 7.10c or 7.10d and bowed/blown envelopes for operators 1 and 2, the result is multiple modulator FM during the attack and decay and then simple FM during the sustain and release when the amplitude of operator 3 is zero (see Figure 7.12).

If we set the f_c:f_{m1}:f_{m2} ratio to be 1:1:1.41, where the 1.41 refers to operator 3, the spectrum will be dense with many inharmonic partials during the attack and decay phases and then will be harmonic during the sustain and release phases (see Figure 7.13). Unlike the simple FM configuration discussed above where the f_c:f_m ratio can be made to change over the course of a note, this multiple modulator version won't have an audible "glissando" of partials when the timbre changes from inharmonic to harmonic. Multiple modulator FM has also been used to successfully imitate the timbral qualities of pianos and bowed strings (Schottstaedt 1977).

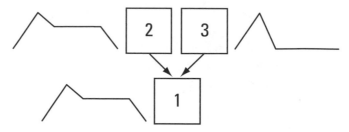

Figure 7.12 Block diagram of parallel modulator FM showing the different envelopes applied to each of the operators. After the attack and decay, operator 3 is off, so the sustain and release will only be simple FM

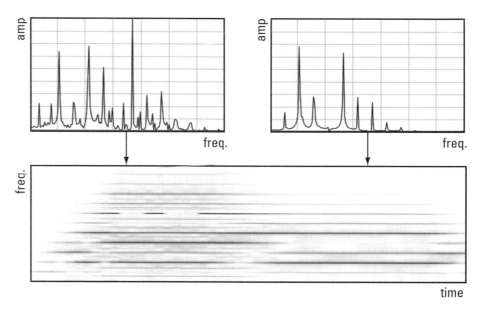

Figure 7.13 The spectrogram (bottom) of multiple modulator FM with a f_c: f_{m1}: f_{m2} ratio of 1:1:1.41 and the second modulator (operator 3) active only during the attack and decay. Spectrum diagrams are shown above the spectrogram as "snapshots" of the frequency content during the inharmonic attack/decay and during the harmonic, simple FM sustain/release

There are many more possible operator configurations, operator envelopes, modulation indexes, and frequency ratios that can be discussed for multi-operator FM. Not only can the modulation be quite complex but it can also vary widely and wildly over the course of an individual note depending on the amplitude envelopes for the individual operators. However, there are only a couple of commercial softsynths that implement multi-operator FM, so some of the more complex details of such configurations are beyond the scope of this book. An excellent primer on DX7-style FM is Chowning and Bristow's *FM theory and applications* (1986), which is out of print but can be found in many college libraries. In addition, Dodge and Jerse (1997) and Roads (1996) are useful references for further details concerning FM.

Table 7.2   Modulation routings for FM

Mapping	Key number → carrier frequency
Effect	When f_c is less than or equal to f_m, this allows the key number to determine the fundamental of the output spectrum if the spectrum is harmonic
Mapping	Velocity → modulation index
Effect	The higher a key is struck the more partials (sidebands) are generated and the brighter the timbre
Mapping	Velocity → envelope → modulation index
Effect	An envelope can alter the modulation index, and thus the brightness of the timbre, over the course of a note. The velocity can determine the strength of that change
Mapping	Envelope → f_c:f_m ratio
Effect	An envelope can alter the spectral makeup of the timbre over the course of a note
Mapping	CC/aftertouch → f_c:f_m ratio
Effect	CC or aftertouch messages can alter the spectral makeup of the timbre over the course of a note or many notes

The modulation routings for simple FM synthesis discussed in this section are summarized in Table 7.2.

PHYSICAL MODELING

The goal of each of the previous synthesis techniques was to create a specific spectrum resulting in the desired timbre. **Physical modeling synthesis**, on the other hand, seeks to mathematically re-create, or model, the physical mechanism by which an instrument produces sound with the expectation that the result of that modeling process will produce a sound closely related to that of the actual instrument. In the end, the desired spectrum/timbre is produced, but almost as a "side effect" of the modeling process.

The idea behind physical modeling is that each individual part of an instrument is modeled mathematically and the results are fed into the next part. The modeling itself involves an in-depth analysis of the mechanism and the way it is played, and thus involves physical and mathematical concepts that are beyond the scope of this book. However, to give you a sense of the process, we will broadly consider some of the factors that would go into modeling a stringed instrument. Later in the chapter, we will discuss the Karplus-Strong algorithm that represents a simplified approach to modeling plucked or struck sounds.

A Physical Overview of a Stringed Instrument

A stringed instrument such as a guitar or violin involves several elements (see Figure 7.14):

1. an excitation to put the string in motion;
2. the string itself;
3. the coupling of the string to a resonating body.

Figure 7.14   Block diagram of a plucked string instrument in which energy is imparted to the string by the pluck and the energy is partially transferred to the resonating body of the instrument and partially reflected back to the string

There are a variety of ways to put a string in motion, including plucking/picking like a guitar, striking like a hammered dulcimer, or bowing like a violin. The effect of a pluck or strike is to create a temporary deformation of the string (see Figure 7.15). This deformation "splits" into two pulses that then travel along the string in both directions away from the site of the plucking or striking until they reach the points at which the string is secured—called the *nut* and the *bridge* on a guitar or violin.

Upon reaching an endpoint, some portion of the pulse is reflected back toward the original pluck/strike point and some portion is transferred to the body of the instrument. It is these traveling pulses that create the vibration in the string. The reflected pulses continue to travel up and down the string until their energy dissipates and the string comes to a rest. The size and shape of the plucking or striking object, the material that the plucking or striking object is made of, the force of the plucking or striking, and where the string is plucked or struck all influence the way the string vibrates.

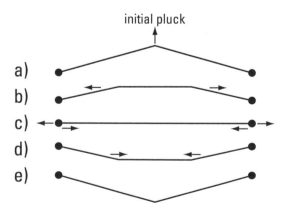

Figure 7.15   A plucked string in motion: a) pluck causes initial displacement of string; b) the deformation splits into two waves traveling on the string in opposite directions; c) the two waves reach the nut/bridge, some energy is transferred to the body of the instrument and some is reflected back to the string; d) the reflected waves travel back toward the center; e) full displacement in the opposite direction from the pluck

Bowing is somewhat different because the exciter—the bow—remains in contact with the string. Bowing involves the rosined hair of the bow pulling the string away from its resting state until the tension from the stretched string causes the bow to slip. As soon as the bow slips and the tension is released, the bow catches the string again and the cycle repeats. This essentially results in many quick plucks that travel down the string away from the bow in both directions.

The position of the plucking, striking, or bowing has an important influence on the way the string vibrates as well. The complex shape of a string's vibration is made up of many simpler motions of the string—referred to as its **normal modes**—occurring at the same time (see Figure 7.16). In its lowest mode, the fundamental, the entire string moves up and down. In its second mode, corresponding to the second harmonic, half of the string moves in one direction, and half in the other, with a **node**, or point of no motion, in the center (see Figure 7.16b). In the third mode, corresponding to the third harmonic, the string vibrates in thirds (see Figure 7.16c). This pattern continues through as many modes as have significant energy, determined by how hard the string was struck, plucked, or bowed, where it was struck/plucked/bowed, what it was struck/plucked/bowed with, and so on. Each mode, except the first, has one or more nodes.

If you pluck a string directly on the node for a given harmonic, that position can no longer be a point of no motion on the string. As a result, the harmonics that have a node at that point won't be part of the resultant spectrum. If you pluck exactly in the middle of a string, then the even-numbered harmonics, which all have a node in the middle, will be eliminated, resulting in a hollow, square-wave-like sound. This is related to the act of playing natural harmonics on a stringed instrument, in which you *create* a

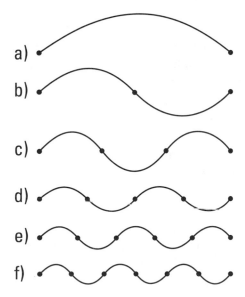

Figure 7.16   a) through f): first six normal modes of a vibrating string. The dots indicate the nodes (position of no displacement) for each mode as well as the fixed ends

node by placing your finger on the string. If you place your finger exactly in the middle of the string, you force a node there and the odd-numbered harmonics, including the fundamental, which don't have a node in the middle, won't be part of the resultant spectrum.

In a related phenomenon, if you pluck, strike, or bow near the bridge, you create a displacement of the string there. All of the modes of a string have a node at the bridge, and the lower modes—lower harmonics—don't have much displacement near the bridge. However, the upper modes—higher harmonics—do have some displacement near the bridge, so plucking, striking, or bowing there excites the higher harmonics. This is the reason for the characteristic glassy sound of bowing sul ponticello (near the bridge) on a bowed stringed instrument. Plucking a guitar near the bridge creates a bright, brittle timbre as a result of exciting those higher harmonics. This also explains the difference in timbre when you strike a drum near the edge rather than in the middle.

The string itself has the physical properties of length, mass, and tension. Each of these properties affects the way the wave caused by the plucking, striking, or bowing travels down the string. This is easy to understand if you think of a guitar string and the cable on a suspension bridge as both being "strings." Clearly using a guitar pick on a suspension bridge cable is not going to have the same effect as it has on a guitar string, just as using a pick on the lowest string of a guitar has a different effect than using it on the highest string. Similarly, the different mass, length, and tension of double-bass strings compared to violin strings necessitate the use of different sized bows for each instrument.

When the traveling waves on the string produced by plucking, striking, or bowing reach the bridge of the instrument, some of their energy is transferred through the bridge to the body of the instrument itself. This energy causes the top and back of the instrument to vibrate in the two-dimensional equivalents of the string's normal modes. It is these vibrations and their interaction with the air inside the body of the instrument that are responsible for most of the sound produced by a stringed instrument. This can be readily understood by thinking of the volume of sound produced by an acoustic guitar as opposed to the volume of sound produced by an un-amplified electric guitar, the body of which is usually too thick to vibrate like the top of an acoustic guitar.

Naturally, the material, the thickness, and the size of the top and back of a stringed instrument body as well as the volume of the air contained in the body affect the volume of sound produced as well as the resultant timbre of the sound. The string itself also interacts directly with the air, but the effect is relatively small compared to that of the vibrating body of the instrument.

Classical Physical Modeling

The physics of a stringed instrument is well known, and the various equations could be directly computed, which would result in a timbre that was dependent on the physical characteristics of the plucking, striking, or bowing object, the string itself, the body of the instrument, and the coupling of those elements. Unlike the previous synthesis techniques discussed, the inputs to such a physical model are based on the physics of the instrument itself rather than being abstract parameters such as the carrier frequency, the index to a wavetable, or the amount of ring modulation. This means that the modulation targets in a physical modeling system will have some physical interpretation such as the position of a pick on a string, the material the string is made of, the position of a pick-up, or the size of the instrument's resonating body.

The drawback to such a physical model is that the calculations are computationally intensive and may not be able to be carried out in real time, particularly if there are many notes being played on many such models simultaneously. A variety of techniques have been developed to make physical modeling more efficient while still having parameters that relate to a physical system, including modal, MSW, and waveguide synthesis. These techniques depart somewhat from the pure modeling of an instrument's physical behavior, but they have the advantage of taking much less computing power to calculate.

Even these "simplified" physical modeling techniques are sufficiently complex as to go beyond the scope of this book. However, to give you a sense of how the ideas of physical modeling have been implemented in computationally efficient ways, we will discuss the basics of an early model for plucked or struck instruments: the Karplus-Strong algorithm.

Karplus-Strong Synthesis

At the heart of the Karplus-Strong algorithm is a delay line. When a delay line is used in sound processing, live or recorded sound is fed into the delay line and sent out some amount of time later. When mixed with the original, non-delayed signal this produces a single echo. If the output of the delay line is fed back into its input, you get a feedback echo that repeats. Delay lines of various lengths with and without feedback are used for echo effects, chorusing, and flanging. These processing techniques will be taken up in the next chapter.

In the Karplus-Strong synthesis algorithm, instead of using live or recorded audio as input, the delay line is pre-filled with noise. When a note is played using this technique, the noise in the delay line is sent out. This little burst of noise by itself isn't very useful, but when the noise is fed back (re-circulated) into the input of the delay line, that burst of noise loops over and over again creating a very complex periodic waveform (see Figure 7.17a). To make this complex wave sound string-like, the amplitude should decay steadily over the course of a note and the sound should get steadily darker over the course of a note.

To achieve these two string characteristics, a low pass filter can be inserted before the output and before the feedback loop (see Figure 7.17b). Each time the output of the delay line is fed back into the input, it first goes through a low pass filter and becomes darker and quieter until finally it dies away completely. The resultant decaying amplitude envelope and bright-to-dark spectrum is characteristic of all struck or plucked timbres. In its simplest form described here, Karplus-Strong synthesis results in plucked string timbres.

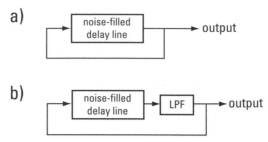

Figure 7.17   Karplus-Strong plucked string synthesis: a) the output of a noise-filled delay line is fed back into its input repeatedly; b) the delay line output is low pass filtered before being fed back into its input

Various extensions have been made to the basic algorithm that correct for some problems relating to pitch and harmonic tuning, but also allow for the simulation of a wide variety of string-like and drum-like timbres. Some of these modifications include filling the initial delay line with a waveform other than pure white noise and using more complex filters in the feedback loop.

Details of the Karplus-Strong algorithm and its various modifications can be found in Karplus and Strong (1983) and Jaffe and Smith (1983). Delay lines are also used extensively in a powerful and efficient physical modeling technique known as waveguide synthesis. Discussions of Karplus-Strong and other physical modeling techniques can be found in Roads (1996), Dodge and Jerse (1997), Cook (2002), Loy (2006), and Smith (2006).

GRANULAR SYNTHESIS

Granular synthesis is a technique that derives from a unique way of looking at sound. In the 1940s, physicist Dennis Gabor postulated that sound can be thought of as both a wave—the traditional model for sound—and a stream of extremely small particles, referred to as "acoustical quanta." This theory paralleled the quantum physics era re-imagining of light as both a wave and a stream of particles. It followed, then, that if existing sounds could be analyzed as streams of particles, then new sounds could be constructed out of streams of particles. From this observation granular synthesis was born.

A stream or cloud of granular particles has two primary aspects: the makeup of the grains themselves and the way those grains are arrayed in time.

Grains

A grain consists of two elements: a waveform with some shape and frequency and an envelope with some shape and duration. At its simplest, the waveform can be a sine wave at some frequency. More complex grains can use waveforms generated by any synthesis technique or drawn from sound files.

The grain envelope can range from simple triangular or trapezoidal shapes to more complex Gaussian or quasi-Gaussian shapes (see Figure 7.18). The length of a grain is typically quite short, ranging approximately from 5 to 50 ms, with some applications calling for durations of hundreds of milliseconds and some for durations of just a few milliseconds. As a result, an individual grain produces only the smallest "pop." However, when tens, hundreds, or thousands of grains are sounded in one second, the result can be a torrent of sound.

The sonic result of many grains is dependent on both the makeup of the grain and the way the grains are used. The effects of various grain waveforms, grain waveform frequencies, grain envelopes, and grain durations are perceived only when many grains are heard in close proximity. The same grain used in different ways can yield very different results. There are two fundamental ways for grains to be organized. Grains can be produced at regular intervals resulting in a "synchronous" granular stream or they can be produced at irregular intervals resulting in an "asynchronous" granular cloud.

Synchronous Granular Streams

If grains are produced at regular intervals, the effect can range from rhythmic pulses to a pitched timbre. Where the granular stream falls in this range depends on the time between the onset of one grain and the onset of the next, referred to as the **inter-onset time** (IOT). Inverting the IOT gives you the density of the grains, or rather grain attacks, measured in grains per second. Implementations of granular synthesis variously use IOT or density as the primary parameter.

If the IOT is less than about 50 ms (grain density = 1/IOT = 1/0.05 = 20 grains per second), the stream will likely be heard as a series of individual pulses. Note that the relationship between the IOT and grain density is the same as that between period (T) and frequency: $f = 1/T$. As the IOT falls below 50 ms—as the pulses get closer together—the stream of pulses begins to transition to a pitch (see Figure 7.19).

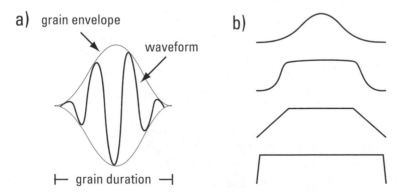

Figure 7.18 Grains: a) basic grain anatomy; b) various grain envelopes, including gaussian (top), quasi-gaussian, trapezoidal, and rectangular (bottom)

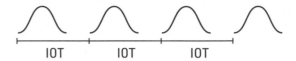

Figure 7.19   Synchronous granular synthesis: the inter-onset time between grains is the same

If the IOT becomes shorter than the grain duration, then the grains will overlap. Some grain overlap results in a smoother texture, with the decay of one grain envelope crossfading with the attack of the next. If the overlap is too complete, the effect of the individual grain envelopes is less pronounced and the grain waveforms and frequencies take on more importance.

The pitch of a granular stream can be unpredictable because of complex interactions between the IOT and the grain parameters. However, treating the IOT as the period of the granular stream is a good starting point for estimating its fundamental frequency ($f \approx 1/\text{IOT}$), bearing in mind that, in the end, this might not be the actual perceived pitch.

The timbre is similarly dependent on all of these parameters. In the simplest case where the grain waveform is a sine wave and the pitch of the granular stream is clear, the grain frequency will impart a peak, or formant, in the spectrum around the grain. The width of this formant is dependent on the specific shape and duration of the grain envelope. Synchronous granular synthesis, then, can be used to impart formant peaks characteristic of various kinds of acoustic sound production.

A form of synchronous granular synthesis called FOF (*fonction d'onde formantique*) utilizes up to five simultaneous streams of sine wave grains, each with the same IOT but different grain frequencies. Having the same IOT ensures that each of the streams will have the same fundamental frequency, while having different grain frequencies causes each stream to create its own formant in the resultant spectrum. In addition, the shape of the grain envelopes is designed to impart a formant shape typical of vocal formants.

When the grain frequencies for the simultaneous streams are chosen to match the five formants of the human singing voice for a given vowel sound, the result is an excellent vocal imitation. If the IOT is held steady but the grain frequencies change from the values associated with one vowel's formants to the values associated with another, the result is a sung pitch with changing vowels. FOF was used extensively in the CHANT program developed at IRCAM (Institut de Recherche et Coordination Acoustique/Musique) (Bennett and Rodet 1989) and has since been incorporated into the widely available Csound synthesis language (Clarke 2000).

The parameters of synchronous granular synthesis that are most readily changeable over time are the inter-onset time and the grain duration. The IOT is particularly useful in creating timbres that build from rhythms into pitches and then "tear apart" as the IOT increases until the grains are again heard as individual entities. During such a "tear apart" process, it is often useful to lengthen the grain as you increase the IOT so that the grains have some body to them when they are heard by themselves. The grain waveform and grain frequency can also be modified to change the timbre over time.

Asynchronous Granular Clouds

Synchronous granular streams are characterized by a regular IOT and stable grain properties. Asynchronous granular clouds, on the other hand, are characterized by fluctuations in these parameters of various magnitudes and distributions that cause the sensation of pitch to dissipate and the orderliness of streams to descend into the chaos of clouds. Granular clouds can range from diffuse, ghostly textures that slither in and through other musical elements to raging torrents of sound that dominate the aural landscape.

Synchronous and asynchronous approaches to granular synthesis really lie on a continuum with synchronous streams able to tolerate some fluctuation and asynchronous clouds in need of some boundaries to their fluctuations. In fact, some fluctuation in synchronous streams lends them a more natural, less machine-like air. It can be interesting sonically to transition between the two, with the synchronous streams becoming unstable or the asynchronous clouds binding together.

In asynchronous clouds, each of the grain parameters and the IOT are characterized by a center value, an amount of deviation above and below that value, and a distribution of the values in between. In the simplest case, a parameter such as the IOT could have a center value of 50 ms, a deviation of +/− 10 ms, and an even distribution throughout that ranges from 40 ms to 60 ms. As with the granular stream, grains in a cloud can overlap as the average IOT becomes smaller than the average grain duration.

As the sizes of the deviations increase, the sense of instability in the cloud increases. Such changes in the IOTs are particularly noticeable at small IOTs (see Figure 7.20). Note that the time distribution of grains in a cloud is often controlled by a grain density parameter, which is the inverse of the IOT. The choice of grain density or IOT is determined by the particular implementation of granular synthesis. In the end they both yield the same result.

The distribution of the values within the range can have an important effect on the resultant cloud. For example, if the deviation in grain frequency is large and the distribution is even, there will be little sense of a central frequency and the cloud will sound more like a band of frequencies (see Figure 7.21a). In that case the cloud would be just as likely to have a grain with a frequency at the top of the deviation as at the center frequency or at the bottom of the deviation.

However, if the distribution is more concentrated around the center value with fewer of the grains having frequencies at the top or bottom of the deviation, the center frequency will take on a more important perceptual role (see Figure 7.21b). It is also possible to have a deviation that is not a simple +/− of some amount but is asymmetrical, with a greater deviation above than below or vice versa (see Figure 7.21c).

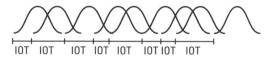

Figure 7.20   Asynchronous granular synthesis: the inter-onset times between the grains are different

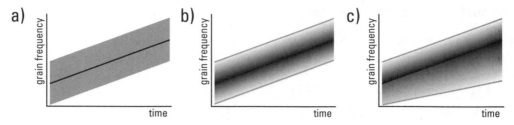

Figure 7.21 Grain frequency distribution examples: a) even distribution of grain frequencies above and below the center value; b) distribution more concentrated around center value (gray boundary lines indicate maximum deviation above and below); c) unequal grain frequency deviation above and below center value, distribution concentrated around center value

The evolution of a granular cloud is dependent on both changing center values and changing deviations. A cloud that starts with small deviations in grain parameters will be a relatively focused granular stream. As the amount of the parameter deviations increases, a granular cloud forms that can be chaotic and unfocused.

Figure 7.22 defines just such a granular stream/cloud as a set of parameter trajectories with changing center values and deviations. The distributions are all assumed to be uniform. As you can see, the IOT grows over the course of the cloud while the deviation increases. The corresponding grain density trajectory—the inverse of the IOT trajectory—is also shown. The grain frequency rises over time with an increasing deviation, while the grain duration also grows along with its deviation. The grain waveform is initially a sine wave, but is eventually randomly chosen from among sine, triangle, square, and sawtooth waves. The result of these parameter trajectories is a pitched granular stream that falls apart as the IOT increases and all of the parameter deviations

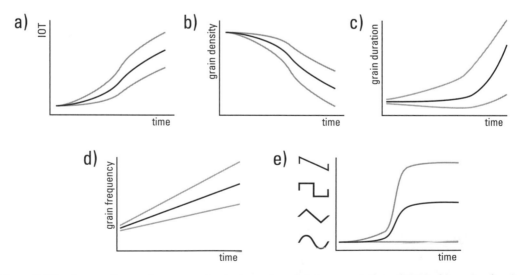

Figure 7.22 A set of granular parameter trajectories: a) inter-onset time (IOT); b) grain density (alternate to IOT); c) grain duration; d) grain frequency; e) grain waveform

increase. In the end the grains in the cloud fluctuate widely, resulting in an unfocused mass of sound.

Granular Processing

When discussing granular streams and clouds, we assumed that the grain waveform was drawn from the standard waveforms or was generated by one of the synthesis techniques discussed above. However, the material inside the grain envelope can just as easily be drawn from a sound file, in which case the grains may have characteristics that will yield complex timbres in granular streams or clouds. Enveloping small chunks of a recorded sound is a special sound processing technique referred to as sound file granulation.

A typical method for executing sound file granulation is to have the audio for successive grains come from successive portions of the sound file. In that way a granular stream or cloud will effectively play back the sound file, undoubtedly with some timbral alterations introduced by the grain duration, envelope, and IOT (see Figure 7.23). The rate at which the grains move through the sound file determines whether the sound file is time-stretched, time-compressed, or remains the same length. This rate can change over the course of the note and be specified as an actual rate or by a changing position value controlled by an envelope or a CC. Regardless of the rate, the pitch of the original material remains unchanged because the actual chunks of audio within each grain are unchanged.

The portions of the sound file within each grain can also be manipulated. If the material inside a grain is played more slowly, then the pitch for that grain will drop. If it is played more quickly, then the pitch for that grain will rise. However, because the grains' progression through the sound file is independent of the playback of each individual grain, this pitch shifting is independent of the time stretching. You could, for example, play through the file more slowly but raise the pitch of the grains resulting in a time-stretched, pitched-up version of the sound file.

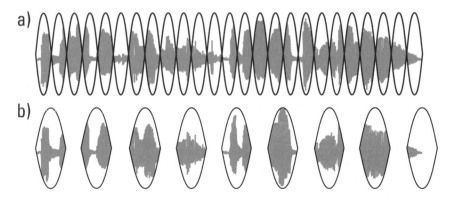

Figure 7.23 A granulated sound file: a) grains are close together so sound file will sound nearly normal; b) grains are spaced far apart so sound file will have gaps

In addition to pitch and time manipulation, the granulation process can also impart interesting timbral effects through the manipulation of the grain envelope, grain duration, IOT, and the magnitude and distribution of their deviations. There are too many combinations of these parameters to list, so I will just mention a few here:

- If these values are chosen so that the grains evenly overlap then the result will be a smooth time-stretching/compression.
- If there are significant gaps between the grains, then the texture will be gritty, particularly if the grain envelope has "sharp edges" (short attack and release).
- If the grains are relatively large and overlap significantly, the result will be smooth and echoey.
- If the grains are short with a high enough IOT and no IOT deviation, the granular stream can impose a new pitch on the sound file that's related to the inverse of the IOT and the original pitch of the sound file.

With all of these possibilities, sound file granulation is a rich, complex, and unique sound processing technique.

Granular synthesis has taken a long time to make its way into commercial software, but there are now a number of softsynths—such as Camel Audio's Alchemy and the Maelstrom synth in Propellerhead Software's Reason—that implement granular synthesis and/or processing in some fashion. Because there are so many variations of granular synthesis/processing, a commercial implementation will likely choose a subset of all of the possibilities to implement and provide parameters specific to that subset. The synthesis parameters suitable as targets for modulation will be specific to each softsynth.

Programmable environments, such as Reaktor, Max/MSP, Pd, SuperCollider, and Csound, allow you to implement granular synthesis in a flexible way. Since you choose the manner of implementation, which parameters can be modulated are up to you.

For more information on granular synthesis, see Roads (1996) and Dodge and Jerse (1997). Granular synthesis, its history, and related techniques are detailed in the excellent *Microsound* by Curtis Roads (Roads 2001).

SYNTHESIS PROGRAMMING APPLICATIONS

Most software synthesizers and samplers have a fixed number of elements (oscillators, filters, envelopes, LFOs, etc.) that can be connected together in a limited number of ways. As a result, they are relatively easy to understand and use, but you are limited to only those resources when creating a synthesis patch. For example, you can't do additive synthesis on a softsynth with only a few oscillators or complex subtractive synthesis on a softsynth with only a few filters. To create a sound using any desired synthesis technique, you need to use a synthesis programming application.

Since you're not given a fixed number of oscillators or filters or anything else within these applications, you can create custom synthesis algorithms that use as many of these functions as you need. As a result, you can create anything in these programs from simple FM to 30-oscillator additive synthesis to brand new synthesis techniques that no one has thought of before. The primary limiting factor on the complexity of your creation is your CPU power, and with modern CPUs you can do quite a bit before you run into any problems.

Though programming sounds like a non-musical task, synthesis programming applications are specially designed for sound synthesis and don't require the same level of programming as computer languages such as C++ or Java do. It certainly takes more effort to program your own synthesizer than it does to use an existing softsynth, but the possibilities in a synthesis programming application are endless. There are two primary types of synthesis programming applications: boxes-and-lines programs and text-based programs.

In boxes-and-lines programs, the various functions that form the basis for synthesis techniques, such as oscillators, filters, delay lines, and envelopes, are represented as boxes that have "inlets" and "outlets." You create a synthesis patch by connecting together the inlets and outlets of these boxes with "patchcords" (see Figure 7.25 on page 178). This type of programming is often referred to as dataflow programming because the flow of the data is graphically depicted.

In text-based programs, the various functions that form the basis for synthesis techniques, such as oscillators, filters, delay lines, and envelopes, are represented as text. These functions, also called unit generators, accept arguments as numbers or variables and output a signal represented by a variable name. A synthesis patch is created by using the variable names output from various unit generators as inputs other unit generators (see Figure 7.24 on page 174).

Table 7.3 shows some examples of boxes-and-lines and text-based synthesis programming applications. Though most of the freeware applications are listed as not being available as plug-ins, there have been various experiments over the years toward that end. An Internet search should uncover any current efforts. It is possible to use technologies such as ReWire to connect some of these applications with traditional

Table 7.3 Representative synthesis programming applications

Application	Type	Plug-in?	Standalone?	Distribution
Max/MSP	boxes/lines	Only in Ableton Live using Max-for-Live add-on	Yes	Commercial
Pd (Pure Data)	boxes/lines	No	Yes	Freeware
Reaktor	boxes/lines	Yes	Yes	Commercial
Tassman	boxes/lines	Yes	Yes	Commercial
ChucK	text-based	No	Yes	Freeware
Csound	text-based	No	Yes	Freeware
RTcmix	text-based	No	Yes	Freeware
SuperCollider	text-based	No	Yes	Freeware

DAW/Sequencers or to use MIDI or OSC (Open Sound Control) routing software for inter-application communication. In addition, at the time of this writing Csound, ChucK, RTcmix, and SuperCollider—all text-based programs—are available as external objects in Max/MSP—a boxes-and-lines program.

A Common Example: Simple FM

It is beyond the scope of this book to explain how to use any of these programs in detail. However, to illustrate the way these programs look and how they work, I will show how simple FM can be realized in a text-based program (Csound) and a boxes-and-lines program (Max/MSP). There are many ways to realize simple FM in both programs; each example given here represents just one possibility.

As discussed earlier in the chapter, simple FM synthesis consists of one oscillator modulating the frequency of another with a modulating frequency in the audio range (> 20 Hz). The modulating oscillator's frequency is the product of the fundamental frequency and the f_m part of the $f_c{:}f_m$ ratio, and its amplitude (peak deviation) is the product of the index of modulation and the modulating frequency. It is typical for the index, and through the index the peak deviation, to be controlled by an envelope. So given a fundamental frequency, an $f_c{:}f_m$ ratio, and an index of modulation, the modulating oscillator's parameters can be calculated.

The carrier oscillator's frequency is the product of the fundamental frequency and the f_c part of the $f_c{:}f_m$ ratio, added to the output of the modulating oscillator. Its amplitude is also typically controlled by an envelope that becomes the overall envelope for the sound. The carrier oscillator's parameters are calculated from the fundamental frequency, the $f_c{:}f_m$ ratio, and an overall amplitude.

This example uses the following parameters:

> fundamental frequency = 440 Hz (A above middle C)
>
> $f_c{:}f_m$ ratio = 1:2 (only odd harmonic partials; likely similar to a square wave)
>
> modulation index = 5
>
> note duration = 5 seconds
>
> maximum overall amplitude = 0.75 (where 1.0 is maximum)

The parameters calculated by each program will be:

> modulating frequency = 2 * 440 Hz = 880 Hz
>
> carrier frequency = 1*440 Hz = 440 Hz
>
> peak deviation = index * modulating frequency = 5 * 880 = 4,400

The ADSR envelopes for the modulating oscillator and the carrier oscillator have the same segment durations for the sake of simplicity:

Attack = 0.5 seconds (500 milliseconds)

Decay = 0.5 seconds

Sustain = 3 seconds

Release = 1 second

The amplitude values for the modulating oscillator's ADSR will be in terms of the peak deviation, and the amplitude values for the carrier oscillator's ADSR will be in terms of the maximum overall amplitude.

Text-based Simple FM in Csound

Figure 7.24 shows the Csound code listing for a simple FM instrument and score. Csound uses an "orchestra" code listing (Figure 7.24a) where the synthesis algorithm for each instrument is defined and a "score" code listing (Figure 7.24b) where specific note information is given. When Csound is run, the data from the score—referred to as parameter fields or p-fields—are passed to the orchestra and the resultant sound is sent to the audio outs of the computer or written to a sound file. These were originally two separate text files, but a single unified orchestra and score file (.csd) is most often used today. Though Csound can run in real time now, Csound was originally a non-real time instrument where one second of sound might take considerably more than one second to calculate.

To keep things simple, there is only one instrument in the example orchestra and there is only one table defining a sine wave and one note in the score. In addition, some header information relating to the sampling rate and number of channels has been left out of Figure 7.24. One of those pieces of header information defines the maximum amplitude for this orchestra as 1.0. Another facet of this code listing to note is that anything following a ";" is a comment and is not acted upon by the program. I've added line numbers to the code listing to keep everything straight in the explanation below— those numbers would not normally appear in the code listing. At first these code listings can be daunting, but they are actually fairly "readable" with a little practice.

Line 01: The simple FM instrument in the orchestra (Figure 7.24a) starts with this line, which indicates the beginning of the code listing for instrument 1. Line 20 indicates the end of the code listing for instrument 1. A Csound orchestra can contain many such instrument definitions beginning with "instr #" and ending with "endin."

Lines 02–07, 24: These lines are a series of assignments in which the p-fields (parameter fields) from Line 24 of the score (Figure 7.24b) are assigned to variables in the orchestra. The very first p-field from Line 24 of the score follows the "i" and determines which instrument the note is used for (instrument 1). The second p-field determines when the note starts (time 0, or as soon as the program is run). The third p-field determines the note duration and this p-field, p3, is assigned to the variable "idur" in the instrument code listing. The "i"s, "k"s, and "a"s at the beginning of

```
a)  01        instr 1
    02        idur    =    p3         ;data from score assigned to variables
    03        iamp    =    p4
    04        ifundHz =    p5
    05        ifc_rat =    p6
    06        ifm_rat =    p7
    07        indx    =    p8
    08        ifc_Hz  =    ifc_rat * ifundHz  ;calculate carrier frequency
    09        ifm_Hz  =    ifm_rat * ifundHz  ;calculate carrier frequency
    10        idev    =    indx * ifm_Hz      ;calcualte peak deviation (d=I*fm)
    11        iatt    =    0.5                ;ADSR attack
    12        idec    =    0.5                ;ADSR decay
    13        irel    =    1                  ;ADSR release
    14        isus    =    idur-iatt-idec-irel  ;ADSR sustain time
    15        kmodamp    linseg  0.2*idev, iatt, idev, idec, 0.7*idev, isus, 0.7*idev, irel, 0.2*idev
    16        amod       oscil   kmodamp, ifm_Hz, 1
    17        kcaramp    linseg  0, iatt, iamp, idec, 0.7*iamp, isus, 0.7*iamp, irel, 0
    18        acar       oscil   kcaramp, ifc_Hz + amod, 1
    19                   outs    acar, acar
    20        endin

b)  21        ;        num   time   size   GEN    p1
    22        f        1     0      4096   10     1
    23        ;        inst  st     dur    amp    freq   fc    fm    index
    24        i        1     0      5      0.75   440    1     2     5
    25        e        ;end of score
```

Figure 7.24 Text-based synthesis programming application. Csound code listing for a simple FM instrument: a) "orchestra" code listing; b) "score" code listing

the variables in Csound all have specific meanings, but we needn't go into that here. P-fields 4 through 8 are subsequently assigned to variables in the instrument.

Lines 08–09, 10: In the first two of these lines, two of the variables defined above are used to calculate the actual frequencies of the carrier and modulating oscillators: ifc_Hz and ifm_Hz, respectively. The peak deviation of the modulator, idev, is then calculated from the index of modulation and the modulating frequency as discussed earlier in the chapter ($I = d/f_m$; $d = I \star f_m$).

Lines 11–14, 15: The next four lines define the time segments for an ADSR envelope that will be used for both the modulating and carrier oscillators. The sustain segment is calculated from the total note duration and the other three segments. These time segments are used to define envelopes in Lines 15 and 17. Line 15 contains the first instance of a "unit generator" in this orchestra. The unit generator here is "linseg," and it simply defines a function made from line segments.

The idea of a unit generator is one of the earliest in computer music. Essentially, a unit generator represents by a single name (a string of letters and numbers) some basic function necessary for various synthesis algorithms. In Csound, unit generators are referred to as "opcodes." They take arguments listed to the right of the opcode and output a signal indicated by a variable to the left of the opcode. In Figure 7.24a, the opcodes are shown in bold typeface. There are only five in this instrument code listing, making this a fairly simple instrument.

The linseg opcode takes a series of arguments that define first a starting value, then a time segment over which that value changes, then the new value to which the first value changes, then a time segment over which that value changes, then the new value to which that value changes, etc. In this line, iatt, idec, isus, and irel just refer to the time durations of the ADSR envelope segments. The first value of 0.2*idev represents the starting value of the envelope, idev represent the peak, 0.7*idev represents the sustain value (on either side of isus so that the sustain level stays constant), and 0.2*idev represents the final value at the end of the envelope.

The output of the linseg opcode is assigned to the variable kmodamp, and whenever kmodamp appears (Line 16), it represents the entire envelope. This envelope starts at a non-zero value because it represents the amount of modulation of the carrier oscillator. Starting out at 0.2*idev causes the resultant sound to start with some frequency modulation, and hence some timbral richness.

Line 16: The oscil (oscillator) opcode takes three arguments: amplitude, frequency, and a wavetable number. This is the modulating oscillator in the simple FM algorithm, so kmodamp is used to represent the modulating oscillator's envelope. The frequency is ifm_Hz, which was calculated in Line 09. The wavetable number is "1," which is defined in Line 22 in the score. This line will be discussed below, but for now it is enough to know that a sine wave is stored in that wavetable. The output of this oscil opcode is assigned the variable amod.

Line 17: This linseg opcode creates the amplitude envelope for the carrier oscillator. This is a more typical amplitude envelope that starts at zero and ends at zero so that the notes that this instrument plays start and end smoothly in silence. The variable iamp, defined by a p-field in the score, represents the overall amplitude of the note, where 1.0 is the maximum. The output of the linseg opcode is assigned the variable kcaramp.

Line 18: This oscil opcode represents the carrier oscillator and takes amplitude, frequency, and wavetable arguments as before. The amplitude is the envelope kcaramp defined in the previous line and the wavetable number is 1, which is a sine wave. The frequency argument is where the FM actually happens. The carrier frequency calculated in Line 09 above is added to the output of the modulating oscillator represented by the variable amod. Since the envelope for amod included the peak deviation value, there is no need to scale the modulating oscillator. The output of the modulated carrier oscillator is assigned to the variable acar.

Lines 19–20: The final opcode in this instrument, outs, simply sends the output of the modulated carrier oscillator to the right and left channels. Here the same signal is being sent to both channels. If the instrument is being played in real time, the signal will go to the audio output of the computer; otherwise it will be rendered as a sound file. Line 20 indicates the end of this instrument's code listing, much like Line 01 represented the beginning.

Line 22: Now that the instrument is fully defined, we can provide performance data for it in the score. The "f" statement is used to create function tables that can be used for a variety of purposes. In this case, we're creating a sine wave "f-table" for use by the oscil opcodes in the instrument code listing. Each f-statement contains a number of p-fields that define how the f-table is created. They all start with the f-table number (number 1 here), the time at which the f-table should be created (time 0, or as soon as the code is executed), and the size of the table (4096 entries in the table in this example).

The next number is the most important, because it determines which "GEN" routine will be used to create the f-table. In this case GEN 10 is used because it generates an f-table that is one cycle of a waveform constructed from harmonic partials. The next p-fields determine the amplitudes of the successive partials. In this case, there is only one p-field after the GEN number indicating that there is only one partial, the fundamental, and it has an amplitude of 1. This, of course, is a sine wave. If the p-fields had instead been 1, 0, 0.333, 0, 0.2, 0, 0.14, 0, and 0.11, then GEN 10 would have created a waveform with only odd partials whose amplitudes are the inverse of the partial number—the recipe for a square wave. Many standard waveforms can be created with this useful generation routine.

Line 24: The "i" statement in this line is the actual bit of code that causes the instrument defined above to generate sound when the program is executed. Like the f-statement, every i-statement has three fixed p-fields that define which instrument will be played (p1, here instrument 1), when the note will start (p2, here time 0), and how long the note will be (p3, here 5 seconds). You determine the remaining p-fields when you create the code listing for the instrument. In this example, Lines 01 through 07 assign the p-field values to variables that are then used in specific ways in the instrument's synthesis algorithm. In this instrument, p4 determines the overall amplitude of the note (1.0 being maximum), p5 determines the fundamental frequency, p6 is the f_c for the $f_c{:}f_m$ ratio, p7 is the f_m for the $f_c{:}f_m$ ratio, and p8 is the index of modulation.

There are many other ways to organize the necessary information, and each number could have taken on a variety of forms. For example, the amplitude can be specified in decibels in the score and then converted to the raw amplitude value in the orchestra. Likewise, the fundamental frequency of the note (provided that p6 is 1) given in p5 can be specified in several different ways that are simpler for musicians than the absolute frequency value. For example, there is an octave.pitch–class notation where 8.00 represents middle C, 8.01 represents C♯, 8.02 represents D, etc. That notation can then be converted into raw frequency values in the instrument code listing.

In addition, to create a more flexible instrument, I could have defined the ADSR time segment values in the score, as well as the starting point for the index of modulation, the sustain level for the carrier oscillator amplitude envelope, and so on, leading to note statements with possibly a dozen or more p-fields. A balance must be struck between the flexibility of the instrument code listing and the need for the note statements to be useable.

Earlier in this chapter and in the previous several chapters, note information such as this would have been provided to a softsynth by MIDI note messages and expressive messages in conjunction with the envelope and LFO settings in the softsynth. Csound instruments can also be controlled by MIDI using the correct codes in the orchestra code listing. MIDI messages can then be supplied live using a controller, by traditional sequencers using MIDI routing software to send messages from the sequencer to Csound, or by using Standard MIDI Files.

Now that we've seen simple FM in a text-based synthesis programming application, let's take a look at the same example in a boxes-and-lines program.

Boxes-and-lines based Simple FM in Max/MSP

Figure 7.25 shows the configuration of boxes-and-lines for a simple FM algorithm in a Max/MSP patch. In Max/MSP, the boxes are referred to as "objects," the lines as "patchcords," and the entire configuration as a "patch." As you can see, most of the objects consist of symbols and text while some are graphical objects. The text residing outside of boxes are comments that don't have any effect on the result. Since this is a dataflow language, I will describe it from the top on down.

At the top left is a checkbox object that starts and stops the audio. Notice that it is connected to the dac~ object at the bottom of the page, which is also where the final audio lines are connected. To the right of the checkbox is a "message box" containing the numbers 440, 1, 2, and 5. You might recognize these from the Csound example as the fundamental frequency, the f_c part of the $f_c{:}f_m$ ratio, the f_m part of the $f_c{:}f_m$ ratio, and the index of modulation. When clicked, a message box outputs its numbers and/or text. This message box operates as the "score" for this patch. The message box is connected to the unpack object box that takes in a list of numbers and/or text and splits it into its separate parts. Comments next to the patchcords leaving the unpack object indicate what the numbers mean.

As in the Csound orchestra, the carrier frequency and modulating frequency are calculated from the fundamental frequency and the $f_c{:}f_m$ ratio, here using "*" (multiplication) objects. The modulating frequency and the index of modulation are then used to calculate the maximum deviation using another "*" object. The modulating frequency is sent to a cycle~ object, which is a cosine oscillator. A cosine wave is the same as a sine wave, just 90 degrees out of phase. The "~" in the name of an object indicates that it is an audio signal rather than just a number. In Csound, this division is indicated by i and k variables for simple and changing regular numbers, and "a" variables for audio signals.

The envelopes for the modulator and carrier are created using graphical function objects. Each of those objects is 5 seconds in length (the duration of the note) and range from 0.0 to 1.0 vertically. When they receive a "bang," the function objects output their values to a line~ object. The output of the modulator envelope is scaled by the peak deviation using a *~ object and is then multiplied by the output of the modulator cycle~ object.

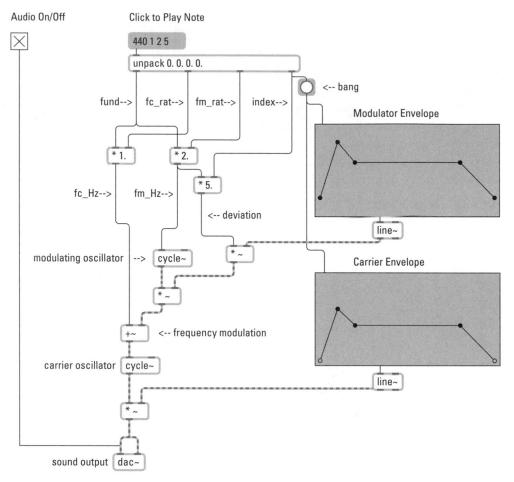

Figure 7.25 Boxes-and-lines synthesis programming application. Max/MSP patch for a simple FM instrument

Once the output of the modulating oscillator has been multiplied by the scaled modulator envelope, it is added to the carrier frequency using a +~ object and becomes the frequency input to another cycle~ object. This, of course, represents the actual modulation of the carrier frequency. The output of the carrier oscillator is multiplied by the carrier envelope, which serves as the overall amplitude envelope for this patch. The output of the *~ object is finally sent to the left and right inputs of the dac~ object, which passes the audio to the audio outputs of the computer.

As with the Csound example, there are many ways to create a patch like this that would allow more note-by-note flexibility. In particular, the basic note information can be generated by a MIDI controller or a sequencer. Max/MSP originated as a real time program, so it is relatively easy to use MIDI note and expressive messages to control a patch. Max/MSP patches can be designed to respond in a very similar fashion to other types of softsynths, just with a far greater variety of synthesis and sampling techniques.

Synthesis programming applications aren't for everyone, but they are the most powerful, flexible programs for digital sound synthesis and sampling. In addition, they can be easily integrated with other types of media and controllers allowing for real time interactivity between movement, sound, and image.

Now that we've explored the creation of rich, dynamic timbres through synthesis and sampling over the last several chapters, we'll discuss in the next chapter how these timbres might be processed with effects in a DAW/Sequencer. The effects are discussed primarily in the context of plug-in effects, but these effects could be external hardware effects, such as rack-mounted effects or guitar "stompboxes," or they could be created in a synthesis programming application such as the ones discussed above.

CHAPTER 8

Effects

The core of this book has focused on synthesis and sampling, generally in the context of virtual instruments in a DAW/Sequencer. The output of these instruments is digital audio that can then be treated in the same way as the other two common sources of audio in a DAW/Sequencer: recorded and imported audio. In this chapter we will explore various audio effects that can be applied to any of these audio sources in interesting and creative ways.

The effects in this chapter can be categorized broadly as dynamics processing effects, filtering effects (including EQ), and time-based effects. Additionally we will look at ring modulation and reverberation. There are many more effects than can be discussed here, and for the effects we will explore, there are many variations. However, if you have a firm grasp of the effects discussed here, you will generally find it easier to understand variants of these effects, unusual effects, or combination effects when you encounter them. Before delving into the effects themselves, we must first understand how signals are routed to effects within a DAW/Sequencer.

INSERTS AND SENDS

You can apply an effect to audio in three different ways: through direct application, as an insert effect, or as a send effect. **Direct application** of an effect is the simplest way, but it is also the least flexible. It typically involves selecting the audio, either as a region in the tracks editor or by using a dedicated sample editor, and then choosing the desired effect from a menu. Once you've set the parameters for the effect in a dialog box, you apply it directly to the audio. Most DAWs will create a new audio file with the effect applied, leaving the original file unchanged, though some may perform the operation "destructively" on the original audio file. To apply an effect directly to the audio produced by a synthesizer or sampler, that audio would first have to be captured as an audio file and appear as an audio region on a track.

An **insert effect** is applied in a mixer window where each track is represented as a channel strip. The recorded, imported, or synthesized/sampled audio goes through the insert effect(s), and then through the pan control and volume fader before being sent to the output. A mixer channel strip with a chorus effect as an insert effect is shown in Figure 8.1a. The signal path that this represents is shown in Figure 8.1b.

Though it appears at first that an insert effect will process 100 percent of the audio signal on that track, there is a "wet/dry" or "mix" setting in some effects that allows you to determine what portion of the audio is processed. This essentially splits up the audio signal into two parts: the dry signal, which is passed through without any processing, and the wet signal that is 100 percent processed. These are mixed together before being sent to the pan and volume controls (see Figure 8.1c).

A **send effect**—also called an "aux send"— is not applied directly in the track, but instead part of the audio signal in a track is sent to the effect using a bus. A **bus** is just a virtual pathway that can carry audio. Even when you're using no effects at all you're using a bus: each track in your DAW/Sequencer is typically routed by default to the output bus, where the audio from each track is mixed together and sent to the main output of the computer. A bus used for a send effect is just another pathway that carries a portion of the audio from a track, or tracks, to the effect.

In a DAW/Sequencer, a send effect is actually an insert effect on a different track, called an **auxiliary track**, or aux track. An aux track is similar to an audio track, but it doesn't store any audio regions—audio just passes through. A portion of the audio from the original track is sent to the aux track on a bus, at which point it becomes the

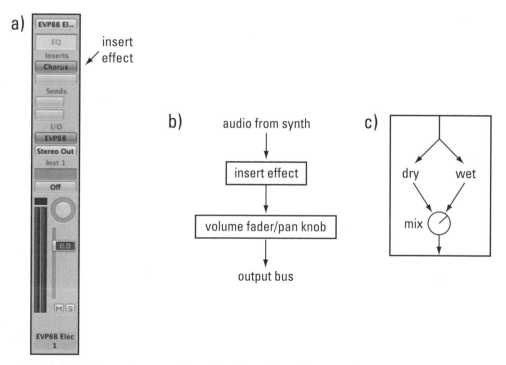

Figure 8.1 Insert effects: a) screen shot of a mixer channel strip with an insert effect (screen shot reprinted with permission from Apple Inc.); b) the signal path for an insert effect; c) an insert effect with a wet/dry mix control

input audio for that track's channel strip. A send knob on the original track determines the amount of audio from that track that is sent on the bus.

The audio is processed by the effect inserted on the aux track, and the processed audio is then sent through the pan and volume controls for the aux track and mixed with the audio from the original track on the output bus. The aux track for the effect is also referred to as the effect's "return."

A mixer channel strip with a send and an auxiliary channel strip with a reverb called "Space Dsn" are shown in Figure 8.2a. The signal path that this represents is shown in Figure 8.2b.

Send effects are used when you want to process multiple sound sources in the same way. For example, you may want all of your tracks to sound like they are in the same reverberant space. Rather than use a reverb insert on each track, you send a portion of the audio from each track on the same bus to an aux track where one reverb plug-in processes all the audio from that bus. This allows you to manipulate only one plug-in to process many tracks, and it also requires the computer to devote processing power to only one plug-in for reverb instead of one plug-in for each track. This is very important when you're using processor-intensive plug-ins such as convolution reverbs (see "Reverberation" later in the chapter).

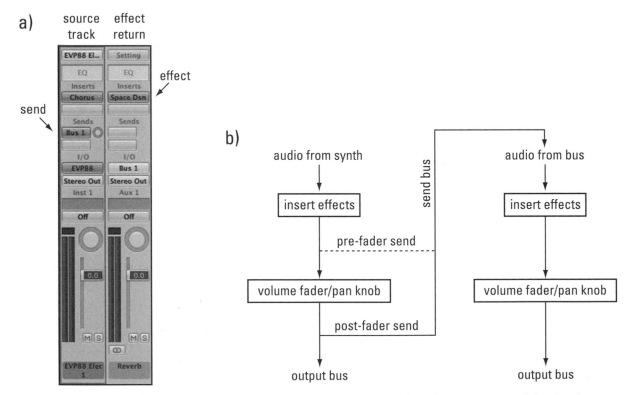

Figure 8.2   Send effects. a) screen shot of a mixer channel strip with a send bus that routes part of the signal to an aux track, which acts as the effect return (screen shot reprinted with permission from Apple Inc.); b) the signal path for a send effect showing the possibility of insert effects on the source track as well as pre- and post-fader routings for the send bus

In addition to controlling how much of the signal is sent to the bus using the send knob, you can also send the signal either post-fader or pre-fader (see Figure 8.2b). In **post-fader** mode, both the send knob *and* the main track fader affect how much of the signal is sent to the effect. Post-fader is generally desirable for effects so that when the main track is faded down the processed part of that signal also goes away. Otherwise, the faded-down track will remain in the mix as a sort of "ghost" that only shows up through the effects. However, if this kind of ghost is desired or the send is going to a stage monitor or headphone mix, then a send might be used **pre-fader**. In some DAW/Sequencers, sends can also be configured as pre- or post-pan. Post-pan sends would require a stereo bus, whereas pre-pan sends could be mono.

For the send effect, we used two buses here: one to route audio to the aux track for the effect and the main output bus where the output for all the tracks, including the effect return aux track, were combined. In practice, you might have a number of buses and aux tracks for send effects, buses and aux tracks for submixes, buses for headphone mixes when recording, and buses for sidechain routing for effects (see below). In addition, these buses and aux tracks may be mono or stereo.

Now that we've seen the various ways in which the signal can be routed to an effect, we'll look at the effects themselves, starting with dynamics processing effects.

DYNAMICS PROCESSING

Dynamics processing involves automatically altering the amplitude of audio in such a way that its dynamic range is changed. The **dynamic range** of an audio signal is the difference between the quietest part of the signal and the loudest part of the signal. This is subtly different than the dynamic range for a digital audio *system* as discussed in Chapter 2, which is the difference between the highest *possible* signal and smallest *possible* signal, or, more practically, the difference between the highest possible signal and the noise in the system. Dynamics processing effects allow you to compress (reduce) or expand the dynamic range. Dynamics processors are generally used as insert effects rather than as send effects, though there are some special techniques, such as parallel compression, that are realized using aux sends.

Dynamics: Compression and Limiting

Compression involves narrowing the dynamic range of an audio signal by reducing its amplitude after it reaches a threshold value. Below the threshold value the amplitude is unchanged, but above the threshold value the amplitude is reduced by some ratio. This has the effect of reducing the amplitude of the loud parts of the audio while leaving the quiet parts alone.

Let's take as an example a compressor whose **threshold** is set to −30 dB FS and whose **ratio** for reducing the audio above that is 3:1. First, it is important to remember that dB FS (full scale) is the amplitude of the digital signal relative to the highest possible amplitude that can be represented in the system. As a result, an audio signal with the highest possible amplitude would be at 0 dB FS and any audio signal with a smaller amplitude would have a negative dB FS value—the logarithm of a number less than one. In our example, any audio input to the compressor below −30 dB FS would be passed unchanged. Any audio input to the compressor above −30 dB would be reduced according to the ratio of 3:1—every 3 dB of increase in the input signal results in only a 1 dB increase in the output signal. If the input signal was −27 dB—3 dB above the threshold—then the output signal would be -29 dB. If the input signal was −20 dB—10 dB above the threshold—then the output signal would be about −27 dB (see Figure 8.3a).

A compressor with a very high ratio— of 10:1 or more—is referred to as a **limiter**. Even large increases in the input signal above the threshold will result in only small increases in the output signal. This allows you to put a near-absolute cap on a signal level.

One of the common uses of a compressor is to increase the overall loudness of the audio signal. To accomplish this, you set the **make-up gain**, or output gain, on the compressor to boost the entire signal after the dynamic range has been reduced. In the example discussed above, if the input audio signal reached a maximum of 0 dB, the output signal would only reach a maximum of −20 dB, because an input signal that was 30 dB above the threshold with a 3:1 ratio would result in an output signal that was only 10 dB above the threshold. This means you could boost the entire compressed signal by 20 dB without clipping, thereby making the entire signal louder. The initial act of compression causes loud and soft sounds to be brought closer together and the application of make-up gain causes the whole thing to get louder. Extremes of compression have led to the "loudness wars" in modern audio production in which producers attempt to out-do each other in the average loudness of their tracks. Figure 8.3b shows a -30 dB threshold, a 3:1 ratio, a −20 dB input signal, and 10 dB of make-up gain resulting in a −17 dB output signal.

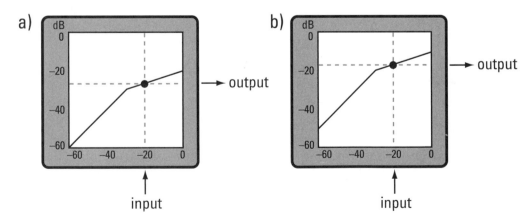

Figure 8.3   Compression: a) threshold of −30 dB, ratio of 3:1, −20 dB input yields −27 dB output; b) same settings and input with 10 dB of makeup gain yields −17 dB output

So far we have assumed that the compressor acts immediately to reduce an audio signal above the threshold. However, a sudden application of compression may sound unnatural. The compressor's **attack** setting determines how quickly the compressor "turns down" the audio above the threshold. This setting allows you to shorten the attack to quickly compress percussive sounds or lengthen it to compress sustained sounds in a less obvious way. You could also use a slightly longer attack to allow some peaks (transients) through before the compression kicks in to retain some of the bite of the original signal while still reducing the dynamic range overall.

The compressor's **release** parameter determines how quickly the compressor stops changing a signal once it drops below the threshold. This can smooth the transition from the compressed to the non-compressed signal, allowing the effect to sound more natural. A heavy compression ratio and a short release time can result in an unnatural "pumping" effect as the signal crosses back and forth over the threshold. A compressor may also allow you to choose a shape for the **knee** at the threshold. A more rounded, "soft" knee can also offer a smoother transition between non-compressed and compressed portions of the audio signal, helping the compressor to do its work less obtrusively. The knee in Figure 8.3 is a "hard" knee.

In addition to affecting an entire input audio signal in the same way, a compressor can be applied differently to separate frequency bands. This is referred to as **multiband compression**. Multiband compression allows you, for example, to apply compression to the lower frequencies—"tighten" them up—while leaving the mid-range and upper frequencies unchanged. Multiband compression is often used as part of the mastering process on an entire mix rather than on a track-by-track basis, though it can be used on an individual track or group of tracks as well.

Dynamics: Expansion and Gating

Where compression is used to reduce the overall dynamic range of an audio signal, **expansion** is used to increase the overall dynamic range. An expander's parameters are very similar to a compressor's: threshold, ratio, attack, and release. With an expander, any signal that falls *below* the threshold is further reduced according to some ratio. This has the effect of reducing the level of the quiet parts of the audio signal while leaving the louder parts alone. It is also possible to have an expander that *increases* the gain *above* the threshold, thereby leaving the quiet parts alone and boosting the loud parts. Both types increase the dynamic range.

Let's take as an example an expander whose threshold is set to −30 dB FS and whose ratio for audio below that threshold is 1:3. Notice that the ratio for an expander is reversed from that of a compressor, because a change in the input signal below the threshold results in a larger change in the output signal. Documentation for some expanders list this ratio as 3:1 with the understanding that the "3" refers to the decrease in output level due to a decrease of "1" in the input level. In our example, any audio input to the expander above −30 dB FS would be passed unchanged. Any audio input to the expander below −30 dB would be reduced according to the ratio of 1:3—every

1 dB of decrease in the input signal results in a 3 dB decrease in the output signal. If the input signal were −31 dB, then the output signal would be −33 dB. If the input signal were −40 dB, then the output signal would be −60 dB (see Figure 8.4a). You can see that the output level below the threshold drops quickly.

An expander can be useful if there is low-level undesirable noise in a sound, such as buzzing from a guitar amp or extraneous sounds from a vocalist. In that example, if the threshold is set properly, when the guitarist stops playing or the vocalist stops singing, the expander will cause the unwanted sounds to quickly fall below audibility. The attack time is the amount of time the effect takes to return to normal, linear behavior above the threshold, and the release time is the amount of time the effect takes to apply the expansion ratio below the threshold. From one perspective, this is opposite the way the attack and release times work for compression, in that the compression attack is the amount of time it takes for the ratio to be applied and the release is the amount of time it takes for the effect to return to normal, linear behavior. On the other hand, attack and release times for both expansion and compression are similar in that attack times apply to signals above the threshold and release times apply below the threshold.

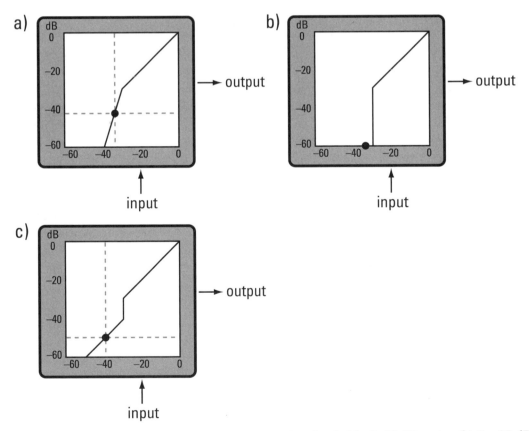

Figure 8.4 Expansion and gating: a) an expander with a threshold of −30 dB, ratio of 1:3, −35 dB input yields −45 dB output; b) a gate with a threshold of −30 dB, input below −30 dB is cut; c) a gate with a fixed drop of 10 dB below −30 dB threshold, input of −40 dB yields a −50 dB output

Just as a high compression ratio results in limiting, a high expansion ratio results in **gating**. Sounds below the threshold drop to essentially nothing (see Figure 8.4b). A gate can also have a settable dB drop so that levels below the threshold are reduced by that number of dB (see Figure 8.4c). Gating can naturally be used to eliminate noise as an extension of the buzzing guitar amp example above, but it can also be used creatively to allow, for example, a percussive sound to suddenly pop out during its attack and quickly disappear before it would naturally die away, creating a tight, punchy sound. In addition to attack and release times that work as they do with expanders—attack above the threshold, release below—gates often have a "hold" time that delays the closing of the gate after the signal has dropped below the threshold by that amount of time. The release time is applied after the hold period.

Dynamics: Sidechains, Keying, Ducking, and Gating

In the discussion of dynamics processing so far, the input audio signal served as both the trigger for the effect—when the threshold was crossed—and as the audio signal to be processed by the effect. However, it is possible to use a *different* signal to trigger the compression/expansion, which can result in some interesting effects. This alternate trigger input to an effect is referred to as a **sidechain input** and it acts to **key**, or trigger, the effect (see Figure 8.5). There are many creative ways to use dynamics processors with sidechain inputs. We will look at two here: ducking and gating.

One common example of using a sidechain input to key a compressor is **ducking**, which means to reduce the level of one audio signal when another audio signal is present. For example, in a podcast you may want to have music playing between segments but have the level of that music drop when you begin to speak—you want the music to "duck under" the voice. This can, of course, be done with volume automation on the

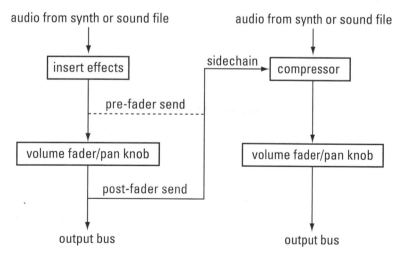

Figure 8.5 Sidechain routing: audio from one track is sent on a bus (pre- or post-fader) to the sidechain input of a compressor. Other types of effects can also take sidechain inputs

music track in a DAW/Sequencer, but it would be more flexible to have the dynamics of the music change automatically when the voice is present.

To accomplish this automatic ducking, you insert the compressor (insert effect) onto the music track and then set the voice track to act as the sidechain input to the compressor. This is usually accomplished by creating a send on the voice track that routes part of the signal to a bus. This bus is then chosen in the music track's compressor as the sidechain input. Now the compressor is comparing the level of the voice track to the threshold and reducing the *music track* when the level of the voice track rises above the threshold and passing the music unchanged when the voice track level drops below the threshold (see Figure 8.6). The compressor uses the ratio and the attack and release times to accomplish the compression. In this case you don't use make-up gain on the compressor because the reduction in overall level of the music track is desirable when the voice track is active.

Another useful example of sidechain routing is to use drum audio to key a gate on a sustained synth pad. The result is a synth pad that only plays when the drums are active, creating a rhythmic synth sound. To accomplish this effect, you insert a gate onto the synth pad track, create a send from the drum track on a bus, and then use this bus as the sidechain input to the gate effect to key the gate (see Figure 8.7). Whenever the drum audio rises above the threshold, the gate is "opened" and the synth pad will be heard. When the drum audio falls below the threshold, the gate is "closed" and the synth pad will be silent.

If the gate has a built-in sidechain filter, you can set it so that only the cymbals or only the kick drum triggers the gate. You can even listen only to the rhythmic synth pad but not the drums by setting the send on the drums to be pre-fader and bringing down the drum track fader. In that instance, the drums are heard only through their gating effect on the synth pad.

FILTERING

Though filters are core elements of synthesizers, some DAW/Sequencers also have filter plug-ins that can be used as insert and send effects. As effects, filter plug-ins can be

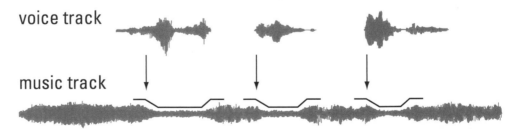

Figure 8.6 Ducking a music track: the voice track acts as the sidechain input to a compressor on the music track. When the voice track exceeds the threshold, it keys the compressor and the amplitude of the music track is reduced

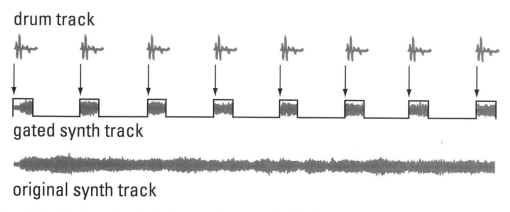

drum track

gated synth track

original synth track

Figure 8.7   Gated synth pad: the drum track acts as the sidechain input to a gate on the synth track. When the drum track exceeds the threshold, it keys the gate and allows the synth pad to come through. The original synth track is shown at the bottom

applied to recorded, imported, and synthesized/sampled audio. Filters are also the primary tools for equalization and we'll discus EQ a little bit later in the chapter.

The basic filter types available in a filter effect are similar to those discussed in previous chapters: low pass with resonance, high pass with resonance, band pass, and notch. The available parameters for these filter types are also the same: cutoff frequency, resonance, and slope for high/low pass and center frequency and bandwidth expressed as a *Q* factor for band pass and notch. The cutoff frequency/center frequency in a filter effect can typically be modulated directly by parameter automation on the audio track or by the effect's built-in envelope and LFO.

Unlike enveloped synth filters, an envelope in a filter effect that is modulating the cutoff frequency won't typically be gated by MIDI note-on and note-off messages. Instead, the envelope can be triggered, or keyed, by the input signal when it exceeds a settable threshold or keyed by a sidechain input when it exceeds the threshold. This is similar to the keying possibilities in the dynamics processing effects discussed above. When the input signal provides the key, the effect is similar to the classic "auto-wah" guitar effect in which each note/chord is modulated by an enveloped filter.

The ability to key the filter effect envelope by an entirely different signal allows for dynamic automated filtering based on another element of the music such as a drum track or vocals. For example, the filter effect could be inserted on a synth pad and then keyed by a drum groove. Every time the drum groove exceeds the threshold value, the filter effect on the synth pad track would be modulated by the envelope. This is a similar setup to the gated synth pad with the sidechain drum groove discussed above, though the resultant effects are quite different.

A filter effect can also be modulated by a built-in LFO whose basic parameters are waveform, rate, and depth. This aspect of a filter effect is very similar to an LFO-modulated synth filter. The rate can be specified as an absolute frequency or it can be synchronized to the DAW/Sequencer's tempo, in which case the rate would be determined by a selected period given in beats or measures. The tempo-synced opening and closing of a filter is common in some forms of electronic dance music.

EQUALIZATION

Filters are also the key elements in **equalization**, or EQ. An EQ plug-in typically consists of several filters of varying types brought together under one plug-in interface with knobs, sliders, and/or graphical objects to control the parameters of the filters. One way to think about the difference between the way that filters are used in synths/effects versus the way filters are used in EQ is that filters in synths/effects are used primarily *creatively*, whereas filters in EQ are used both *correctively* and creatively. Used correctively, EQ can help to eliminate or reduce unwanted buzzes or hums or adjust parts of the frequency spectrum on one or more tracks to reduce conflicts between instruments that share the same frequency range. Corrective EQ goes largely unnoticed because we no longer hear the problem that it was used to fix. Used creatively, an EQ plug-in can help to boost or reduce different portions of the spectrum in unique and perhaps extreme ways. Creative EQ is meant to be noticed.

Peaking and Shelving Filters

When discussing synth filters, we encountered several different types: resonant low pass, resonant high pass, band pass, and notch. EQs use low pass, high pass, and notch filters, along with peaking filters and shelving filters (the low pass and high pass filters in EQs don't typically use resonance). As we saw in Chapter 6, a peaking filter is similar in shape to a band pass filter. However, where a band pass filter attenuates (reduces) frequencies outside of the pass band, a peaking filter leaves them unchanged (see Figure 6.16 on page 137 and Figure 8.8). This allows you to use a peaking filter to affect only a narrow range of frequencies rather than broadly affecting the entire frequency range.

In EQs, peaking and notching filters are a single type with a variable gain: positive gain yields a peaking effect and negative gain yields a notching effect (see Figure 8.8). The parameters for a peak/notch, then, are center frequency, bandwidth, and gain, with the bandwidth determined by the Q factor along with the center frequency. The Q factor was discussed in some detail in Chapter 6.

As the name indicates, shelving filters create a flat shelf of gain above or below a cutoff frequency. A **high shelf filter** either boosts (positive gain) or attenuates (negative gain) frequencies *above* a cutoff frequency (see Figure 8.9a). On the other hand, a **low shelf filter** boosts (positive gain) or attenuates (negative gain) frequencies *below* a cutoff frequency (see Figure 8.9b). Simple tone controls on a home or car stereo that allow you to boost/cut the treble or boost/cut the bass are often implemented with shelving filters.

Shelving filters have two parameters: cutoff frequency and gain. Just like all of the other filters discussed, shelving filters don't cause a sudden jump or fall at the cutoff

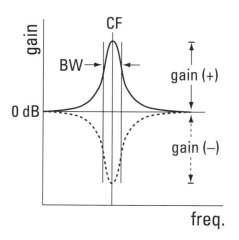

Figure 8.8 Peak/notch filter showing center frequency (CF), bandwidth (BW), and gain (notch shown with dashed lines). Peak and notch are different only in the sign of their gain

frequency, but rather have a transition from the unaffected frequency range to the affected one. Some EQ plug-ins have different types for shelving and other filters that affect the shape of this transition.

Graphic and Parametric Equalizers

There are two basic types of EQs: graphic and parametric. **Graphic equalizers** split up the frequency spectrum into some number of perceptually equal bands. Since the frequency spectrum encompasses approximately ten octaves, an "octave band" graphic

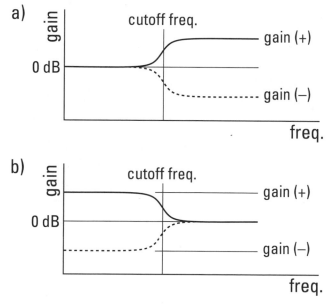

Figure 8.9 Shelving filters: a) high shelf showing cutoff frequency and gain; negative gain shown with dashed lines; b) low shelf filter

equalizer will have ten bands that are an octave wide and a "one-third octave band" equalizer will have thirty bands that are one-third of an octave wide. Each of the bands in a graphic EQ is a peak/notch filter with a fixed center frequency, fixed Q, and variable gain on the order of +/−6 dB or +/−12 dB controlled by a slider or knob.

Graphic equalizers are the quintessential corrective EQs. They are often used in sound reinforcement to correct for frequencies that are emphasized in a performance space and in fancier car stereos to emphasize essential parts of different radio programs that might be covered up by road noise. An example of the latter might be to emphasize the upper midrange when listening to talk radio so that consonants in speech aren't obscured by road noise.

Parametric equalizers use one or more filters of various types—low pass, high pass, shelving, and peak/notch—and are often characterized by the number of filters as one-band EQs, two-band EQs, eight-band EQs, etc. Many EQ plug-ins divide up the spectrum into five bands—low, low-mid, mid, high-mid, and high—and each band can be manipulated using a peak/notch filter. Unlike the graphic EQ, these peak/notch filters have variable center frequencies and Qs so that they can be used quite precisely. In addition, a variable-slope high pass filter at the low end of the spectrum and a variable-slope low pass filter at the high end of the spectrum are often available. To add to the flexibility, one of the bands on either end of the spectrum can usually be switched

Figure 8.10 Masterworks parametric EQ in Digital Performer 6 (courtesy of MOTU). There are five bands of peak/notch filters covering low, low-midrange, midrange, high-midrange, and high frequencies, plus a high-pass filter at the low end of the spectrum and a low pass filter at the high end of the spectrum. The low-midrange band can be switched to a low shelf and the high-midrange band can be switched to a high shelf

between peak/notch and shelf. Figure 8.10 shows an EQ plug-in with each of these features.

The parametric EQ described above is configured to fill a fundamentally corrective purpose, but you can also think of such a multiband EQ plug-in as just several useful filters gathered in the same place. One possible creative use of such a collection of filters is to use the peaking filters to impose a series of formants on the input signal. This could become a form of do-it-yourself formant filter as described in Chapter 6. By positioning the center frequencies of the peaking filters at the appropriate frequencies for the formants of a particular vowel and adjusting the gain and Q, you could impose a voice-like character on the sound being processed. Because peaking filters pass everything outside of the affected band unchanged, this would not be as extreme an effect as if they were bandpass filters.

To change vowel types over time, you could use track automation to automate the center frequencies of the peaking filters. Of course, for this to work at all, the sound must have some energy in that part of the spectrum to be shaped by peaking filters at those frequencies. As mentioned in Chapter 6, you can find tables of vowel formant frequencies in Bennett and Rodet (1989) and Dodge and Jerse (1997).

You could also use the peaking filters to impose arbitrary formants that are related by the overtone series or that outline a particular chord. The formants could also be somewhat arbitrary: high gain, high Q peaking placed at various places in the spectrum, can cause unexpected resonances when the partials for the affected sound stray into those frequencies. These resonances can also lead to distortion, so care must be taken to reduce the overall volume as necessary when using positive gain with peaking filters. Using the high and low pass filters to roll off substantial portions of both ends of the spectrum can remove much of the "body" from the incoming sounds, making it sound "low-fi." Combining this with the unusually placed resonances can create a strange and wonderful effect. Turning those peaks into notches by reversing the gain can create anti-resonances, or "holes," in the affected sound.

In its corrective capacity, an EQ plug-in might be used as an insert effect on a track to EQ a specific instrument, on a sub-mix channel strip to EQ a group of tracks, or on the output channel strip to EQ the overall mix. In the case of the creative EQ applications discussed above, an EQ plug-in could be used as an insert effect on a track to change the timbre of just that track, as an insert on an aux-track that's being used to sub-mix several tracks, or possibly as a send effect in order to control the mix of the affected and unaffected sound (the wet/dry mix). As a send effect, the EQ could be followed by a reverb so that some of the unusual effects described above would seem to be part of the reverb forming a strange sort of halo around the unaffected sound.

TIME-BASED EFFECTS

So far in this chapter we've discussed dynamics processing effects, which are based on amplitude, and filtering/EQ effects, which are based on frequency. The effects in this section are based on time, and include delay/echo, chorusing, flanging, and phasing. These effects are typically used as insert effects either on individual tracks or on aux tracks being used to sub-mix several tracks. In addition, many softsynths include one or more of these effects in the synth itself. In the latter case, their parameters can be modulation targets for any of the modulators in a synth. At the heart of these time-based effects is the delay line.

A delay line is a memory space that stores incoming audio for some period of time—usually no more than a few seconds and often much less—and then sends it to the output. A time-based effect is the result of combining the delayed signal with the un-delayed signal in some proportion determined by the wet/dry mix. Which of the effects is heard is partially dependent on how long the delay is. Longer delays yield clear echoes while shorter delays cause the delayed signal to fuse with the un-delayed signal.

Time-based Effects: Delay/Echo

When the delay in an effect is more than about 50 milliseconds, the result, when combined with the un-delayed signal, is a single **echo**. A single echo could be useful in some situations, but it is common to feed back some portion of the delay output back into the input of the delay, resulting in a series of echoes. The higher the feedback amount, the more echoes will be created at the time interval of the delay (see Figure 8.11). As long as the feedback multiplier is less than one, the echoes will eventually die away. The feedback signal can often be phase inverted either by clicking a phase button or by using negative feedback values. This phase inversion usually has a subtle timbral effect on the output.

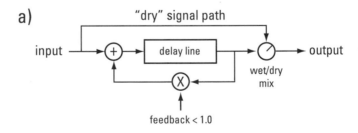

Figure 8.11   Delay/echo effect: a) signal routing showing the delay line, the feedback loop, and the feedback multiplier along with the "dry" signal path and wet/dry mix knob; b) a short sound processed by feedback delay

There are several enhancements to the simple **feedback delay** that are commonly found in DAW/Sequencer plug-ins. One common option is that the delay time can be specified as a musical duration, rather than in milliseconds, so that it can be tempo-synced to your DAW/Sequencer. A second option is a **stereo delay** in which the right and left channels can have different delay times and feedback amounts. Also in a stereo delay, the output of the left channel can often be fed back to the right channel and vice versa to create a more complex stereo image. This is referred to as **cross-feedback**. A third option is to have a filter of some type in the feedback and cross-feedback loops to alter the timbre of the repeated echoes. Using a low pass filter in this situation darkens the timbre on each echo, which mimics the acoustic behavior of echoes in which more high-frequency energy than low frequency energy is lost when a sound bounces off of a surface.

Another type of delay effect is the **multitap delay**. In the delay effect discussed above, there was a single delay value, which was the total length of the delay line. However, some delay effects use a relatively long delay line and then **tap** that delay line at one or more places in the line, resulting in multiple delay times (see Figure 8.12). For example, a 2,000 ms (2 second) delay line could have delay taps at 500 ms, 1,000 ms, and 1,500 ms. The result is three separate delays that are then added to the dry signal. These specific tap times—500 ms, 1,000 ms, and 1,500 ms—could actually be created with a simple feedback delay because they are all multiples of a single delay time of 500 ms. One useful aspect of a multitap delay is that it allows you to have multiple echoes that are not simply related to another. For example, you could choose taps of 500 ms, 710 ms, and 1,150 ms, which would create a delay pattern not possible with a simple feedback delay.

Like the simple feedback delay, a multitap delay may have tempo-synced delay values specified in musical durations, feedback for individual taps or for all of them combined, stereo crossfeedback, and filtering in the feedback loops. In addition, the gain of each tap can be specified so that the echoes don't have the constant decrease in amplitude of the simple feedback delay.

Time-based Effects: Chorus

As the delay time falls below about 50 ms, the delay sounds less like an echo and more like "fattening" of the sound. It is important to note that the change in effect due to delay time is continuous and the 50 ms value that I've been using is only a rough approximation. For sharp percussive sounds, values quite a bit smaller than 50 ms may still sound like echoes, whereas for more continuous sounds the "fattening" may start to happen at larger delay times. An effect that utilizes this "fattening" effect is **chorus**.

In general, a chorus effect is used to obtain a richer sound than the synth or audio recording produces. The term itself derives from the chorus effect of multiple similar singers performing the same melody. In that situation, there will be small variations in timing and pitch that give the ensemble its massed sound. A group of any similar instruments playing the same music will also have these small variations.

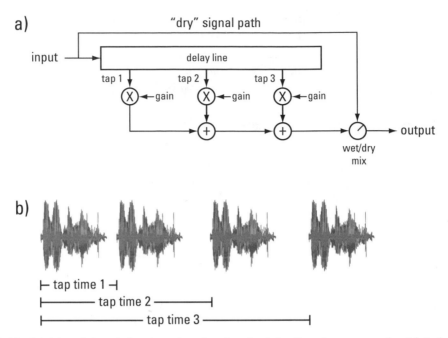

Figure 8.12   Multitap delay: a) signal routing showing the delay line, three taps each with independent gain, and the "dry" signal path with wet/dry mix knob; b) a short sound processed by a multitap delay (all gain factors are 1.0 in this illustration)

One way to achieve a chorus effect is to use a delay of approximately 10–50 ms, modulate that delay time with a built-in LFO, and mix the modulated delay with the original dry signal (see Figure 8.13a). As before, the 10–50 ms range is merely a rough guideline; a chorus may allow for larger or smaller values. The modulated delay produces changes in both timing and pitch due to the changing delay length. A more complex chorus effect might use multiple time-varying delays or a multitap delay with time-varying taps (see Figure 8.13b).

The parameters for the simple version of this effect (Figure 8.13a) include the starting, or center, delay time, the depth or amount of the modulation of delay time due to the LFO, the LFO rate, and the mix between the dry and wet signals. A stereo chorus may allow for independent panning of the dry and wet signals to increase the apparent size of the instrument or voice. Larger LFO depth values increase how much the delay time changes above and below the starting value, producing larger timing and pitch changes. Larger LFO rates increase the pace of those changes. For a natural chorus, a 20–30 ms delay time, a modest LFO depth of 10–30 percent, and an LFO rate of 0.5–3 Hz are reasonable values. More extreme values can be used to create unusual effects. A mix value of 100 percent wet can be used to impose a vibrato of sorts on the signal, because the output would be just the modulated delay line that is fluctuating in pitch according to the LFO rate and depth. Though not strictly part of the chorus concept, some plug-ins also allow for feedback.

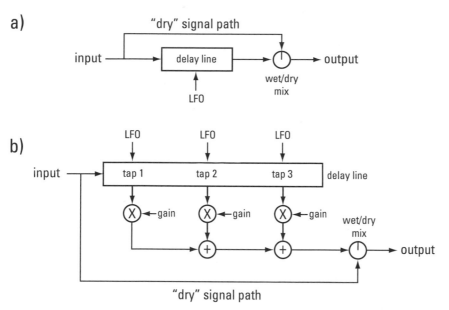

Figure 8.13 Chorus effect: a) a simple chorus in which the dry signal is mixed (50 percent wet/dry mix) with the output of an LFO-modulated delay line; b) a more complex chorus using a multitap delay (only three taps are shown), each of which is modulated by an LFO

Time-based Effects: Flanging

A delay of less than about 10 ms results in the spectral "combing" effect described in Chapter 6 when discussing the comb filter (see page 138). As you recall, a comb filter utilizes a very short delay that creates a number of evenly spaced peaks or notches in the spectrum of the input signal when it is combined with the un-delayed signal (see Figure 6.17 on page 138). The spacing and positioning of the peaks is determined by the delay time. Shorter delays yield wider peak/notch spacing and a first peak/notch at a higher frequency; as the delay time grows, the peaks/notches get closer together and shift down in the spectrum. The notch depth is determined by the wet/dry mix. If the phase of the delayed portion of the signal is inverted, the position of the peaks/notches shifts. A comb filter becomes a **flanging** effect when the delay time is modulated with an LFO, resulting in shifting peaks/notches as the spacing between them periodically widens and narrows (see Figure 8.14).

Most of the primary parameters in a flanger plug-in are similar to those of a simple chorus, including the delay time (less than 10 ms for a flanger), the LFO depth, the LFO rate, and the wet/dry mix. The LFO rate can usually be specified either in absolute time (ms) or as a musical duration that would sync the flanger LFO to the tempo of your DAW/Sequencer. Tempo-synced flanging is a common effect in some kinds of electronic dance music. In addition, the flanger plug-in includes a feedback value, which sharpens the comb peaks and imparts a distinctly metallic tinge at high feedback values. As with the basic feedback delay above, the portion of the signal being fed back can

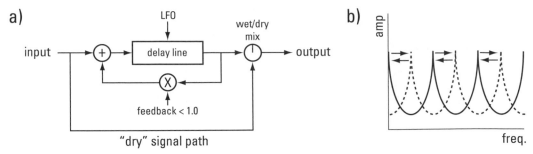

Figure 8.14 Flanger effect: a) signal routing showing a feedback delay with an LFO-modulated delay time; b) flanger spectrum with high feedback value showing the comb-filter-like peaks shifting due to the LFO (frequency axis is linear)

be inverted, using negative feedback values or a dedicated button, which results in a timbral change that can range from subtle to pronounced depending on the audio being flanged.

Notice that as the delay times have gotten smaller and smaller in this discussion, time-based delay effects have gradually become filter effects as with the flanger, which can be thought of as an LFO-modulated comb filter. As discussed in the "Technically Speaking . . . a little filter theory" sidebar in Chapter 6 (see page 140), filters are actually composed of one or more very small delays—some as small as the time between individual samples in a digital audio signal ($1/44,100 \approx 0.023$ ms).

Time-based Effects: Phasing

Phasing is similar to flanging in that both create shifting peaks/notches in the spectrum of the input signal. However, phasing is produced not by using a delay line but rather by using several special filters called **all-pass filters**. Where a low pass filter passes low frequencies and a high pass filter passes high frequencies, an all-pass filter passes all frequencies with their amplitudes unaltered. What all-pass filters do change are the *phases* of the partials. When the output of this series of all-pass filters is combined with the unaffected signal, phase cancellations occur, resulting in notches in the spectrum. These notches differ from those created by comb filtering in that phasing produces fewer notches that are not evenly spaced. Phasing takes on its characteristic sound when the notches are swept through the spectrum using an LFO (see Figure 8.15).

The parameters of a phaser typically include controls over the notch spacing and position, the LFO rate, LFO depth, feedback, and dry/wet mix. Implementation of phaser effects varies widely among plug-ins from different companies, so there may be additional parameters as well. As with the flanger and echo effects, the LFO rate for some phaser plug-ins can be set using musical durations, rather than absolute time values (ms), so that the effect is tempo-synced with the DAW/Sequencer. A dry/wet mix of 50 percent (equal parts dry and wet) yields the most pronounced phasing.

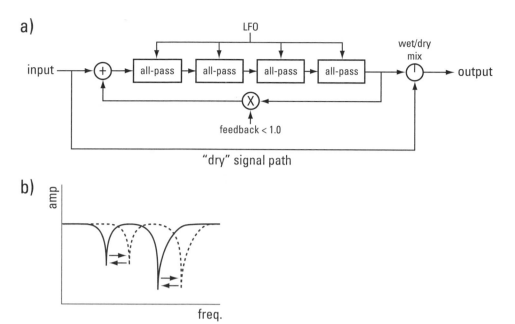

Figure 8.15 Phaser effect: a) signal routing showing four LFO-modulated all-pass filters and a possible feedback loop; b) phaser spectrum with no feedback showing the unevenly-spaced notches shifting due to the LFO. Feedback causes the "humps" between the notches to sharpen into peaks

RING MODULATION

We discussed **ring modulation** in Chapter 6 as a possible interaction between two oscillators in a synth (see page 124). As a plug-in effect, the basics of ring modulation are the same: two sound sources are combined such that their partials are added and subtracted to form a new spectrum. With fixed waveforms—sine, triangle, square, sawtooth—the resultant spectrum has a certain amount of regularity. When the sources are complex recorded, imported, or synthesized/sampled audio, the spectrum can be quite chaotic.

When inserted on a track, a ring modulation plug-in uses the audio from the track as one sound source and either an internal oscillator or a sidechain input as the other sound source. When the plug-in's internal oscillator is being used, the partials from the track's audio are reflected around the oscillator's partials. If the oscillator waveform is a simple sine wave, then the resultant spectrum is the spectrum of the track's audio shifted up by the oscillator's frequency plus a mirror of that spectrum below the oscillator's frequency. If the oscillator's waveform is more complex than a sine wave, then each partial in the waveform acts as a center around which the spectrum of the track's audio is mirrored.

Ring modulation can be used for any type of sound, but it is particularly effective processing speech, in part because speech can often be recognized even when it has been heavily processed. When speech is ring modulated with the plug-in's internal oscillator at a frequency of around 30 Hz, the result is a sort of mechanical growl. If the oscillator's frequency is around 1,000 Hz, the result is reminiscent of distorted radio communications.

Figure 8.16a shows the spectrum of a moment in a speech sound file with no processing. Figure 8.16b shows the spectrum at that same moment as processed by a ring modulator using an internal sine wave oscillator with a frequency of 1,000 Hz. Notice the mirroring in Figure 8.16b with a center at 1,000 Hz.

When the plug-in uses a sidechain input as the second sound source, the resultant spectrum has the partials of the sidechain input mirrored around the partials of the track's audio. When both are of even moderate complexity, the results are not as regular as with the internal oscillator, but they can be quite interesting. Synth pads and other sounds with sustained frequency content can provide some degree of regularity when ring modulating a rapidly changing sound source such as speech.

REVERBERATION

One of the more common and useful effects is reverberation, or **reverb**, which simulates the effects of a sound in a room or hall. Reverb can be used as an insert effect, but it is probably best used as a send effect, which allows multiple tracks to be processed by the same plug-in to save CPU power and apply a common reverb to those tracks. The reverb on the aux track (reverb return) would be set to 100 percent wet, and the wet-dry mix would be controlled by the fader for the source track (dry) and the fader for the reverb aux track (wet). You might use reverb as an insert effect to process a track with its own unique settings. In that case, you would use the wet/dry mix control on the reverb plug-in to balance the direct and reverberated sound.

In general, reverb can be thought of in three parts: direct sound, early echoes, and dense echoes (see Figure 8.17). The **direct sound** component is the sound that travels directly from the stage to your ears without bouncing off of anything. If you were trying to simulate sound sources at different distances from the listener, you could delay the

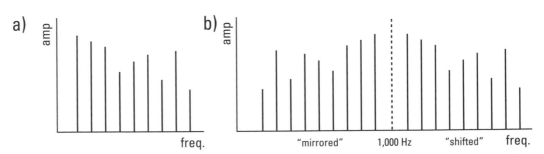

Figure 8.16   Ring modulation effect: a) unprocessed spectrum; b) spectrum after ring modulation with a 1,000 Hz sine wave

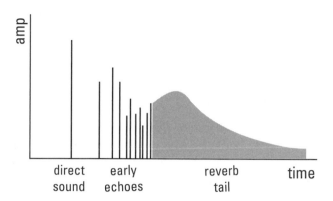

Figure 8.17   Parts of reverberation: direct sound, early echoes, and dense echoes (reverb tail)

direct sound for a source based on the amount of time it would take sound to travel the distance you are simulating.

The **early echoes** represent the source sound bouncing just once or a few times off of the walls, floor, and ceiling of the room and then reaching your ears. By bouncing off a surface these echoes travel farther to get to you and some of their energy, particularly high frequency energy, is absorbed by the surface materials. As a result, the early echoes are both quieter and darker than the direct sound. The degree to which they are quieter and darker is different for different types of surfaces. Highly absorbent materials, such as fabric curtains, would dampen and darken the sound quite a bit, whereas more reflective materials, such as bathroom tiles, would dampen the sound very little and leave much of the high frequency energy in the reflected sound. The early echoes take more time to reach you than the direct sound. The specific amount of time is based on the distance from the sound source to you.

The later, **dense echoes** represent multiple bounces of the source sound off the various surfaces before it reaches you—this stage of reverb is also referred to as the **reverb tail**. With an even longer travel path and more contact with surface materials, the dense echoes are quieter and darker than the early echoes. The level and darkness of these echoes are dependent on the surface materials just as the early echoes were. Naturally, these echoes also take more time to build up than the early echoes.

Overall, the reverberation of short sounds dies away and becomes darker over a period of time referred to as the reverberation time. The response of a reverb to a quick short sound, or impulse, is referred to as the reverb's impulse response.

There are two basic types of reverb plug-ins: artificial reverb and convolution, or sampling, reverb.

Artificial Reverb

Artificial reverbs use elements such as all-pass filters, comb filters, and delays to mimic the effect of a source sound reflecting off the walls, floor, and ceiling of a room or hall.

To simulate the various reverb stages, artificial reverb plug-ins provide a variety of controls. The specific controls depend on the details of the reverb algorithm being used and vary widely from reverb to reverb. One simple example is Averb in Logic Pro, which is the simplest of the six different reverb plug-ins in Logic. Averb has the following parameters: pre-delay, reflectivity, room size, density/time, and wet/dry mix (see Figure 8.18a).

The pre-delay in Adverb sets the delay time between the direct sound and the early echoes. The reflectivity value is related to the type of the materials in the room or hall. This parameter affects how much overall energy the source sound loses with each bounce off of a surface along with the amount of high frequency energy that is lost with each bounce—this is the dampening and darkening discussed above.

The room size influences the time it takes for bounced sounds to reach you and is used to set the internal values of the comb filters, all-pass filters, and delays. The density/time control determines how dense the reverb tail will become and how long it will take to die out. The terms density and diffusion are sometimes used interchangeably, though some reverbs make the distinction between the density of the late echoes and how they're distributed (diffusion). More complex artificial reverbs provide more

Figure 8.18   Artificial reverb plug-ins: a) simple reverb (Averb in Logic Pro 9); b) more complex reverb (Goldverb in Logic Pro 9) (screen shots reprinted with permission from Apple Inc.)

refined control over each of the reverb stages along with features specific to the reverb algorithm being used (see Figure 8.18b).

The reverb time parameter found in many reverb plug-ins determines how long the reverberated signal takes to fall to 1/1,000 of its peak amplitude. This is referred to as the RT60 value because it represents a 60 dB drop from the peak of the reverb response. We can verify this by using the decibel formula for amplitude discussed in Chapter 1. Here, A_p refers to the peak amplitude of the reverb response:

$$\text{Decibel reduction} = 20 \log_{10} (0.001 A_p / A_p) = -60 \text{ dB}$$

The natural application of a reverb plug-in is to simulate an acoustic space around your source sounds. However, there are a number of interesting effects that can be achieved by thinking of a reverb unit as a complex sound processor. One of the most basic approaches to finding out what a reverb plug-in can do is to explore extreme settings, both high and low, for the various parameters. Since we're exploring reverb for its unusual effects, it would be better used as an insert rather than send, unless you want the entire mix or a sub-mix to be processed in this unusual way.

Using the parameters of the Averb discussed above, we can set the following parameter values (your reverb plug-in will likely have different parameters, so you'll have to translate this discussion to your reverb): pre-delay = 0, reflectivity = 100 percent, room size = 100 percent, density/time = 0, wet/dry mix = 100 percent (all wet). These settings effectively remove the reverb tail from the result, and you get a complex set of "early" echoes in a very large, highly reflective hall. A very different result can be gotten with the following settings: pre-delay = 0, reflectivity = 100 percent, room size = 10 percent (minimum), density/time = 100 percent, wet/dry mix = 100 percent (all wet). In this case, the room is tiny, maximally reflective, and the density is at maximum, so you'll hear mostly the reverb tail. This yields a ringing effect because the internal elements of the artificial reverb are set to produce very short delay times (small room) with high feedback levels (high density). If you now set the room size to maximum, you'll hear mostly a very dense reverb tail that doesn't much sound like reverb at all. Naturally, you can combine these unusual reverbs with other effects discussed above such as dynamics processors, filters, phasers, and flangers.

Convolution, or Sampling, Reverb

Convolution reverbs, also called **sampling reverbs**, take a very different approach to reverberation. Instead of using elements such as comb filters, all-pass filters, and delays to simulate the early echoes and reverb tail of a simulated space, convolution reverbs utilize impulse response recordings from actual spaces. Several DAW/Sequencers have a convolution reverb plug-in as part of the basic installation and there are a number of third-party plug-ins available (see Figure 8.19).

Originally, an **impulse response** recording was made by making a sharp sound—an impulse—from the stage of a performance hall and then recording the sound from

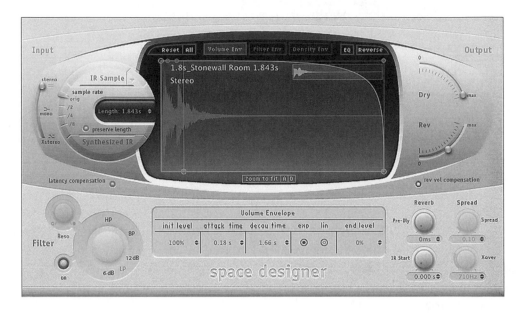

Figure 8.19 Space Designer convolution reverb from Logic Pro 9 (screen shot reprinted with permission from Apple Inc.). The impulse response for this setting is shown in the middle

somewhere in the seating area of the hall. The recording then consisted of the impulse along with the early echoes and reverb tail of the hall. More modern techniques involve playing a sine wave sweeping through the entire frequency range in the hall, recording the sine wave sweep, and then mathematically constructing the impulse response recording from it.

To apply the reverberation properties represented by the impulse response to a source sound, sampling reverbs use a mathematical technique known as convolution. The result of the process is the source sound with the reverb of the hall in which the impulse was recorded. This process allows you to apply reverb from any space in the world to your sounds. There are many impulse responses available on the Internet.

So far we've been assuming that the impulse response was created in a performance hall. However, just about any recording can be used in a convolution reverb. This includes recordings made in unusual spaces such as subway stations or drainage tunnels as well as recordings of instrument notes and drum beats. Recordings that look like impulse responses—basically a struck/plucked envelope—will have more reverb-like results, but others can be used to generate unique sounds.

There are many more effects available in most DAW/Sequencers than those discussed here, but these represent a core collection that can result in many interesting timbres. The key to discovering the possibilities in unfamiliar effects plug-ins is to use your knowledge of the plug-ins discussed here to guide your experimentation. The core chapters in this book on synthesis and sampling techniques can help you to generate rich, powerful timbres that can then be processed in creative ways using the effects described in this chapter.

CHAPTER 9

MIDI in Detail

Chapter 3: MIDI, Sequencing, and Software Instruments Overview introduced MIDI **channel messages**, including note messages, expressive messages, and program messages, along with a brief mention of **system messages**. Subsequent chapters explored the use of these messages to control the parameters of software synthesizers and samplers. In this chapter we will explore MIDI messages in detail.

As we delve into the details of these messages, it is important to remember that the value of MIDI messages lies in the control that they allow us over synthesizers and samplers. The reason for understanding these details, then, is that it allows us to make more effective use of these electronic resources.

STATUS BYTES AND DATA BYTES

MIDI messages are digital, and the information contained in them is split up into separate **bytes**, each consisting of eight binary digits, or **bits**. There are two types of bytes in MIDI: status bytes and data bytes.

The information in a **status byte** indicates what **type of message** it is, such as note-on, note-off, pitch bend, or aftertouch, as well as the **channel** for channel messages. The status byte for system messages indicates the type of message (system) and then which specific system message it is. Because system messages are not directed to any channel, there's no channel indicated in the status byte. Due to the way the status byte is constructed, there are a total of only eight message types in MIDI—a small enough number that we can learn at least the basics of each.

The channel information in a channel message status byte is used by a multitimbral synth to direct the message to the appropriate timbre on the synth. Most hardware synths and samplers are multitimbral and thus make use of channel information. A number of software synths and samplers are also multitimbral, but many are monotimbral. There are also still some specialized hardware synths and legacy hardware synths that are monotimbral. Those synths have either a single receive channel or will receive messages on all channels (omni mode). A synth with a single receive channel will read the channel number of an incoming MIDI message and ignore the message if it doesn't match its receive channel. Hardware synths set to receive in omni mode act on all messages regardless of channel.

Status bytes are followed by some number of **data bytes** that provide the synth with the actual information it needs to generate sound. The message type contained in the status byte tells the synth how to interpret the data bytes that follow. We've already encountered a number of pieces of information that are encoded as data bytes, including the key number, velocity, pressure value, and pitch bend value. System messages can have from zero to many data bytes, but channel messages have only one or two data bytes.

Technically Speaking

TECHNICALLY SPEAKING . . . MIDI BYTES

Technically speaking . . . MIDI bytes are made up of eight bits (binary digits), which can take on values of only 0 or 1. Status bytes and data bytes are differentiated in MIDI by their most significant bit (MSB), or the bit with the greatest place value. MSB can also stand for most significant *byte* in other circumstances, so it is important to keep track of whether we're talking about bits or bytes. The MSB for a status byte is always 1 and the MSB for a data byte is always 0.

Status bytes for channel messages indicate the type of message and the channel number. The highest four bits—the bits with the highest value—are used for the message type and the bottom four bits are used for the channel number (see Figure 9.1). Since eight bits is a "byte," four bits is sometimes referred to as a "nibble" (really!). Because the MSB in a status byte is always 1, only three of the highest four bits can change. This means that there are actually only *three* bits available to indicate the message type. Three bits form eight unique combinations ($2^3 = 8$): 000, 001, 010, 011, 100, 101, 110, and 111. Those eight combinations represent the eight possible MIDI message types—seven channel messages and the system messages.

The lowest four bits indicate the channel number for MIDI channel messages and the specific system message type for system messages. Four bits can form sixteen unique combinations ($2^4 = 16$): 0000, 0001, 0010, 0011, 0100, 0101, 0110, 0111, 1000, 1001, 1010, 1011, 1100, 1101, 1110, and 1111. This is the origin of the sixteen-channel limitation in MIDI, which derives directly from the binary structure of its messages. If the creators of MIDI had foreseen the demand for more than sixteen MIDI channels they might have chosen to give the channel number its own data byte, which would have increased the possibilities from 16 to 128. However, there were few signs in 1983 that such a demand would develop. Since these same four bits are used to indicate the specific system message, there are also sixteen possible system messages, though not all are in use.

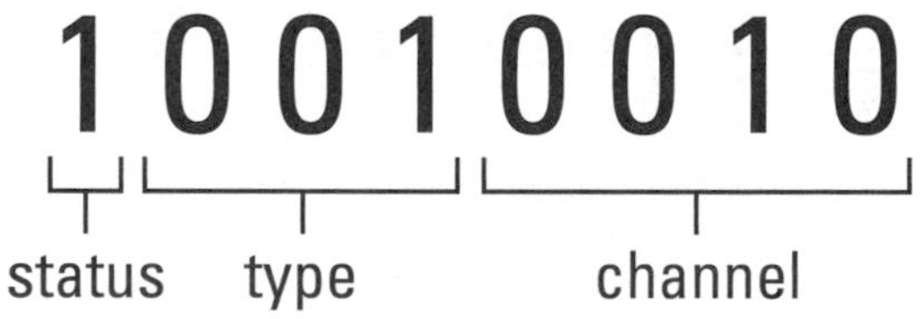

1 0 0 1 0 0 1 0

status   type   channel

Figure 9.1 Anatomy of a status byte: most significant bit of "1" indicates a status byte, message type shown is note-on, and channel shown is 3

As you can see above, the MIDI channel numbers range, in binary form, from 0000 to 1111, which translates to 0 to 15 in base-10 numbering. Counting from 0 is standard in computing, but unusual elsewhere, so MIDI channels are usually numbered from 1 to 16. For example, if a status byte has the lower four bits of 1100, that would be converted into decimal value and then channel number as follows:

Place value	$2^3 = 8$	$2^2 = 4$	$2^1 = 2$	$2^0 = 1$
Bit value (0 or 1)	1	1	0	0

Decimal equivalent = $(1 \times 8) + (1 \times 4) + (0 \times 2) + (0 \times 1) = 12$

Value of 0 = Channel 1, so

Value of 12 = Channel 13

This "off by one" counting issue occurs in several instances in MIDI practice, such as with patch numbers. However, it's not consistent, so you have to be aware of when you start counting from 1 and when you start counting from 0.

Of the eights bits in a **data byte**, the most significant bit (MSB) is always a 0 (see Figure 9.2). This tells the receiving device that this byte is supporting information for the message type indicated in the previously received status byte; no new message is starting. The remaining seven bits can form 128 different combinations ($2^7 = 128$), ranging from binary 00000000 to 01111111, or 0–127 in decimal. You can derive the maximum decimal value for a data byte from the binary representation as follows:

Place value	$2^7 = 128$	$2^6 = 64$	$2^5 = 32$	$2^4 = 16$	$2^3 = 8$	$2^2 = 4$	$2^1 = 2$	$2^0 = 1$
Bit value (0 or 1)	0	1	1	1	1	1	1	1

Decimal equivalent = $(0 \times 128) + (1 \times 64) + (1 \times 32) + (1 \times 16) + (1 \times 8) + (1 \times 4) + (1 \times 2) + (1 \times 1) = 127$

As you can see, the 0–127 range that we've been seeing all along derives directly from the binary structure of MIDI data bytes. There are some MIDI messages, such as bank change

Technically Speaking

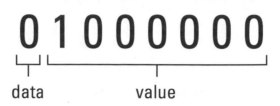

data   value

Figure 9.2 Anatomy of a data byte: most significant bit of "0" indicates a data byte; the value shown is 64 (2^6)

and pitch bend, that combine two data bytes together to create a larger data range. This will be discussed a little later in the chapter.

We've been using binary numbers in this sidebar in order to understand the basic structures of status bytes and data bytes. However, you will never encounter binary numbers while working with a DAW/Sequencer or synth and they are seldom seen even in detailed documentation. There is one non-base-10 type of counting system that is used regularly in detailed documentation: the hexadecimal system or base 16.

In MIDI, you encounter hexadecimal numbers with two hex digits: the 16's place and the 1's place (16^1 and 16^0). Since each hex digit can accommodate sixteen different numbers, the numbers 0–9 plus the letters A, B, C, D, E, and F (which are stand-ins for 10, 11, 12, 13, 14, and 15) are used. Hex numbers are often indicated as such by a preceding "0x" or a trailing "H". So 7FH and 0x7F are the same hexadecimal number.

To convert to decimal, you multiply each digit by its place value and add them together. For example, the hexadecimal number 7F has a decimal equivalent of $(7 \times 16) + (15 \times 1) = 127$. The maximum value that can be represented by two hex digits is 0xFF = $(15 \times 16) + (15 \times 1) = 255$. Thus two hex digits are equivalent to a standard eight-bit byte whose values also range from 0 to 255.

As you can see, 0x7F (127) would be the maximum value for MIDI data bytes, which range from 0x00 to 0x7F. The hex numbers 0x80 to 0xFF are MIDI status bytes. Since half of a status byte is used for the channel in a channel message, the channel is indicated in hex in the rightmost hex digit. So, 0x80 is a note-off on channel 1, 0x81 is a note-off on channel 2, . . . , 0x8F is a note-off on channel 16. Note the off-by-one issue discussed previously. The left-most hex digit indicates the type of MIDI message:

- 0x80–0x8F are note-off status bytes.
- 0x90–0x9F are note-on status bytes.
- 0xA0–0xAF are poly pressure status bytes.
- 0xB0–0xBF are control change status bytes.
- 0xC0–0xCF are program change status bytes.
- 0xD0–0xDF are channel pressure status bytes.
- 0xE0–0xEF are pitch bend status bytes.
- 0xF0–0xFF are system message status bytes.

OVERVIEW OF MIDI CHANNEL MESSAGES

Of the eight MIDI messages, seven of them are channel messages, each of which has a status byte that indicates the message type and the channel followed by one or two data bytes that provide the necessary information for that type of message. There are some exceptions to this one-or-two-data-bytes rule that will be discussed later in the chapter. Table 9.1 provides an overview of the status bytes and data bytes for each of the MIDI channel messages. Each message will be discussed in detail below.

NOTE MESSAGES

As discussed previously, note-on messages contain a channel number, a key number, and a velocity value. The type of message (note-on) and the channel are contained in the status byte, the key number is the first data byte following the status byte, and the velocity is the second data byte following the status byte. As with all data bytes, the key number and velocity each range from 0 to 127:

Status byte	Data byte 1	Data byte 2
Note-on/channel (1–16)	Key number (0–127)	Velocity (0–127)

The note-off message is similar to the note-on message except that the second data byte represents the release velocity. Receiving synthesizers seldom utilize this value when generating sound and many keyboards don't transmit it, sending a "dummy" value (usually 64) instead.

Status byte	Data byte 1	Data byte 2
Note-off/channel	Key number	Release velocity

Table 9.1 MIDI channel messages

Status byte	Data byte 1	Data byte 2
Note-on/channel	Key number	Velocity
Note-off/channel	Key number	Release velocity
Program change/channel	Program number	[none]
Control change/channel	Control number	Control value
Channel pressure/channel	Pressure value	[none]
Poly pressure/channel	Key number	Pressure value
Pitch bend/channel	Fine value (LSB)	Coarse value (MSB)

In order for a note-off message to actually turn off a previous note-on message, the channel and key number must match. For example, you might generate the following messages when playing and releasing a note on a keyboard:

Note-on/channel 3	72	80
Note-off/channel 3	72	64

The first message indicates the C above middle C was struck with medium speed (127 being the maximum possible). Key number 60 is middle C, so key number 72 would be "C4" if middle C were defined as "C3." This message was sent to channel 3 of the receiving device. The second message indicates that C4 was lifted either with a medium release speed or the keyboard does not generate release velocity values (so 64 would be a "dummy" value). This message was also sent to channel 3 of the receiving device.

The release velocity is one of those good ideas in MIDI that doesn't get used much. The velocity value in a note-on message allows you to shape the volume and attack of a note during performance. The release velocity was designed to allow you to also shape the end of a note (the release) during performance. If you were to lift a key quickly, you could indicate that the note should release quickly (staccato). If you were to lift the key slowly, you could indicate that the note should release slowly (legato). This is a potentially powerful idea, but today very few synths respond to the release velocity. Regardless of the value, the sound engine of the synthesizer usually ignores the release velocity.

In fact, many controllers, keyboard synths, and sequencers don't send note-off messages at all. Instead they substitute a note-on message with a velocity of 0, which is defined in the MIDI specification as being the equivalent of a Note-Off message. So both of the following combinations of messages do the same thing:

Note-on/channel 5	66	45
Note-off/channel 5	66	64

Or:

Note-on/channel 5	66	45
Note-on/channel 5	66	0

The reason for this equivalency is related to the speed with which MIDI messages are transmitted and the concept of running status. See the sidebar "Technically Speaking . . . the MIDI data rate."

TECHNICALLY SPEAKING . . . THE MIDI DATA RATE

Technically speaking . . . MIDI messages are transmitted down a MIDI cable at a speed of 31,250 bits per second (bits per second is also referred to as the "baud rate"). As we saw in the sidebar "Technically Speaking . . . MIDI bytes," both status bytes and data bytes are made up of eight bits each. However, during transmission two additional bits are added to each byte, a "start" bit and a "stop" bit, bringing the bit total to ten for each status and data byte. You can determine how long it takes to transmit a MIDI status byte or data byte as follows:

$$10 \text{ bits} \div 31{,}250 \text{ bits per second} = 0.00032 \text{ seconds} = 0.32 \text{ ms (milliseconds)}$$

This means that a note-on message, which consists of three bytes—status byte, data byte for key number, and data byte for velocity—would take:

$$3 \text{ bytes} \times 0.32 \text{ ms per byte} = 0.96 \text{ ms} \approx 1 \text{ ms}$$

One millisecond is, of course, an exceptionally short amount of time, but since MIDI messages are transmitted serially, one bit at a time, each additional MIDI message adds 1 ms to the time delay. The note-on messages for a ten-note chord would take 10 ms from the time the first note-on was received until the time that the last note was received and then another 10 ms once the note-offs were transmitted. If pitch bend messages or modulation wheel messages are also sent at the same time, the delay between the notes could become perceptible. Perceptibility of such a delay will depend in part on the characteristics of the particular timbres. For example, delays on a patch with a long attack will be harder to perceive than delays on a patch with a short attack.

One way to reduce these delays is through the use of **running status**. Running status allows transmitting devices to skip sending a status byte when it is a repeat of the status byte in the immediately preceding message: the status is allowed to "run." The receiver is programmed to process a long stream of data bytes as if each one- or two-data byte group has been preceded by that status byte. This is particularly valuable for messages such as pitch bend, aftertouch, and control change messages where the performance gestures (e.g. moving the pitch bend wheel) can generate dozens or hundreds of messages in a short span of time. In fact, many controllers and sequencers have a function that allows them to "thin" controller data by eliminating some percentage of those messages.

As we saw in the discussion of note messages, it is common for a controller to send a note-on message with a velocity of zero instead of an actual note-off message. Since these two messages have the same status bytes, running status can be used. Thus the following two sets of messages are equivalent:

| Note-on/channel 5 | 66 | 45 |
| Note-on/channel 5 | 66 | 0 |

Or:

Note-on/channel 5	66	45
	66	0

Over the course of many notes, pitch bend messages, aftertouch, and control change messages, the data reduction due to running status approaches about one-third. This could be the difference between perceivable delay and unperceivable delay and thus the difference between acceptable and unacceptable playback for devices connected by MIDI cables.

PRESSURE (AFTERTOUCH) MESSAGES

Aftertouch messages are usually sent from a synth when you play a key and then press down further, activating a sensor beneath the keys. These messages allow you to perform with both hands on your keyboard and still cause the kinds of modifications to the sound that usually require you to move a wheel, slider, or knob. Not every keyboard controller is equipped to send aftertouch messages and some controllers assign a slider or knob to send aftertouch instead. There are two types of aftertouch messages: channel pressure and polyphonic key pressure.

Channel pressure messages contain a channel number and a pressure value:

Status byte	Data byte 1	Data byte 2
Channel pressure/channel	Pressure value (0–127)	[none]

Channel pressure messages set the pressure value for the entire channel. If you're playing a chord and press down to send channel pressure—also known as "monophonic aftertouch"—only one value will be sent at a time for the whole channel regardless of how many keys are pressed. As mentioned in Chapter 3: MIDI, Sequencing, and Software Instruments Overview, channel pressure messages can be mapped to any sound parameter of the synth, but they are often used to control vibrato (controlling an LFO that is mapped to pitch) or the cutoff frequency of a filter. Some alternate controllers such as wind controllers can send channel pressure messages in response to breath pressure on the instrument.

Polyphonic key pressure messages—also known as "polyphonic aftertouch" or "poly pressure"—contain a channel number, a key number, and a pressure value:

Status byte	Data byte 1	Data byte 2
Poly pressure/channel	Key number (0–127)	Pressure value (0–127)

The addition of the key number allows you to send different pressure values for each key that you're pressing. This means that you can modify the sound on a key-by-key basis, such as playing a chord in which each note has a somewhat different amount of vibrato or different values for the filter cutoff. This message has had some interesting applications in experimental circles, but it is not widely used: very few keyboard controllers send this message and very few synthesizers are programmed to respond to it.

PITCH BEND MESSAGES

The pitch bend message probably has the most obvious function: it bends the pitch. Pitch bend is usually sent from a dedicated wheel or from a joystick that combines modulation control change and pitch bend. The pitch bend message contains a channel number and a pitch bend value that is split between two data bytes—a coarse value (most significant byte, or MSB) and a fine value (least significant byte, or LSB):

Status byte	Data byte 1	Data byte 2
Pitch bend/channel	Fine value or LSB (0–127)	Coarse value or MSB (0–127)

Each data byte ranges from 0 to 127, but when they are combined, the value ranges from 0 to 16,383 (see the "Technically Speaking . . . MSB and LSB" sidebar on page 214). This is true of all MIDI messages whose values are expressed as an MSB and an LSB. A value of 0 represents the pitch bent all the way down, a value of 8,192 represents no pitch bend, and a value of 16,383 represents the pitch bent all the way up. Often these values are shown in a sequencer centered around 0 so that −8,192 will be all the way down, 0 will be no change, and 8,191 will be all the way up. This is a much more intuitive display than having to remember that 8,192 represents no pitch bend.

Pitch bend is separated out for this special treatment because we are more sensitive to changes in pitch than we are to changes in other sound parameters. Because the pitch bend values are digital, pitch bend is always going to be a series of steps up or down in pitch, but by using the larger data range, it will sound as if it's a continuous change.

The other motivation for the large range of values is that the response to pitch bend (pitch bend sensitivity) is up to the receiving device. A synth may interpret pitch bend fully up/down as +/−2 semitones, +/− two octaves, or anything else determined by the synthesizer manufacturer. This response can be set globally on a synth, on a

TECHNICALLY SPEAKING . . . MSB AND LSB

Technically speaking . . . by combining two data bytes into a single composite number, the data range for that parameter can be expanded from 0–127 to 0–16,383. Pitch bend is the most common use of this data byte combining, but a similar principle is at work in bank change messages and other high-resolution controllers (see "Control Change Messages" later in the chapter).

Each data byte by itself consists of a 0 in the most significant bit followed by seven bits that can be ones or zeroes. The binary range, then, is 00000000 to 01111111, which we saw converted to decimal values of 0–127 in the "Technically Speaking . . . MIDI bytes" sidebar. When two data bytes are combined, one byte is defined as the most significant byte (MSB) and the other the least significant byte (LSB). The seven bits in each that can change are combined into one 14-bit number with the bits from the most significant byte (MSB) taking on the higher place values and the bits from the least significant byte (LSB) taking on the lower place values. You should note that the "B" in MSB and LSB is used variously to refer to "bit" or "byte" depending on the context. The MSB/LSB combination for the minimum, midpoint, and maximum value works as follows:

	Most significant byte (MSB)							Least significant byte (LSB)						
Original place	2^6	2^5	2^4	2^3	2^2	2^1	2^0	2^6	2^5	2^4	2^3	2^2	2^1	2^0
Value	64	32	16	8	4	2	1	64	32	16	8	4	2	1
Combined	2^{13}	2^{12}	2^{11}	2^{10}	2^9	2^8	2^7	2^6	2^5	2^4	2^3	2^2	2^1	2^0
Place value	8,192	4,096	2,048	1,024	512	256	128	64	32	16	8	4	2	1
Minimum bit values	0	0	0	0	0	0	0	0	0	0	0	0	0	0
Midpoint bit values	1	0	0	0	0	0	0	0	0	0	0	0	0	0
Maximum bit values	1	1	1	1	1	1	1	1	1	1	1	1	1	1

- For the minimum bit values, each byte has a value, according to the original byte place values of 0, and the decimal equivalent of the combined bytes is 0.
- For the midpoint bit values, the MSB has a value, according to the original byte place values, of 64, the LSB has a value, according to the original byte place values, of 0, and the decimal equivalent of the combined bytes is $1 \times 8,192 = 8,192$.
- For the maximum bit values, each byte has a value, according to the original byte place values, of 127, the decimal equivalent is:

Maximum bit value decimal equivalent = $(1 \times 8,192) + (1 \times 4,096) + (1 \times 2,048) + (1 \times 1,024) + (1 \times 512) + (1 \times 256) + (1 \times 128) + (1 \times 64) + (1 \times 32) + (1 \times 16) + (1 \times 8) + (1 \times 4) + (1 \times 2) + (1 \times 1) = 16,383$

Technically Speaking

For pitch bend messages where the data byte order is LSB then MSB, the minimum, midpoint, and maximum would be represented as follows:

Bent all the way down: LSB = 0, MSB = 0

No bend: LSB = 0, MSB = 64

Bent all the way up: LSB = 127, MSB = 127

The MSB is referred to as the "coarse" value and the LSB the "fine" value. The reason for this is that between each MSB value there are 128 LSB values, so the LSB is seen as a fine-tuning of the MSB value. This is similar conceptually to the way that changes in semitones and octaves are "coarse" modifications to pitch while changes in cents are "fine" modifications to pitch.

patch-by-patch basis, or changed by an RPN message where supported (see "Control Change Messages" below).

If a synth's up/down response to pitch bend is +/−2 semitones and pitch bend has only the standard 0–127 range, then each semitone will only be divided into 32 steps, which is one-third of the usual division of a semitone into 100 cents, resulting in minimum steps in the pitch bend message of 3 cents. Steps that are 3 cents in size are pretty small, but might be hearable to sensitive ears. If the up/down range is +/−24 semitones and the PB range is only 0–127, then each semitone will only be divided into 3 steps resulting in steps of 33 cents, which everyone would be able to hear. However, with an up/down setting of +/−24 and a PB range of 0–16,383, then each semitone is divided up into 341 steps, or about 0.3 cents per step, a step far too small for even sensitive ears to detect.

PROGRAM CHANGE MESSAGES

Program change messages contain a channel number and a program number. The type of message (program change) and the channel are contained in the status byte and the program number is contained in the subsequent data byte. There is no second data byte for a program change message.

Status byte	Data byte 1	Data byte 2
Program change/channel	Program number (0–127)	[none]

This message causes the receiving synth to access a program, or "patch," from a memory location indicated by the program number. On a hardware synth, this memory is often referred to as "parameter RAM" (PRAM) or "parameter ROM" (PROM) depending whether the program parameters are stored in changeable ("user") or permanent ("preset") memory respectively.

The program number data byte, which ranges from 0 to 127, allows you to select a patch from 128 different possibilities numbered in the synth from 0 to 127 or from 1 to 128. This is the same "off by one" problem we encountered earlier in the "Technically Speaking . . . MIDI bytes" sidebar when discussing the numbering of MIDI channels. The decimal equivalent of the actual binary digits sent in a program number data byte ranges from 0 to 127. However, regular people (and musicians) are generally more comfortable counting objects such as channels and patches from 1 than counting from 0, so the first patch in some synthesizers is patch 1 while in others it's patch 0. You just have to be aware of which counting scheme your synthesizer uses. This is most critical when creating or modifying the patchlists used by sequencing software.

Program messages are most important when you're using hardware synthesizers or samplers. In software synthesizers and samplers, the patch is most often called up from the instrument's interface or through the DAW/Sequencer. Program messages are also used to call up presets on devices that are not sound generators, such as lighting boards and audio processors.

At the time MIDI was created, few synthesizers had large preset memories. The DX7, which came out in 1983, had a relatively large memory space for its time—thirty-two programs with sixty-four more available on a cartridge—so the 128 memory locations that could be addressed by the program change message would have seemed more than sufficient. However, as in all areas of computing, memory size has expanded dramatically so that the 128-program limitation in the program change message is no longer sufficient to address the number of patches available on the average synthesizer. To accommodate this, two control numbers from the control change message were assigned to be bank change messages: 0 and 32. Control change messages will be discussed more thoroughly later, but it is useful to discuss bank change messages in the context of the program change message.

Bank Select Messages

Control change messages contain a channel number, a control number, and a control value.

Status byte	Data byte 1	Data byte 2
Control change/channel	Control number (0–127)	Control value (0–127)

The control number data byte allows the control change message to be split into 128 "sub-messages," each with its own control number. The two "sub-messages" of concern here are control number 0 (abbreviated as CC0) and control number 32 (CC32)—the bank select messages.

Each of these messages takes on a control value in the second data byte. Some synthesizers require only one bank change message (CC0) plus the program change message to call up a program (patch) on the synth. In that case, these two messages would be sufficient to call specify a patch:

Control change/channel #	0	4
Program change/channel #	82	

In the above messages, the control change message indicates the bank 4. This bank is actually the 5th bank because 0 would indicate the first bank—the same off-by-one problem as the program change message itself above. The program change message then indicates program number 82—the 83rd program using the same logic. This combination allows for 128 banks of 128 patches each, which yields $128 \times 128 = 16,384$ different patches.

Some synths require both bank select messages (CC0 and CC32) in addition to the program change message to properly indicate the storage location of a patch. In that case these three messages would be required:

Control change/channel #	0	0–127
Control change/channel #	32	0–127
Program change/channel #	0–127	

Here the MSB provided by the CC0 control value combines with the LSB provided by the CC32 control value to allow for 16,384 banks (see the "Technically Speaking . . . MSB and LSB" sidebar earlier in the chapter). Each of those banks can have 128 patches selected by the program number of the program change message, yielding 16,384 banks × 128 patches = 2,097,152 different patches that can be addressed by this scheme. That would certainly seem to be enough patches for the foreseeable future!

It is worth noting that had the creators of MIDI chosen to add a second data byte to the program change message, one data byte could be used to choose the bank and the second data byte used to choose the program (patch) within that bank. This scheme would have been able to address 128 banks of 128 programs each allowing for a total of $128 \times 128 = 16,384$ separate patches. This would have made the bank change messages largely unnecessary, because the number of patches available now on even high-end hardware synthesizers is fewer than 16,384.

Patchlists

A DAW/Sequencer that is transmitting bank change and program change messages doesn't really "know" ahead of time what program is stored at that location on the receiving device, despite the fact that you usually choose the desired patch by name. The names are provided to the DAW/Sequencer through a patchlist, which is a simple file on your computer that lists patch names and their associated bank change and program change values.

This provides the illusion that your DAW/Sequencer "knows" what patches are on your synth or that the patches on your synth come from the DAW/Sequencer itself. If you were to change the name of the patch on the hardware synth itself, your DAW/Sequencer wouldn't know that it had changed until you went in and actively changed it in the patchlist on your computer. In general, you choose patches for software synthesizers from the main window of the software synth itself, so details of patchlists are only of concern when you're dealing with a hardware synthesizer.

Figure 9.3 shows an excerpt from a patchlist for a Korg Triton synthesizer in the .midnam patchlist file format. Near the top of this listing are the CC0 and CC32 values required to call up patches in this bank. The rest of the list provides patch names in the bank and their associated program numbers. In your DAW/Sequencer, you would select the patch by patch name, and the DAW/Sequencer would read this patchlist file and send the necessary CC0, CC32, and program change messages to call up the chosen patch.

```
<PatchBank Name="Program Bank C" >
    <MIDICommands>
        <ControlChange Control="0" Value="0" />
        <ControlChange Control="32" Value="2" />
    </MIDICommands>
    <PatchNameList>
        <Patch Number="C000" Name="Techno Phonic" ProgramChange="0" />
        <Patch Number="C001" Name="Warm E.Grand" ProgramChange="1" />
        <Patch Number="C002" Name="Rave &lt;Ribbon&gt;" ProgramChange="2" />
        <Patch Number="C003" Name="Stereo Strings" ProgramChange="3" />
        <Patch Number="C004" Name="WAcKy HiPHop Kit" ProgramChange="4" />
        <Patch Number="C005" Name="Spanish Guitar" ProgramChange="5" />
        <Patch Number="C006" Name="Phat Bass" ProgramChange="6" />
        <Patch Number="C007" Name="Dirty 'B'" ProgramChange="7" />
        <Patch Number="C008" Name="Super Sweeper" ProgramChange="8" />
        <Patch Number="C009" Name="DynaBrassStereo1" ProgramChange="9" />
        <Patch Number="C010" Name="&lt;ReverseVoxBox&gt;" ProgramChange="10" />
        <Patch Number="C011" Name="Vocalscaping" ProgramChange="11" />

                        . . .

        <Patch Number="C124" Name="Brian's Sync" ProgramChange="124" />
        <Patch Number="C125" Name="PanFlute" ProgramChange="125" />
        <Patch Number="C126" Name="Glass Vox" ProgramChange="126" />
        <Patch Number="C127" Name="Bottle-Bell" ProgramChange="127" />
    </PatchNameList>
</PatchBank>
```

Figure 9.3 Excerpt from the patchlist for a Korg Triton

General MIDI

Different receiving synths often have different patches stored at a given memory location, so program number 35 in a particular bank on a Korg synth might be a string sound while program 35 in the same numbered bank on a Yamaha might be a "whoosh" sound. At first, this may seem chaotic, but a selling point for many synths, particularly in the professional market, is a unique sound set. Standardizing sound sets removes that uniqueness.

Nevertheless, there are cases where a predictable sound set is more important than a unique one. This is particularly true in educational settings, videogame music, cell phone ring tones, and when transferring files between differing studio setups. The General MIDI System Level 1 (GM or GM1, adopted in 1991) and the General MIDI System Level 2 (GM2, adopted in 1999) were developed as additions to the MIDI specification to provide just such consistent sound sets between synths that are labeled as GM1 or GM2 compatible. GM1 and GM2 in particular also specify consistent responses to a certain subset of MIDI messages and consistent sound production capabilities.

The General MIDI System Levels 1 and 2 specifications include:

- a minimum number of simultaneous voices (polyphony): 24 for GM1 and 32 for GM2;
- support for sixteen simultaneous MIDI channels (sixteen-part multitimbral) with channel 10 as a dedicated "rhythm" channel (percussion) in GM1 and both channel 10 and 11 available as rhythm channels in GM2;
- a minimum of 128 (GM1) or 256 (GM2) programs (patches) in which program numbers are mapped to specific program names;
- a minimum of forty-seven preset percussion sounds in the standard drum kit for GM1 and sixty-one for GM2 conforming to the "GM Percussion Map";
- one Standard drum kit for GM1 and ten for GM2;
- a standard octave definition (key 60 is middle C), standard pitch bend range (+/−2 semitones), standard definitions for several controllers, response to velocity, aftertouch (channel pressure), and support for several universal system exclusive messages including messages to turn the GM1 or GM2 modes on and off.

Though the key element of GM is often considered the standardized sound set, GM, and GM2 in particular, also represents an effort to create common standards for the ways in which a synthesizer responds to MIDI messages. In this respect, GM2 can be seen as some of the most up-to-date thinking about how a synth should respond to MIDI messages. However, only GM2 synths are *required* to implement those more standardized responses.

CONTROL CHANGE MESSAGES

The bank change messages discussed above are specific instances of the control change message (CC). Control change messages contain a channel number, a control number, and a control value.

Status byte	Data byte 1	Data byte 2
Control change/channel	Control number (0–127)	Control value (0–127)

Of all the channel messages, control change is the most complex and flexible in that it really contains 128 "sub-messages" selected by the control number. These messages can be combined to create a wider data range than is available with the single control value data byte or to indicate still more "sub-messages" in the form of Registered Parameter Numbers (RPNs) and Non-Registered Parameter Numbers (NRPNs). Control change messages have the same status byte as another group of messages known as channel mode messages. Though they are structured like control change messages, channel mode messages change the way a receiving device responds to channel messages. Channel mode messages will be discussed in a later section of the chapter.

It is important to note that not all sound-producing devices implement all of these messages. As with all things MIDI, it is up to the receiving device what it does with the messages it receives. Only GM1 or GM2 compatible synths are required to respond in specific ways to control change messages, and even they are not required to respond to all of them.

To accommodate this fact, the MIDI specification includes instructions for manufacturers to create a **MIDI implementation chart** that details what messages are transmitted and what messages can be received by a particular device. This chart is typically included in a device's manual. A "version 2" of the MIDI implementation chart has been created that is three pages long and provides a clearer format for indicating the device's support for transmitting and receiving each of the MIDI messages. If your synth doesn't respond to MIDI messages as expected, the MIDI implementation chart should be the first resource for determining the cause of the problem.

Commonly Used Controllers

There are many controllers, but only a handful of them are used on a day-to-day basis and are interpreted predictably by most synthesizers. These include the bank select messages (bank change, CC0 and CC32), Modulation Wheel (CC1), Channel Volume (CC7), Pan (CC10), Expression (CC11), and Sustain (CC64). A few other controllers such as Data Entry (CC6) and Breath Control (CC2) also get used from time to time, but their effect on the synth patch is less predictable. The bank select messages (bank change, CC0 and CC32) were discussed in detail above.

The **Modulation Wheel** controller (CC1) is typically assigned to a physical wheel or joystick on a synth. Its effect on a patch varies from patch to patch, but it is often used to add vibrato or to control the cutoff frequency of a filter (see Chapter 4: Synthesis, Sampling, and MIDI Control and Chapter 5: Modulation and Dynamic Sound). A value of 0 typically represents no effect and 127 maximum effect, though there is nothing to prevent it from being implemented the other way around on the synth. What constitutes the "maximum" effect (for example, the maximum amount of vibrato or maximum cutoff frequency for the filter) is usually programmed in the patch itself as part of a modulation routing (see Chapter 5: Modulation and Dynamic Sound), but it can also be set using a Registered Parameter Number (discussed later). In practice, you typically use however much of the CC1 range is expressively useful and change the programming of the patch if the maximum effect needs to be increased.

The **Pan** controller (CC10) sets the position of the timbre in the left–right stereo field for a given channel (pan is short for "panorama"). This allows the user to manage the stereo position of the timbres assigned to each of the sixteen MIDI channels independently. Pan messages can be sent by a knob on a controller or by using the virtual knobs in a DAW/Sequencer. The control value for CC10 ranges from 0 to 127 with 0 representing hard left (all the sound coming out of the left speaker), 64 representing the middle (equal amounts of sound coming out of both speakers), and 127 representing hard right (all the sound coming out of the right speaker). Some software and some synthesizers indicate pan positions as −63 for left to +63 for right or 63L to 63R.

The simplest way for a synth to implement panning would be to multiply the amplitude of the signal in the left and right channels by the following:

Left: multiply by (127 − CC10)/127

Right: multiply by (CC10/127)

If CC10 was 0, then the left channel would be multiplied by one ((127 − 0)/127) and the right channel by 0 (0/127), making the signal panned hard left. If CC10 was 64, then each side would be multiplied by $64/127 \approx 0.5$, making the signal panned to the center. If CC10 was 127, then the left channel would be multiplied by 0 and the right by 1, making the signal panned hard right. This is "linear" panning, because when the curve is plotted it forms a straight line (see Figure 9.4a).

Though this seems logical, this type of panning results in a "hole" in the middle of the stereo field where the sound is quieter than at either of the edges. The solution to this is to utilize **equal power panning**. This involves using the trigonometry functions sine and cosine so that the amplitude curves for each channel cross at a higher point in the middle, thereby alleviating that "hole." Fig 9.4b shows equal power curves for the amplitudes of the left and right channels. Similar equal power curves are used for crossfades in audio editing.

The **Channel Volume** controller (CC7) modifies the volume of a given channel on a synthesizer. This allows the user to manage the volume for each of the sixteen MIDI channels on a device independently. The volume knob on a hardware synthesizer controls that synthesizer's overall volume, but it may or may not cause main volume messages to be sent out. As a result, CC7s are most often set in a sequencing program using virtual fader automation or by using sliders on a controller that are mapped to CC7.

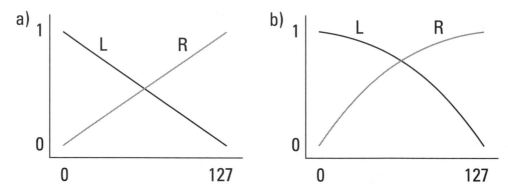

Figure 9.4 Panning curves: a) linear panning results in a "hole" in the middle (the amplitude curve for the right channel is shown in gray); b) equal-power panning results in a smooth transition from left to right

The control value for CC7 determines the gain for the channel, with 127 being no reduction in gain, resulting in maximum volume, and 0 an infinite gain reduction, resulting in no sound. If CC7 is being used to control the fader of an audio track in a DAW/Sequencer, the response of the fader due to CC7 may be set so that a value of 127 provides some positive gain, such as +6 dB, as would be typical for the maximum fader position on a mixing board.

Because CC7 controls the *gain*, or the change in loudness, rather than the absolute volume level, there is not necessarily a predictable relationship between the CC7 control value and the resultant loudness for given channel. An inherently loud sound, such as a sample of an explosion, on a channel with a CC7 value of 64 could easily be louder than an inherently quiet sound, such as a sample of a kitten's meow or a heavily filtered waveform, on a channel with a CC7 value of 127. For many synths (hardware and software), CC7 is the primary control of volume for a given channel, so that crescendos or diminuendos are created by a series of CC7 messages with changing control values. However, for some synths and samplers, the expression controller is also used.

The **Expression controller** (CC11) was designed to be used in conjunction with CC7 to allow you to set the overall volume modification on a channel with CC7 and then make expressive volume modifications to that with CC11. In a synth or sampler that recognizes CC11, you would use CC7 to create a volume balance between instruments on different channels, and then use CC11 to create crescendos and diminuendos on each individual channel (see Figure 9.5).

CC11 operates by *reducing* the gain set by CC7. For example, if CC7 was set to 80 for a particular channel, setting CC11 to 127 would result in an effective volume value of 80 (no change). If CC11 was set to 64 (the half-way point in its range) on that channel, the effective volume value would be $0.5 \times 80 = 40$. If CC11 were set to 32 (a quarter of the way through its range), the effective volume value would be $0.25 \times 80 = 20$. The formula is:

Effective volume setting = (CC11 value ÷ 127) × CC7 value

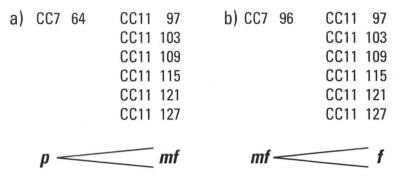

Figure 9.5   The change in CC7 from a) to b) causes different beginning and ending dynamics for the crescendo created by the CC11 messages. The jump between CC11 values is for graphical convenience

Table 9.2 shows the effective volume value for various CC11 values given a CC7 value of 110 (moderately high). The relationship between CC7 and CC11 is detailed in the General MIDI 2 specification, so it is only strictly in force in synths that are General MIDI 2 compatible.

The combination of CC7 and CC11 determine the gain for the channel, but the effective volume value is not itself a "gain" value, which is usually measured in decibels. The mathematical formulas as found in the General MIDI 2 standard are discussed in the "Technically Speaking . . . CC7 and CC11 gain" sidebar.

The **Sustain Pedal** controller, CC64, determines whether the notes on a given channel are held after their keys have been released. In other words, if the sustain pedal on a synthesizer is depressed while the performer is holding down one or more keys, those note-off messages will be deferred until the sustain pedal is released. This is referred to as a damper pedal on an acoustic piano because the pedal causes the dampers to be held away from the strings.

CC64 is a different type of controller from CCs 1, 7, 10, and 11. Those controllers are referred to as "continuous" controllers because their control values can range from 0 to 127. CC64 is a switch controller: it is either on (control value 127) or off (control value 0). The values between 0 and 63 are usually interpreted as "off" by a receiving

Table 9.2   The effective volume value when CC7 and CC11 are combined

CC11 value	Resultant multiplier	CC7 value	Effective volume value
127	1.00	110	110
96	0.75	110	83
64	0.50	110	55
32	0.25	110	28
0	0.00	110	0

TECHNICALLY SPEAKING . . . CC7 AND CC11 GAIN

Technically speaking . . . the gain change due to CC7 is given in the General MIDI 2 specification by the following formula:

$$\text{Gain in dB} = 40 \times \log_{10} (\text{CC7}/127)$$

When CC7 has a value of 127, the argument of the logarithm is 1 and the gain will be 0 dB, or no change in the output of the synthesizer or sampler. As the CC7 value falls below 127, the ratio of CC7 to 127 becomes smaller than 1 and hence the logarithm becomes negative. For example, a CC7 value of 96 yields a gain of –4.9 dB, or a reduction of 4.9 dB. When CC7 is 0, the equation is actually undefined, but as CC7 approaches 0, the equation approaches $-\infty$ dB, resulting in no sound, as we would expect.

The formula above is similar to the amplitude dB formula for dB FS that we saw in Chapter 2, except that the multiplication factor there was 20 instead of 40 and the reference amplitude was the maximum possible amplitude value for the system:

$$\text{dB FS} = 20 \times \log_{10} (A_{sig}/A_{max})$$

The GM2 spec states that the amplitude (they say "volume") is proportional to the square of the CC7 value. Making that substitution and inserting a value of 127 for the maximum value, we get:

$$\text{Gain in dB} = 20 \times \log_{10} (\text{CC7}^2/127^2) = 20 \times \log_{10} (\text{CC7}/127)^2$$

Using the exponent rule for logarithms, we get back the original equation:

$$\text{Gain in dB} = 40 \times \log_{10} (\text{CC7}/127)$$

The combination of CC7 and CC11 is given in the GM2 spec by the following formula:

$$\text{Gain in dB} = 40 \times \log_{10} (\text{CC7}/127) + 40 \times \log_{10} (\text{CC11}/127)$$

As you can see, the maximum gain in dB when both CC7 and CC11 are 127 is still 0 dB. Because CC7 is to be used for channel volume and CC11 for diminuendos and crescendos, the first term in that equation represents the gain reduction due to the channel volume and the second term a *further* reduction due to CC11. As a result, CC7 values determine the maximum volume for the channel and CC11 values below 127 reduce that volume.

In the main body of the text, I interpreted CC11/127 as a factor that reduces the effective CC7 value. You can derive that interpretation from the above equation by applying the addition rule of logarithms:

$$\text{Gain in dB} = 40 \times \log_{10} (\text{CC7}/127) + 40 \times \log_{10} (\text{CC11}/127)$$

$$\text{Gain in dB} = 40 \times \log_{10} ((\text{CC11}/127) \times (\text{CC7}/127))$$

This last equation can be seen as the same as the original equation for CC7 alone where the CC7 value is modified by the CC11/127 factor, yielding the same results shown in Table 9.2.

synth, and the values between 64 and 127 are usually interpreted as "on." As many pianists have noticed, this is a less refined control than the damper pedal on an acoustic piano, which allows half-pedaling and gradual pedaling.

Though the above CCs are the most common, there are many other useful control change messages. The following several sections detail the rest of the CCs.

Continuous Controllers

The first 32 of the 128 possible control numbers are typically referred to as continuous controllers because they can be sent as a series of messages with the same control number, but with changing control values that alter some parameter of the receiving synth in a continuous manner. Table 9.3 lists the first 32 control numbers (referred to as CC0 to CC31), notes any functions that are assigned, and comments on any unique features or typical usage.

Several of these control numbers imply a physical implementation of them on a synth: the Modulation Wheel controller (CC1) is associated with a wheel or joystick on the controller, the Breath Control (CC2) is associated with a device that fits in your mouth and is plugged into a controller which measures your breath pressure (also may be used for wind controllers), the Foot controller (CC4) is a continuous pedal that is plugged into the controller, the data entry controller (CC6) may be associated with a slider on the controller. Not all of these physical controllers are implemented on every MIDI controller.

High Resolution Controllers

Each of the next 32 controllers, CC32 to CC63, combines with its counterpart in the first 32 controllers to form a high-resolution controller (see Table 9.4). You've already seen that the control values for CC0 and CC32, the bank select messages, combine to allow for 16,384 banks (each of which can have 128 patches) and the two data bytes from a pitch bend message combine to allow for 16,384 different values.

Similarly, the control values for CC1 and CC33 combine to increase the possible modulation values from the 128 that are possible with just CC1 to 16,384 values. The control value for CC1 represents the most significant byte (MSB) and the control value for CC33 is the least significant byte (LSB). See the "Technically Speaking . . . MSB and LSB" sidebar earlier in the chapter for a detailed look at combining data bytes.

Despite the greater degree of control over parameters that MSB/LSB combinations allow, they are seldom used. The most significant exceptions to this are the bank change messages that you've already encountered: CC0 is the bank change MSB and CC32 is the bank change LSB. The MSB/LSB concept also figures prominently in the concept of Registered and Non-registered Parameters Numbers that will be discussed below.

Table 9.3   Continuous controllers CC0 to CC31

Control number	Control function	Notes
0	Bank select	Typically used along with CC32 to select a bank of patches. The program change message (patch change) then selects the specific patch within the bank.
1	Modulation wheel	Associated with a physical wheel or joystick on a synth/controller. Often controls vibrato.
2	Breath control	Associated with a wind controller or a breath control device that plugs into a jack on a synth/controller. Can control various parameters.
3	Undefined	
4	Foot controller	Associated with an expression pedal that plugs into a jack on a synth/controller. Can control various parameters.
5	Portamento time	Controls the amount of time that a synth "glides" between notes. Lower values create shorter portamento times (or faster portamento rates). Portamento is turned on/off by switch controller CC65.
6	Data entry	Sometimes associated with a slider on a synth/controller. Can control various parameters; used to set the value for Registered Parameter Numbers (RPNs) and Non-Registered Parameter Numbers (NRPNs).
7	Channel volume	Sometimes associated with a slider on a synth/controller. Modifies main volume for a channel.
8	Balance	Sets the balance between two different sounds sources with 0 giving full volume to one sound, 127 giving full volume to the other, and 64 giving each equal volume.
9	Undefined	
10	Pan	Sets position of sound in stereo field. 0 is hard left, 64 is in the middle, and 127 is hard right.
11	Expression	Modifies the volume of a channel as set by CC7 to allow temporary changes such as crescendos and diminuendos.
12	Effect control 1	Changes some parameter of a synth's built-in effects. Depends on specific synth programming.
13	Effect control 2	Changes some parameter of a synth's built-in effects. Depends on specific synth programming.
14	Undefined	
15	Undefined	
16	General purpose controller 1	Can be used to control some synthesizer parameter. Depends on specific synth programming.
17	General purpose controller 2	Can be used to control some synthesizer parameter. Depends on specific synth programming.
18	General purpose controller 3	Can be used to control some synthesizer parameter. Depends on specific synth programming.
19	General purpose controller 4	Can be used to control some synthesizer parameter. Depends on specific synth programming.
20–31	Undefined	

Table 9.4   Continuous controllers CC32 to CC63 (LSBs to CC0 to CC31)

Control number	Control function
32	LSB for CC0 (bank select)
33	LSB for CC1 (modulation wheel)
34	LSB for CC2 (breath controller)
35	LSB for CC3 (undefined)
36	LSB for CC 4 (foot controller)
37	LSB for CC5 (portamento time)
38	LSB for CC6 (data entry)
39	LSB for CC7 (channel volume)
40	LSB for CC8 (balance)
41	LSB for CC9 (undefined)
42	LSB for CC10 (pan)
43	LSB for CC11 (expression)
44	LSB for CC12 (effect control 1)
45	LSB for CC13 (effect control 2)
46	LSB for CC14 (undefined)
47	LSB for CC15 (undefined)
48	LSB for CC16 (general purpose controller 1)
49	LSB for CC16 (general purpose controller 2)
50	LSB for CC16 (general purpose controller 3)
51	LSB for CC16 (general purpose controller 4)
52–63	LSBs for CCs 20–31 (undefined)

Switch Controllers

There are several control numbers that correspond to switch controllers. Where continuous controllers are designed for synthesizer parameters that can take on the full 0–127 range of values, switch controllers are designed for synth parameters that are just on or off. Typically any control value between 0 and 63 will be interpreted as "off" and any value between 64 and 127 will be interpreted as "on." However, when sending messages from a sequencer, it is better to stick to just 0 or 127 as the values. Table 9.5 lists the switch control numbers (CC64 to CC69), any functions that are assigned, and makes note of any unique features or typical usage.

Table 9.5   Switch controllers CC64 to CC69

Control number	Control function	Notes
64	Sustain pedal	Sustains all notes attacked, but not yet released, before the pedal is depressed and all notes attacked while the pedal is depressed, regardless of whether the notes have been released (i.e. note-off messages have been sent). Similar to damper pedal on piano. Control values 0–63 indicate "off" and values 64–127 indicate "on" for all switch controllers.
65	Portamento on/off	Turns on/off the "glide" between successive notes. The amount of portamento is set by CC5 (see above).
66	Sostenuto on/off	Sustains notes that are already sounding when pedal is depressed, but does not sustain any notes subsequently attacked. Similar to sostenuto pedal on a piano.
67	Soft pedal on/off	Reduces volume of notes played while pedal is depressed. Similar to soft pedal on a piano.
68	Legato footswitch	Turns on/off monophonic legato mode on receiving device such that if a note is attacked before the previous note is released the synth will change the pitch without re-triggering the volume envelope.
69	Hold 2	Prolongs the release of sounding notes.

Sound and Effects Controllers

There are a variety of control change messages that are designed to control specific aspects of a synthesizer's sound or a synthesizer's effects. If your synth utilizes these messages, they can be very effective in shaping a performance. Effects controllers 1 and 2 and general purpose controllers 1–4, all listed with continuous controllers above (CC12–13, CC16–19), could fall into this category, though they don't have default definitions that specify just what they control. General purpose controllers 5–8 (CC80–83) are listed here for numerical convenience, but they also lack any specific default definition. Note that the effects controllers 1–2 and the general purpose controllers 1–4 can have associated LSBs (CC44–45 are the LSBs for CC12–13, and CC48–51 are the LSBs for CC16–19), and thus a potential data range of 0–16,383, whereas the controllers discussed here cannot.

The sound controllers, with the exception of number 10, have default definitions as shown in Table 9.6. However, their destinations can be changed by the Universal System Exclusive message "Controller Destination Setting" (system messages are discussed later in the chapter). In addition, the sound controllers, with the exception of sound controller 1, are recommended in the General MIDI 2 specification (GM2) to be *relative* controllers. A control value of 64 leaves the designated synth parameter unchanged, values less than 64 reduce the synth parameter, and values greater than 64 increase the synth parameter.

Table 9.6   Sound and effects controllers CC70 to CC95

Control number	Control function	Notes
70	Sound controller 1	Default: Sound Variation. The control value will select a variation programmed into the current patch (it doesn't change patches). Examples include muted vs. strummed guitar or bowed vs. pizzicato strings. There may be multiple levels of variation mapped across the 0–127 range.
71	Sound controller 2	Default: Timbre/Harmonic Intensity. The parameter this changes is dependent on the sound production architecture of the receiving synth. The resonance control on a filter is one application. GM2 defines this as a relative parameter.
72	Sound controller 3	Default: Release Time. GM2 defines this as a relative parameter.
73	Sound controller 4	Default: Attack Time. GM2 defines this as a relative parameter.
74	Sound controller 5	Default: Brightness. May be implemented by controlling the cutoff frequency of a low pass filter. GM2 defines this as a relative parameter.
75	Sound controller 6	Default: Decay Time. GM2 defines this as a relative parameter.
76	Sound controller 7	Default: Vibrato Rate. GM2 defines this as a relative parameter.
77	Sound controller 8	Default: Vibrato Depth. GM2 defines this as a relative parameter.
78	Sound controller 9	Default: Vibrato Delay. This sets the delay after the attack of the note before the vibrato begins. GM2 defines this as a relative parameter.
79	Sound controller 10	Default: Undefined.
80	General purpose controller 5	Can be used to control some synthesizer parameter. Depends on specific synth programming.
81	General purpose controller 6	Can be used to control some synthesizer parameter. Depends on specific synth programming.
82	General purpose controller 7	Can be used to control some synthesizer parameter. Depends on specific synth programming.
83	General purpose controller 8	Can be used to control some synthesizer parameter. Depends on specific synth programming.
84	Portamento control	Allows for one-time use of portamento (as opposed to CC65 which turns portamento on until it is released). The control value in this message specifies the key number that is the start of the portamento glide. The next note-on message causes the pitch to glide from the key number in the portamento control message to the key number in the note-on message. No subsequent note messages are affected. The rate for this could be preset in the patch or set by CC5.
85–87	Undefined	
88	High resolution velocity prefix	The control value for this control number effectively represents an LSB for the velocity value in the next note-on message, providing a high-resolution velocity value. This expanded velocity ranges from 128 to 16,384 for a total of 16,256 values. The 128 lower limit stems from technical reasons related to running status.
89–90	Undefined	
91	Effects 1 depth	Default: Reverb Send Level. A control value of 127 would be a send level of 100 percent.
92	Effects 2 depth	Formerly: Tremolo Depth. Can be used to control the depth of an effect or any other sound parameter.
93	Effects 3 depth	Default: Chorus Send Level.
94	Effects 4 depth	Formerly: Celeste [Detune] Depth. Can be used to control the depth of an effect or any other sound parameter.
95	Effects 5 depth	Formerly: Phaser Depth. Can be used to control the depth of an effect or any other sound parameter.

What these controllers all have in common is that they are designed to be used "on-the-fly" during performance (even if the "performance" is the playback of a sequence) and don't change the patch's programming. Also listed for numerical convenience in Table 9.6 are several undefined control numbers and a couple of others.

RPNs and NRPNs

Registered Parameter Numbers (RPNs) and Non-Registered Parameter Numbers (NRPNs) allow the set of control change messages to be greatly expanded. Several RPNs have been defined and, when implemented, can be expected to behave in a consistent manner from synth to synth. NRPNs are all officially undefined, but can be defined by a manufacturer for any given synth. RPNs and NRPNs have an MSB and an LSB to specify the actual parameter number, so each can address 16,384 different parameters for a possible effective total of 32,768 additional control numbers! Table 9.7 lists the RPN and NRPN control numbers. The undefined controllers CC102–119 are listed here for numerical convenience.

To change the value of a particular registered parameter, you would send the RPN MSB and LSB control numbers (CC101 and CC100) each with the appropriate control

Table 9.7   RPN- and NRPN-related controllers

Control number	Control function	Notes
96	Data increment (+1)	Indicates an increase of 1 relative to an existing value. This is typically used to change RPN and NRPN values. The actual control value is usually ignored since the control number already indicates +1.
97	Data decrement (−1)	Indicates a decrease of 1 relative to an existing value. This is typically used to change RPN and NRPN values. The actual control value is usually ignored since the control number already indicates −1.
98	Non-Registered Parameter Number (NRPN) LSB	Along with CC99 this is used to choose a parameter to change. The value would then be set by CC6/CC38 (as MSB/LSB), CC96, or CC97. See discussion in the text in this section.
99	Non-Registered Parameter Number (NRPN) MSB	Along with CC98 this is used to choose a parameter to change. The value would then be set by CC6/38 (as (MSB/LSB), CC96, or CC97. See discussion in the text in this section.
100	Registered Parameter Number (RPN) LSB	Along with CC101 this is used to choose a parameter to change. The value would then be set by CC6/CC38 (as MSB/LSB), CC96, or CC97. See discussion in the text in this section.
101	Registered Parameter Number (RPN) MSB	Along with CC100 this is used to choose a parameter to change. The value would then be set by CC6/CC38 (as MSB/LSB), CC96, or CC97. See discussion in the text in this section.
102–119	Undefined	

values to select a particular parameter (see Table 9.8). Then you would send either a CC6 (data entry) message to set the parameter value, or a CC6 plus a CC38 if the parameter value requires both. To change the value of a parameter relative to its current value, you could instead send a CC96 message to increment the value by one, or a CC97 message to decrement the value by one. Their control values are ignored since the control numbers already indicate increment and decrement.

Similarly, NRPN messages consist of the NRPN MSB and LSB (CC99 and CC98), each with the appropriate control values to select a particular parameter (as defined by the manufacturer). You would send a CC6 or a CC6 plus a CC38 to set the parameter value, or CC96/97 messages to increment or decrement the existing value.

Table 9.8 lists the currently defined RPNs (NRPNs are defined differently by each manufacturer) and their associated CC6 and/or CC38 values (CC96 and CC97 effects will be discussed below).

Table 9.8 List of Registered Parameter Numbers (RPNs)

RPN	CC101 value	CC100 value	Data entry values
Pitch bend sensitivity	0	0	CC6 value: +/− semitones CC38 value: +/− cents GM2 default value is 02/00 for 2 semitones up and 2 semitones down
Channel fine tuning	0	1	Tuning change in cents above or below A3 (440 Hz). Examples: CC6 0 and CC38 0 = −100 cents; CC6 64 and CC38 0 = no change; CC6 127 and CC38 127 = +100 cents.
Channel coarse tuning	0	2	Tuning change in cents above or below A3 (440 Hz): CC6 0 = −6400; CC6 64 = no change; CC6 127 = +6300
Tuning program change	0	3	CC6 value selects the tuning program number
Tuning bank select	0	4	CC6 value selects the tuning bank number
Modulation depth range	0	5	CC6/CC38 values sets modulation depth range. This RPN was added to be a part of GM2
3D sound controllers	61	0–8	CC6/CC38 set the value of the parameter specified by the LSB (CC100). These concern the simulated movement of sound in 3D space
Null setting	127	127	This resets the parameter number. After this CC6, CC38, CC96, and CC96 can be used independently of RPNs. This is also true for NRPNs when the CC98 and CC99 values are set to 127

As an example, to set the channel fine tuning down 50 cents (down a quarter tone) you would send the following messages:

Control Change/Ch. #	101	0
Control Change/Ch. #	100	1
Control Change/Ch. #	6	32
Control Change/Ch. #	38	0

Since this RPN uses both the MSB and LSB for the data entry controller, the range for the value of this parameter is 0 to 16,383 with 0 representing 100 cents down, 8,192 representing no change, and 16,383 representing 100 cents up. In the example, the combination of the CC6 and CC38 values results in a value of 4,096, which would indicate 50 cents down (see the "Technically Speaking . . . MSB and LSB" sidebar earlier in the chapter). The formula for determining the results in cents of the fine tuning RPN using the combined CC6 and CC38 value as the argument is:

Fine tuning change in cents = 100/8,192 × (combined_value − 8,192)

If you were done changing the channel fine tuning and weren't going to change some other RPN or NRPN, you would then want to send these messages to reset the parameter number and free CC6 and CC38 to be used by themselves:

Control Change/Ch. #	101	127
Control Change/Ch. #	100	127

As mentioned above, in addition to using the CC6/38 controllers to set the value for a parameter, it is also possible to use CC96 and CC97 to change the value relative to the existing value by incrementing or decrementing by one respectively. For the pitch bend sensitivity and channel fine tuning RPNs, CC96 and CC97 change the LSB value by one. For the RPNs that use only the MSB (CC6) for a value (RPNs 02, 03, and 04), they would change the MSB. For future RPNs, they affect the LSB unless specified otherwise.

CHANNEL MODE MESSAGES

The channel mode messages are used to change the way in which the receiving synth responds to channel messages. Mode messages have the same status byte and structure as control change messages and contain a channel, control number, and control value:

Status byte	Data byte 1	Data byte 2
Control change/channel	Control number (0–127)	Control value (0–127)

Of these messages, the most useful controllers are probably CC121 and CC123. CC121 can be used at the beginning of each track of a sequence to ensure that there are no settings on a synth's channels that are undesirable, such as any non-zeroed pitch bend or non-zeroed mod wheel. This is generally only necessary with hardware synthesizers and samplers. CC123 (or CC120) can be used by a sequencer as a "panic" function to stop any "stuck" MIDI notes that are sounding. Table 9.9 lists the channel mode messages by control number.

The last four channel mode messages combine to form the four modes found in the MIDI specification:

Mode 1: Omni On, Poly

Mode 2: Omni On, Mono

Mode 3: Omni Off, Poly

Mode 4: Omni Off, Mono

Table 9.9 Channel mode messages

Control number	Control function	Notes
120	All sound off	Immediately silences all sounding notes on the receiving device and turns the notes off. Control value data byte should be 0.
121	Reset all controllers	Resets controllers, pitch bend, pressure values, etc. to the *receiving device's* ideal state. Usually this means at least mod wheel to 0 and pitch bend to center. Control value data byte should be 0.
122	Local control on/off	Breaks the connection between a synth's keyboard and sound engine—used particularly in sequencing situations. A control value of 0 turns the local control off and a control value of 127 turns the local control on.
123	All notes off	Turns all sounding notes off. Unlike CC120, the notes' envelopes will go through their normal release. The control value data byte has no effect. This message shouldn't affect notes being played on the synth's keyboard or any notes being held by the sustain pedal.
124	Omni Mode Off	Puts the synth into Omni Off mode and turns all notes off. Control value is 0.
125	Omni Mode On	Puts the synth into Omni On mode and turns all notes off. Control value is 0.
126	Mono Mode On	Puts the synth into Mono mode and turns all notes off. Control value can indicate the number of mono channels to be used (in Omni Off) or is set to 0 (Omni Off) if the number of channels is equal to the number of voices in the receiving synth.
127	Poly Mode On	Puts synth into Poly mode and turns all notes off. Control value is ignored.

These modes were essentially conceived for synths that could play only a single timbre at a time (monotimbral), though they can be applied to multitimbral synths by thinking of those instruments as multiple synths, each with its own possible mode, packaged together.

A synth set to Omni On will receive messages from any channel and play them polyphonically (multiple notes at once). A multitimbral synth placed into Omni On mode will receive messages from any channel and play them with the same timbre. This essentially renders the device monotimbral.

In Omni Off, the synth will respond only to messages on a "basic channel" that is set on the synth itself. For early monotimbral synths, this was a way of ensuring that a synth connected in a daisychain would only respond to messages intended for that synth. Each synth in the daisychain could have a different basic channel. A multitimbral synth responds to messages on more than one channel, with each channel responding only to messages directed to it. A sixteen-part multitimbral synth, then, is like sixteen separate Omni Off synths in the same box. This is the multi mode—also called combi mode or performance mode—in which modern multitimbral synths operate. Multi mode is not a true MIDI mode, but it is the standard operating mode for multitimbral synths.

The Poly On message causes a synth to play multiple notes on a timbre at the same time. When combined with Omni On (Mode 1), messages received on any channel would be played polyphonically on a single timbre. When combined with Omni Off (Mode 3), messages received only on the synth's basic channel would be played polyphonically. For a multitimbral synth, each part would play notes on its channel polyphonically.

Mono On and Poly On are mutually exclusive: setting a synth to Mono On turns Poly Off and vice versa. Monophonic, of course, indicates one voice at a time. When combined with Omni On (Mode 2), a synth with Mono On behaves as you would expect, accepting notes from any channel (Omni On), but playing only one note at a time (Mono On). However, when combined with Omni Off (Mode 4), the behavior can become more complicated.

In Mode 4, messages are received starting from the basic channel up to the basic channel plus the number of voices specified in the control value data byte of the Mono On message minus one. Using the terminology from the MIDI specification, if the basic channel is N and the number of voices specified in the Mono On message is M, then the synth receives messages on channels N through N+M−1. Each of those channels would utilize a single voice (monophonic).

This mode would be useful in conjunction with a guitar controller where it would be desirable for the note messages for each string to be played with independent pitch bend and other characteristics so that, for example, one string could be bent while the others are not. In this case, the guitar would send the note and pitch bend data for each string on separate channels (transmitting in Mode 4), and a receiving synth set to Mode 4 would play the messages on each channel independently.

In the GM2 spec, which in many ways represents some of the more up-to-date thinking about how a synth should respond to MIDI messages, Omni is not supported and the only recognized "M" in the control value of the Mono On message is 1, so that only the channel receiving the Mono On message changes to Mono mode and other channels are not affected. This would still work fine with a guitar controller, or other controller sending messages on multiple channels, because a sixteen–part multitimbral GM2 synth would respond to each channel (messages from each string) independently anyway.

SYSTEM MESSAGES

Unlike channel voice messages, MIDI system messages are not directed at a specific channel, but rather apply to the entire receiving MIDI device. System messages start out, as all MIDI messages do, with a status byte that indicates what type of message is being sent—in this case a system message. Because system messages are not directed at a specific channel, the four bits in the status byte that determine the channel in channel messages are used in system status bytes to determine which system message is being sent (see the "Technically Speaking . . . MIDI bytes" sidebar earlier in the chapter). As a result, there are a total of sixteen possible kinds of system messages, though not all are in use. These messages are organized into three groups of system messages: System Exclusive, System Common, and System Real Time.

System Exclusive Messages

System Exclusive, or **SysEx**, messages are designed to allow you to communicate with a single, specific synth to send it information that is unique to that synth, and hence perhaps not useful to other synths. For example, you may want to change a particular parameter of a program (patch) on a synth, such as the kind of filter being used in the patch or the basic sample set for the patch. The specific data and the format for that data contained in a SysEx message are defined by each manufacturer and published as part of the user's manual or other documentation. A sub-class of system exclusive messages, called Universal System Exclusive messages, behave differently and are discussed a bit later.

A SysEx message starts with a SysEx status byte and ends with an end-of-exclusive, or **EOX**, status byte. In between are any number of data bytes as determined by the manufacturer. The first data byte is always the **ID number**, which usually indicates the manufacturer of the target device. When a device receives the start of a SysEx message, it looks at the ID number and decides whether the message is intended for it. For example, if a Roland synth receives a SysEx message with a Yamaha ID number, it completely ignores the rest of the message. The manufacturer determines all of the data between the ID number and the EOX. Many manufacturers also include a **model number** and a **device ID** with the SysEx message so that it can be directed to a specific device made by that manufacturer. For example, using a model number and device ID, a SysEx message could be aimed at not just any Yamaha Synth, but the Yamaha Motif, and not just any Yamaha Motif, but the Yamaha Motif whose device ID is 1. The device ID is typically settable from the front face of the synth.

One of the more common uses for SysEx messages has been to allow patch-editing software to communicate with a hardware synth. Patch-editing software provides a graphical interface for the user to change all of the available parameters of a patch and communicate those changes directly to the synth. At that point, you can send note messages and expressive messages to be played by your newly modified timbre. SysEx messages also allow you to "dump" patch information from your hardware instrument to your sequencing software as a backup and transfer it back to the synth to restore the patch later. This allows you to store modified patches that you used for a particular project on the computer instead of relying on the parameter memory (PRAM, or parameter RAM), which can be erased by you or other users, or lost if the internal battery were to run down.

These applications are quite hardware-centric and are less relevant when you're using software synths and samplers to generate sound. In that case, you are more likely to make patch parameter modifications by moving a knob or slider on the interface of the software synth/sampler and to save your modified patches as new patch files on the computer.

Universal System Exclusive messages share the same status byte as regular SysEx messages, but are instead used for extensions to MIDI that are *not* exclusive to a particular manufacturer. In regular SysEx messages, the ID number indicates a specific manufacturer that was assigned that number. In Universal SysEx messages, on the other hand, the ID numbers are either 126 or 127, which are reserved for this purpose and not assigned to any manufacturer. ID 126 is used for Non-Real Time Universal SysEx messages and ID 127 is used for Real Time Universal SysEx messages.

Non-Real Time Universal SysEx messages are not designed to be sent "on the fly" as a sequence is playing, and they include commands to turn General MIDI mode on and off, requests to transmit (dump) samples, and requests to transmit (dump) tuning tables. Real Time Universal SysEx messages are designed to be acted upon immediately by the receiving device and include master tuning, global parameter control, single note tuning change, some kinds of MIDI Time Code (MTC) messages, MIDI Machine Control (MMC) messages, and MIDI Show Control messages (MSC). MMC and MSC are additions to the MIDI standard that allow for MIDI control of such equipment as audio recording decks, live performance systems, and theatrical systems.

System Common Messages

System Common messages include the EOX message that tells all of the synths in a MIDI network that a system exclusive message is over and the **MIDI Time Code** quarter frame message. MIDI Time Code quarter frame messages allow MIDI hardware and software to send and receive messages indicating a point in time as measured in a form of time code created by the Society of Motion Picture and Television Engineers (SMPTE; pronounced "Simp-tee"). This is used most often when MIDI software must be slaved to an external clock usually associated with video. In the project studio, transmission of SMPTE time code has been largely superseded by the use of digital video files, which can be viewed and synchronized directly in sequencing software, but time code is still used in certain high-end applications.

In a situation where it is desirable to synchronize a DAW/Sequencer with an external SMPTE source, such as a video deck, a device is needed to convert SMPTE time code into MIDI Time Code (MTC). Fortunately, many of the larger multiport MIDI interfaces will accept SMPTE input and deliver MTC to the computer and the DAW/Sequencer. With the DAW/Sequencer set to synchronize or "slave" to MTC, pressing play on the video deck will cause the DAW/Sequencer to start playing from the same time location as the video. The DAW/Sequencer will then pass its note messages and expressive messages to software synths/samplers or attached hardware synths and samplers, and thus the music will be synchronized with the video (see Figure 9.6).

In SMPTE time code, time is encoded as hours, minutes, seconds, and film frames. MTC encodes each of those four time fields into two separate messages, thus requiring eight total messages to represent a single SMPTE location. These are called "quarter frame" messages, because the messages are sent every quarter of a frame. As a result, the full data for a single SMPTE location is sent every two frames.

MTC quarter frame messages are used when the SMPTE source is playing steadily either forward or backward. However, when the device is in fast forward or rewind, the rate of the quarter frame messages could exceed the MIDI bandwidth (31,250 bits per second) and thus "clog" or "choke" the MIDI stream. In those circumstances, a Real Time Universal SysEx message called MIDI Time Code Full Message is sent.

The MTC Full Message encodes all four time fields in one message. This allows a SMPTE source that is fast-forwarding or rewinding to send out a single SMPTE time location message when it's done and have the MTC slave device cue itself to that point

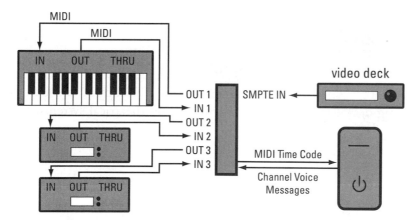

Figure 9.6   Synchronization through MIDI Time Code: a video deck generates SMPTE time code, and a MIDI interface with SMPTE capability converts the SMPTE time code into MIDI Time Code and sends it to the computer over a USB cable. A DAW/Sequencer slaved to MTC sends MIDI channel voice messages to MIDI devices

and prepare for MTC quarter frame messages when the SMPTE source begins playback. Both the MTC quarter frame messages and the MTC Full Message contain a code that indicates the SMPTE frame rate.

System Real Time Messages

System Real Time messages allow MIDI software and hardware to maintain the same tempo, through the use of the **Timing Clock** message, and to start and stop at the same time, through the use of the start, continue, and stop messages. These tempo and transport (**start**, **stop**, **continue**) synchronization messages might be used between sequencing software and MIDI hardware such as drum machines or workstations that have their own tempos and note patterns. Pattern-based workstations, such as the Akai MPC series, are particularly popular in hip-hop music production and performance. In addition, these messages can be used in conjunction with synthesizers that have arpeggiators or modulation effects that can be tempo synchronized.

Unlike MIDI Time Code discussed above, the timing clock message doesn't provide a fixed time location, but instead is sent twenty-four times per beat (*not* second) providing a tempo-based pulse that can be used by the slave device to maintain the same tempo as the master—often a software sequencer (see Figure 9.7). The start, stop, and continue messages allow slave devices to start and stop their clocks based on the actions of the master.

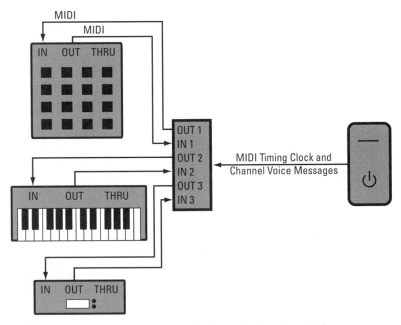

Figure 9.7 Synchronization through MIDI Timing Clock: a DAW/Sequencer produces MIDI Timing Clock messages along with channel voice messages. Receiving devices synchronize internal sequencers or tempo-based effects to the clock messages

System messages can be quite powerful, but they have not been used as frequently in recent years, particularly with the proliferation of software-based synthesizers and samplers, which don't need some of these specialized messages. Table 9.10 gives an overview of the MIDI system messages discussed here.

Table 9.10   Selected system messages

System messages	Notes
System Exclusive	
SysEx	Only devices manufactured by the company indicated in the ID number of this message will respond to it. Ends with EOX (System Common message). Data in between is determined by the manufacturer.
Universal SysEx	Messages that extend the MIDI standard. Grouped into Real Time and Non-Real Time messages. Includes General MIDI On/Off, MIDI Machine Control (MMC), and MIDI Show Control (MSC).
System Common	
MTC Quarter Frame	Allows for absolute time synchronization between devices in the form of eight messages over two frames that indicate a specific time location in SMPTE format (hours, minutes, seconds, frames).
EOX	End of Exclusive, concludes a SysEx message.
System Realtime	
Timing Clock	Synchronizes the tempo of slaved devices with the master device by sending 24 clock messages per beat.
Start	Starts the clocks (play) of slaved devices at the beginning of the song or sequence.
Continue	Continues the clocks of slaved devices from the current location in the song or sequence.
Stop	Stops the clocks of slaved devices.

Bibliography

Aikin, Jim. 2004. *Power tools for synthesizer programming: the ultimate reference for sound design.* San Francisco, CA: Backbeat Books.

ASHA (American Speech-Language-Hearing Association). No date. Noise and hearing loss. www.asha.org/public/hearing/Noise.

Ballora, Mark. 2003. *Essentials of music technology.* Upper Saddle River, NJ: Pearson Education, Inc.

Ballou, Glen. 2008. *Handbook for sound engineers.* 4th ed. Oxford: Focal Press.

Bennett, Gerald and Xavier Rodet. 1989. "Synthesis of the singing voice," in Mathews, Max V. and John R. Pierce, eds. *Current directions in computer music research,* pp. 19–44. Cambridge, MA: MIT Press.

Boulanger, Richard Charles. 2000. *The Csound book: perspectives in software synthesis, sound design, signal processing, and programming.* Cambridge, MA: MIT Press.

Bristow-Johnson, Robert. 1996. "Wavetable synthesis 101, a fundamental perspective," 101st AES Convention (Los Angeles, California), Audio Engineering Society (AES). Available at: www.musicdsp.org/files/Wavetable-101.pdf and www.aes.org/e-lib/browse.cfm?elib=7379.

Chowning, John. 1989. "Frequency modulation synthesis of the singing voice," in Mathews, Max V. and John R. Pierce, eds. *Current directions in computer music research,* pp. 57–63. Cambridge, MA: MIT Press.

Chowning, John, and David Bristow. 1986. *FM theory and applications.* Tokyo: Yamaha Music Foundation.

Clarke, Michael. 2000. "FOF and FOG synthesis in Csound," in Boulanger, Richard, ed. *The Csound book,* pp. 293–306. Cambridge, MA: MIT Press.

Cook, Perry R. 1999. *Music, cognition, and computerized sound: an introduction to psychoacoustics.* Cambridge, MA: MIT Press.

Cook, Perry R. 2002. *Real sound synthesis for interactive applications.* Natick, MA: A.K. Peters.

De Poli, Giovanni. 1983. "A tutorial on digital sound synthesis techniques," *Computer Music Journal* 7(4). Reprinted in Roads, Curtis, ed. 1989. *The music machine,* pp. 429–447. Cambridge, MA: MIT Press.

Dodge, Charles, and Thomas A. Jerse. 1997. *Computer music: synthesis, composition, and performance.* 2nd ed. New York: Schirmer Books.

Donahue, Thomas. 2005. *A guide to musical temperament.* Lanham, MD: The Scarecrow Press.

Fletcher, Neville H., and Thomas D. Rossing. 1998. *The physics of musical instruments.* 2nd ed. New York: Springer.

Gelfand, Stanley A. 2010. *Hearing: an introduction to psychological and physiological acoustics,* 5th ed. London: Informa Healthcare.

Guérin, Robert. 2006. *MIDI power!* 2nd ed. Boston, MA: Thomson Course Technology.

Hall, Gary S. 2002. "Cramped quarters," *Electronic Musician* 18, No. 4 (April). Available at: http://emusician.com/tutorials/emusic_cramped_quarters/.

Helmholtz, Hermann von. 1954. *On the sensations of tone as a physiological basis for the theory of music.* 2nd English ed. Trans. Alexander John Ellis. New York: Dover Publications.

Holmes, Thom. 2008. *Electronic and experimental music: technology, music, and culture.* 3rd ed. New York: Routledge.

Huber, David Miles, and Robert E. Runstein. 2005. *Modern recording techniques.* 6th ed. Boston, MA: Focal Press/Elsevier.

Isacoff, Stuart. 2001. *Temperament: the idea that solved music's greatest riddle.* New York: Alfred A. Knopf.

Jaffe, David A. and Julius O. Smith. 1983. "Extensions of the Karplus-Strong plucked-string algorithm," *Computer Music Journal* 7(2). Reprinted in Roads, Curtis, ed. 1989. *The music machine,* pp. 481–494. Cambridge, MA: MIT Press.

Johnston, Ian D. 2009. *Measured tones: the interplay of physics and music.* 3rd ed. Boca Raton, FL: CRC Press.

Karplus, Kevin and Alex Strong. 1983. "Digital synthesis of plucked-string and drum timbres," *Computer Music Journal* 7(2). Reprinted in Roads, Curtis, ed. 1989. *The music machine,* pp. 467–479. Cambridge, MA: MIT Press.

Keen, R.G. 1999. "The technology of phase shifters and flangers." Available at: www.geofex.com/Article_Folders/phasers/phase.html (accessed January 10, 2011).

Lebrun, Marc. 1977. "A derivation of the spectrum of FM with a complex modulating wave," *Computer Music Journal* 1(4), pp. 51–52. Reprinted in Roads, Curtis and John Strawn, eds. 1985. *Foundations of computer music,* pp. 65–67. Cambridge, MA: MIT Press.

Lehrman, Paul D., and Tim Tully. 1993. *MIDI for the professional.* New York: Amsco Publications.

Leider, Colby. 2004. *Digital audio workstation.* New York: McGraw-Hill.

Loy, D. Gareth. 1985. "Musicians make a standard: the MIDI phenomenon," *Computer Music Journal* 9(4) (Winter), pp. 8–26. Reprinted in Roads, Curtis, ed. 1989. *The music machine,* pp. 181–198. Cambridge, MA: MIT Press.

Loy, D. Gareth. 2006. *Musimathics: the mathematical foundations of music.* Vols 1 and 2. Cambridge, MA: MIT Press.

Manning, Peter. 2004. *Electronic and computer music.* Revised and expanded ed. New York: Oxford University Press.

MIDI Manufacturers Association. 2003. *General MIDI 2.* Version 1.1. Los Angeles, CA: MIDI Manufacturers Association.

MIDI Manufacturers Association. 2006. *The complete MIDI 1.0 detailed specification: incorporating all recommended practices.* Los Angeles, CA: MIDI Manufacturers Association.

Moog, Robert A. 1965. "Voltage-controlled electronic music modules," *Journal of the Audio Engineering Society* 13(3) (July), pp. 200–206.

Moog, Robert A. 1986. "Musical instrument digital interface," *Journal of the Audio Engineering Society* 34(5) (May), pp. 394–404.

Moore, Brian C.J. 2003. *An introduction to the psychology of hearing.* 5th ed. San Diego, CA: Academic Press.

Moore, F. Richard. 1988. "The dysfunctions of MIDI," *Computer Music Journal* 12(1) (Spring), pp. 19–28.

Moore, F. Richard. 1990. *Elements of computer music.* Englewood Cliffs, NJ: Prentice Hall.

Morrill, Dexter. 1977. "Trumpet algorithms for computer composition," *Computer Music Journal* 1(1), pp. 46–52. Reprinted in Roads, Curtis and John Strawn, eds. 1985. *Foundations of computer music,* pp. 30–44. Cambridge, MA: MIT Press.

Pejrolo, Andrea, and Rich DeRosa. 2007. *Acoustic and MIDI orchestration for the contemporary composer.* Boston, MA: Focal Press.

Pellman, Samuel. 1994. *An introduction to the creation of electroacoustic music.* Belmont, CA: Wadsworth Pub. Co.

Pierce, John Robinson. 1992. *The science of musical sound.* Revised ed. New York: W.H. Freeman.

Pohlmann, Ken C. 2005. *Principles of digital audio.* 5th ed. New York: McGraw-Hill.

Puckette, Miller. 2007. *The theory and technique of electronic music.* Available at: http://crca.ucsd.edu/~msp/techniques/latest/book-html/ (online book, accessed January 10, 2011).

Richmond Sound Design, Ltd. 2010. "WaterWorld show and sound control refit." Available at www.richmond sounddesign.com/ (accessed January 10, 2011).

Roads, Curtis. 1996. *The computer music tutorial.* Cambridge, MA: MIT Press.

Roads, Curtis. 2001. *Microsound.* Cambridge, MA: MIT Press.

Roederer, Juan. 2008. *The physics and psychophysics of music: an introduction.* 4th ed. New York: Springer.

Rumsey, Francis, and Tim McCormick. 2006. *Sound and recording: an introduction.* 5th ed. Boston, MA: Elsevier/ Focal Press.

Sallows, Kevin. 2001. *Listen while you work: hearing conservation for the arts.* Vancouver: SHAPE (Safety and Health in Arts Production and Entertainment). Available at: www.actsafe.ca/wp-content/uploads/resources/pdf/ listen.pdf.

Schottstaedt, Bill. 1977. "The simulation of natural instrument tones using frequency modulation with a complex modulating wave," *Computer Music Journal* 1(4), pp. 46–50. Reprinted in Roads, Curtis and John Strawn, eds. 1985. *Foundations of computer music*, pp. 54–64. Cambridge, MA: MIT Press.

SHAPE (Safety and Health in Arts Production and Entertainment). 2005. *Noise and hearing loss in musicians.* Vancouver: SHAPE. Available at: www.actsafe.ca/wp-content/uploads/resources/pdf/noisehearingloss musicians.pdf.

Smith, J.O. 2006. *Physical audio signal processing.* Available at: http://ccrma.stanford.edu/~jos/pasp/ (online book, accessed January 10, 2011).

Steiglitz, Kenneth. 1996. *A DSP primer: with applications to digital audio and computer music.* Menlo Park, CA: Addison-Wesley.

Thompson, Daniel M. 2005. *Understanding audio: getting the most out of your project or professional recording studio.* Boston, MA: Berklee Press.

Woram, John M. 1989. *Sound recording handbook.* John Woram Audio Series. Indianapolis, IN: Howard W. Sams & Co.

Young, Robert W. 1939. "Terminology for logarithmic frequency units," *Journal of the Acoustical Society of America* 11(1) (July), pp. 134–139.

Index

ONE WEEK LOAN

Renew Books on PHONE-it: 01443 654456
Help Desk: 01443 482625
Media Services Reception: 01443 482610

Books are to be returned on or before the last date below

0 9 JAN 2009

Treforest Learning Resources Centre
University of Glamorgan CF37 1DL